Uranus

The Constant of Change

Eric Meyers, M.A.

Astrology Sight Publishing

Uranus
The Constant of Change

Published by ASP:

Astrology Sight Publishing
4401 Redmond Dr.
#22–105
Longmont, CO 80503
(303) 684-8264

ISBN Number: 978-9747766-3-7

Printed in the United States of America

Cover Art by Evelyn Terranova
www.moonbeamgallery.com

Order online at:
www.AstrologySight.com
info@AstrologySight.com

Also by the author:

The Arrow's Ascent:
Astrology & The Quest for Meaning

Between Past & Presence:
A Spiritual View of the Moon & Sun

Dedicated to everything we don't know,
the people we've never met,
and the times that are eternally coming,
but never arrive.

"Come mothers and fathers
Throughout the land
And don't criticize
What you can't understand
Your sons and your daughters
Are beyond your command
Your old road is
Rapidly agin'.
Please get out of the new one
If you can't lend your hand
For the times they are a-changin'."

--Bob Dylan

Contents

Part 1 – Individuation

Part 2 – Revolution

Part 3 – The Intelligence of Nature

Foreward
by Bill Streett

A herald of the Aquarian Age, Ram Dass, stated, "Across planes of consciousness, we have to live with the paradox that opposite things can be simultaneously true." Although one always wants to counter the temptation of assuming intrinsic meanings in the course of evolution, it is difficult to resist the belief that one of the central messages of our time—as world views, religions and civilizations clash—is that paradox seems to be built into the nature of things. Moreover, as we throttle through a time of significant change, those that will thrive will be able to live with the unsettling proposition that "opposite things can be simultaneously true."

As Eric Meyers suggests, paradox is not only indicative of the astrological Uranus, but it is a major thread that runs throughout this book. From the subtitle to the concluding page, *Uranus: The Constant of Change* is fraught with the disconcerting higher truth that opposites and contradictions are interwoven into the cosmic condition. Though it is true that an emphasis on paradox is bound to appear in a study of Uranus, the prominence placed on paradox found in Meyers' work is more the result of his thorough and thoughtful treatment of this astrological archetype. Meyers admirably takes us from Uranus's manifestation in the individual, to the collective, to the transpersonal. Additionally, Meyers doesn't succumb to the easy lure of viewing Uranus either as solely a malevolent, destructive force that threatens the ego's need for constancy and security or as a purely positive energy, sprinkling creativity, liberty, vitally, and vibrancy in the wake of its magic wand. This breadth of scope and depth of understanding leads to one of the most comprehensive works devoted to any one astrological symbol.

Since Meyers presents a complete mandala of the astrological Uranus, one could simply use certain sections for one's individual pursuits: As a tool for inner exploration, a guide for predictive trends, or a starting point in historical or biographical research. In honoring Uranus, you are free to use this work as you wish. However, a full appreciation of Uranus (and of this work) can really only come from the number of vantage points that Meyers has constructed. And with a thorough reading of *Uranus: The Constant of Change*, you will perhaps arrive at one of the book's greatest paradoxes: In order to understand how the astrological Uranus works through you as an individual, you must fully know and understand how Uranus impacts other individuals, historical cycles, the collective, and, in Meyers' words, the "intelligence of nature" itself.

A book on Uranus is the perfect vessel for Meyers voice, which, as he has established with his previous works, is full of novel connections, verbal gymnastics, and stylistic improvisations. Perhaps this natural fit between the subject matter and author was the result of accident and whimsy, whereby the choice to write this book was merely the outcome of the author's inspiration and imagination. However, if there is any truth in the maxim declared by many astrologers—"You do not pick astrology; astrology picks you"—then perhaps we can extrapolate the same logic and assume that Meyers' original impetus to pen this book was not solely personal but "picked" by the transpersonal force that is the subject matter of these pages.

Individuals who are awake realize that the winds of change are set to blow, making the publication of this work prescient as well as instructive. However, rather than become a manual to navigate the "psychospiritual weather conditions" of the current time, *Uranus: The Constant of Change* should provide a wealth of material and insights beyond the current cultural climate and become a resource for astrologers, or the astrologically curious, in times to come.

Introduction
Shock to the System

Imagine the excitement felt by the group of revolutionaries who decided to overthrow the British monarchy and demand self-rule in the formative days of the United States. Picture Jackie Robinson taking the field as the first African-American to play Major League baseball. Think of Albert Einstein, who must have been in ecstatic wonder when the idea of relativity began to coalesce. Visualize Janis Joplin singing to a sea of hippies, all of them drunk on radical notions of how society must change. Remember the image of the courageous student in Tiananmen Square, refusing to cede ground to an armored tank.

There are many names for these types of behavior: trailblazing, rebellious, inventive, anti-establishment, or audacious. A common thread is the desire to align with a vision of something new, to throw out the rulebook and steer toward potentials not yet fully realized. What is motivating such *fools*? Why do these people stubbornly forge ahead, completely willing to face ridicule or worse from the dominant factions in society? Perhaps part of this answer is being in the grips of some sort of force that requires this level of bravado. In the astrological system this energizing spirit is associated with the planet Uranus, planet of liberation, progress, breakthroughs, metaphysics, revolution, de-conditioning, innovation, multi-dimensional understandings, psychic interconnectedness, synchronicities, and the overarching intelligence within nature. Uranus pertains to the ongoing flux of energy that awakens all of us to new realities. Uranus is the constant of change.

Many have made the observation that the "only thing that remains stable is change." This wonderfully paradoxical statement captures the essence of this trickster planet. Along with its association with the fixed sign Aquarius, the Uranus principle relates to the variability of all form—the everlasting dynamism of this existence. We can learn to see patterns pertaining to growth, a method to the "madness." From the standpoint of the individual, we see that change fosters developmental progress—the claiming of self-awareness and individuation. A bit wider lens yields more general cycles and time periods, how collectively we are joined in an organized evolutionary project. Using the widest lens we notice the intelligence of nature itself, how all changes serve to bring us into alignment with unity consciousness and interconnectedness. These three levels—the personal, social, and transpersonal—compose this book.

Depending on how it's harnessed and utilized, change can bring progress, but also disorder and chaos. Sometimes change is unwarranted and uninformed, and could lead to dismal outcomes. These changes also invite new responses and necessary adjustments. However managed, change is a force that continually breaks up what has been concretized. Uranus/Aquarius is associated with the future because change (and ideally a conscious response to it leading to collective progress) allows us to unfold this sweeping evolutionary situation we find ourselves in.

The bristling energy of Uranus is transpersonal or metaphysical like a teeming network of potentials. It must find an outlet through the physical world in order to have potency. The realm of ideas and possibilities is unlimited but not manifest. It endlessly invites us to seek, to break through, to latch on to a moment of insight that could change the world. There is a part of us that innately knows there is always more to the story. What we do with it in the familiar or physical realms is completely up to us.

When we are *foolish* enough to attempt to capture lightning in a bottle, we become the personal instigators of change. And like a lightning bolt searing the ground, the moment of impact has both a "before" and an "after." Who could blame the owner of the land by being irked by such an intrusion? And here we have the great dilemma: change intrudes upon the status quo. It is often unwelcome, usually perplexing and always disruptive. Those who prefer to guard against such an imposition view change as deviant, ornery and uncalled for. Central to our discussion is the dynamic between the established order (Saturn) versus change (Uranus). This is a tension that takes on multiple forms in every possible domain, be it personal, social, environmental, political, or spiritual.

The necessary closing in to solidify order and maximize utility (Saturn) and the obliteration of worn-out structures for progressive reasons (Uranus) illustrates the dynamic of narrowness versus inclusiveness. Whereas the calcification of routine and the generation of rules promote stability, this limit-setting also draws distinctions between what is preferred and what isn't. This takes the form of social norms and customs, as well as the paradigms and prevailing attitudes of the day. At best, this process of discernment separates the wheat from the chaff; at worst, it manifests as rank discrimination. Uranus is about the whole, the oneness of humanity and the universe. It forever challenges us to reach toward a cohesive, unified vision. Though separation may serve a temporary aim, in the larger view, it severs the underlying unity.

The movement toward wholeness begins at the personal level. Uranus relates to the part of the individual that refuses to be tamed, to "sell out" or compromise its authenticity in any way. The wider orbit of Uranus in relation to Saturn suggests an expansion into unfamiliar or untried areas that are filled with novel experiences and insights for self-revelation. Uranus, being the first *transpersonal* planet, connects the personality to processes that reside within the larger matrix of spiritual interconnectedness. These processes are unadulterated by the norms, parameters and methods of everyday functioning. Uranus relates to the process of de-conditioning: finding who we really are beyond the societal encasement of age, sex and culture definitions—even the time period in which we live. When we grasp Uranus, the personal identity is shattered, only for the self to claim its spiritual purity and therefore truly find itself. In Part 1, we'll address Uranus in the individual birth chart: the sign it's in and the planets it aspects, as well as several examples of particularly Uranian people.

All individuals are part of groups, communities, societies, and all of humanity. We band together to instigate larger movements and trends, to shape the social, political, and environmental landscape we are inexorably a part of. Part 2 comprises Uranian functions at the collective level. We'll review a collection of Uranian events: individuals and social occurrences altering the collective consciousness. The interplay of Uranus with the other social and transpersonal planets (Jupiter, Saturn, Neptune, and Pluto), specifically how these cycles correlate with societal shifts, will be addressed. We are about to enter a particularly Uranian time frame (2008-2012 and beyond). Part 2 concludes with a discussion of the major astrological events starring Uranus in the years to come.

Collectively we are part of an energetic web that envelops us. In Part 3, we'll explore the transpersonal facets of Uranus as it pertains to nature, cosmos and Spirit including the interconnection of souls and how the universe itself participates in evolution. We'll also review some ground-breaking scientific information regarding the oneness of nature and how the planets play a role within a larger matrix. When we leave all personal concerns behind and attempt to peer through the widest of lenses, what emerges is nothing less than miraculous, paradoxical and bewildering—the marks of Uranus.[1]

Chapter 1
About Uranus

Uranus was officially discovered on March 13, 1781, by Abraham Herschel. It is the seventh planet from the Sun, with a revolution of about 84 years. Its average distance from the Sun is 1784 million miles. Unlike any other planet, it rotates on an axis that faces the Sun; therefore, it appears to roll rather than spin. The Earth's axis tilts at about 23 degrees, while Uranus rotates at 98—this makes it difficult to determine which would be its North Pole. The diameter at its equator is about 32,560 miles, making it over four times larger than the Earth. The average temperature is below 200 degrees Centigrade. Uranus' atmosphere is about 83% hydrogen, 15% helium and 2% methane.

Uranus' blue color is the result of absorption of red light by methane in the upper atmosphere. Uranus radiates less heat than it receives from the Sun, unlike the other gas planets. For example, Jupiter (considered a fire planet) radiates more heat than it receives and is likened to the Sun for this quality, as well as for its colossal size. Unlike titanic Jupiter, Uranus is barely visible on a clear night, and can usually be seen only with a visual aid, such as a telescope or binoculars. This is most curious since the planet wasn't officially spotted until the eighteenth century, despite leagues of stargazers studying the heavens. Perhaps we weren't *ready* to discover it until that time. The "character" of Uranus is detached, lurking just beyond conscious visibility, elusive, cold, and it has a most unusual rotation.

Uranus is named for Ouranos, father of Cronos (Saturn) and husband to the Earth Goddess Gaia. Ouranos is known as a "sky god," and is male, ruler of the heavens and removed from the daily happenings on Earth. Ouranos wasn't much of a father as he was absent from his many children, dissatisfied with and even hostile to them. He had them remain in the womb of Gaia, condemned to the conditions of Earthly existence. In a climactic moment, Cronos uses his scythe to castrate his father, separating

Earth from sky and rendering Ouranos impotent. As the tale continues, the severed genitals are flung into the sea and transform into Aphrodite (Venus), the goddess of love. This metaphor illustrates the point that brilliant ideas must be born into this world, then develop through hands-on resourcefulness and aesthetic sensibility (Venus).

Several astrologers, most prominently Richard Tarnas, have argued that the astrological Uranus we have grown accustomed to shows little resemblance to Ouranos other than the mythic lineage to Cronos and the famous tale mentioned previously. The god Prometheus, emblematic of freedom, brilliance, innovation, non-conformity, and revolution, has many qualities that have become associated with Uranus. Is it possible that two (or more) mythological gods could be associated with this archetype? Considering that Uranus pertains to multi-dimensional understandings, this seems appropriate. Furthermore, Uranus does play the role of trickster, so having a Promethean quality would seem fitting. Perhaps Prometheus may represent our personal relationship to the planet/archetype, as each individual latches onto greater freedom and self-understanding, while Ouranos could pertain to its structural and metaphysical component, the overriding intelligence of nature.

Range of Expression

A central variable to consider in examining any factor in the astrological system is range of expression. Any planet, sign, house, or aspect has a spectrum of potential that is accessed by the quality or level of consciousness that enlivens it. There are muddled, sub-optimal expressions and there are effective and favorable ones. To simplify the range, the terms "low" or "high" are often employed.

The archetype and energy of Uranus mixes with the state of consciousness of a person, or on the global scale, the state of our collective consciousness. When managed well, there are breakthroughs, advances and a fascination with possibilities. A resistant response to Uranus tends to bring breakdowns or breakups, unexpected dilemmas or other shocks to one's system. In either scenario, the energy stimulates awareness to address new or previously ignored phenomena. Achieving a new level of perspective or adjusting to life in a wheelchair both awaken dormant faculties and focus attention in novel ways.

Uranus does shake things up. In order not to be personally shaken too much, a cooperative attitude towards growth is essential—this is the "high" end. Some might see an approaching Uranus transit to natal Venus as an ominous sign of relationship crises, which stems from fear, the "low" end. There is no guarantee how the event will play out—the event is *thematically* rather than literally predictive. Therefore, it is likely that new relational awareness regarding self and/or partner will force the connection to integrate such awareness or collapse trying. The transit may trigger many beneficial changes that bring the relationship into greater alignment with its inherent promise. It may also deliver shocking or disruptive events that may seem overwhelming, leading to the more unfortunate outcome of alienation or breakup. Much depends on the attitude and intentions that interact with the transit.

Some have taken to viewing Uranus in malevolent terms, for it does instigate necessary adjustments or recalibrations to new ways of being. For those interested in stability, continuity and ease, Uranus is a most formidable force of disruption. Those willing and able to grow, to stretch and detach from personal agendas and stories of how life *should* unfold, have a far easier time rolling with the punches. Uranus is only malevolent to resistance.

The Cool Planet

Just as the actual planet doesn't radiate as much heat as it takes in, the defining psychological condition of Uranus is nonattachment. Instead of participation, there is observation. Uranus takes us away from the blinding spotlight to a place of dispassion. Contrast the image of a cool, removed planet orbiting beyond the perimeter of the familiar, with the extravagant and generous Sun providing light and heat to all living things. We may consider the Sun to be *charged* and Uranus to be *neutral*. This characteristic simply means that Uranus is not invested in ego concerns and favors more global or transpersonal considerations—it cares about the individual's *truth*, which may be quite threatening to the ego.

This condition of neutrality does allow for greater objectivity, but those who align too closely with Uranus are prone to disengagement or even alienation. The disposition of not investing personally, the tendency toward aloofness or the adoption of a style that pressures the status quo to stop and take a good look at itself is considered "cool" in the modern parlance. The outsider, rebel or maverick who just doesn't care to be included carries the "cool" mystique. Wearing sunglasses hides the eyes and allows observation to proceed without being noticed personally. They are a central accouterment to the "cool" attire.

Those who behave selflessly, help a friend in need or anonymously give of themselves to a cause are also "cool." Volunteering or recycling are "cool things to do," and when we drop a coin in a homeless person's cup, we may hear a "Cool Man!" for a thank you. In contrast, extreme selfishness and acting without concern for others are "not cool." Those who maintain composure under trying circumstances are "cool as a cucumber" while those who act impulsively are "hotheaded."

"Cool" is also applied to items that fascinate and enthrall, such as our gadgets and technological discoveries. Science fiction, time travel and similar "far out" phenomena achieve the "cool" label. The Internet is a medium potentially shared by all and is an apt metaphor to the overarching connective Uranian web that transcends the interests of any singular person. Anything "new" that goes beyond the parameters of what we are used to and informs a broader, multidimensional understanding and perspective qualifies as being "cool" and also informs us of a broader reality. From quantum mechanics and relativity to temporarily surpassing ego limits in pursuit of unusual peak experiences: all are prized as being "cool." If it breaks the rules, it is "cool."

The Uranian style is typified by James Dean wearing his leather jacket, smug look on his face with a cigarette hanging out of his mouth. The neutrality and connective functioning is captured by the Internet. The fascination of Uranus is noted in phenomenal scientific discoveries that recalibrate awareness to new plateaus. The spirit of the planet is witnessed in revolutions that topple repressive empires. The selfless altruism is noticed in the philanthropist. Everything associated with the planet is what we would call "cool."

Aquarius and the 11th House

Uranus rules the sign of Aquarius and is linked to the 11th House—together planet, sign and house compose the themes of individuation, revolution and the overarching metaphysical structure that envelops us. Although this book focuses specifically on Uranus, the accompanying sign (Aquarius) and house (11th) are understood as being part of the scope.

To distinguish the difference among planet, sign and house, consider again the Sun. We have a direct energetic relationship with this massive giver of light and heat. Sunshine is immediate and palpable. The Sun rules Leo, which like the other signs denotes a process, style or developmental goal. Leo concerns the process of developing a unique personality, displaying a talent and being open to joy. The actual energy a person radiates, the essential life force, is one's solar energy or Sun. The 5th House involves areas where we naturally socialize, perform or express the self in some way.

Planets are immediate and energetic (what), signs are styles and processes (how), and houses are areas (where). I like to think of them as primary (planet), secondary (sign) and tertiary (house). Planets are primary because they are the direct energy in the system, like the Sun. Signs are secondary because they deal with attributes, skills and goals that become activated by a planet—planets *rule* signs. Houses are tertiary since they are the areas in which a planet, modified by a sign process, can extend itself into the world.

Uranus is an actual energy in this solar system. Aquarius is the psychospiritual process of aligning with one's unconditioned, authentic inner truth and developing the awareness that the self is a vehicle for collective progress. I find it best to think of the 11th House as a series of concentric circles, similar to a target. The scope of the 11th ranges from an immediate group—such as a clique, gang or fellowship—to acquaintances and audiences, to more distant allies made through networking, to one's community, to society, to the global community, to the solar system, to the universe itself. Membership in something larger than the self, which envelops the self within it, would apply to this target analogy. Traditionally considered the "house of friends," this should not be confused with personal relationships, which are more suited to the relational houses (5-8). In Aquarian terms, "friends" are the people, groups or allies who support us. The 5th House is about individual expression. The polarity is the 11th House, which concerns how an individual is part of larger frameworks.

As the 11th House and Aquarius follow the 10th House and Capricorn theme, another facet is how we harvest the returns of our work. Often discussed in terms of "hopes and wishes," there is a future orientation to the 11th House. What do we want to receive from the world? This does include how we desire to impact the world (10th House), then have the world reflect back its appreciation (11th House), but the more "evolved" essence transcends the personal. The 10th represents the peak years of achievement, and the 12th is akin to retirement. The 11th House is how we begin to transcend ambition and status (10th House) in order to contribute to a selfless vision of humanitarian progress. This selflessness often maximizes the harvest (11th House) of what we might possibly receive when we learn to join together. The final stage of release is in the 12th House. Just as Uranus orbits outside of Saturn, so too does Aquarius follow Capricorn, and the 11th House builds upon the 10th. Uranus, Aquarius and the 11th House compose the theme of moving away from the personal story and (re)joining with the underlying unity. The 12th further integrates this wisdom into the soul

Part 1 – Individuation

Many have used the term "higher self" when discussing one's innate potential and spiritual possibilities. This term, though, is somewhat nebulous, which makes for a poorly marked road in achieving such heights. In the astrological system, the planet Uranus does suggest what a more individuated self could aspire to, and clearly delineates the qualities available when realized.

Busting through limitations and arriving at liberation is a classic Uranian theme. Although this theme is evident in social movements or advances in metaphysical understandings, it's also applicable for personal growth. In order to be secure and viable beings, it's imperative to learn the rules of life and abide. Undoubtedly, many concessions are made in this process. Uranus invites us to latch on to the unfiltered brilliancy of what we could be independently of social conditioning.

In addition to overcoming social expectations that might hinder self-realization, the interplay of Uranus with Saturn also involves overcoming personal obstacles. Saturn represents inhibitions that require discipline to master. If we don't take on the challenge of Saturn, we feel overpowered and defeated. Upon rising to the challenge, a whole new area of potential is opened.

Uranus in the natal chart indicates what has been out of bounds, things that have introduced disruptions, or looming issues that we must attend to in order to develop greater consciousness or self-insight about them. Ideally, what was previously inaccessible becomes integrated into the parameters of the growing self. This bridges the boundary of the personal, indicated by Saturn, with the limitless expanse of the transpersonal, which begins with Uranus.

Thus, the "higher self" includes phenomena that have been out of reach and invite greater advancement when addressed. The complete profile of Uranus, including sign, house, and aspects, clearly denotes the cutting edge of personal innovation and progress. Claiming the Uranian territory is by its nature unfamiliar and pushes the edge of what is comfortable. In order to reinvent the self, one must pass a series of tests to demonstrate that a newer self can actually become manifest.

Chapter 2
Uranian Contacts with the Planets

Through its aspectual relationships with the planets, Uranus enlivens the other energies and catalyzes them to develop. Any planet(s) in aspect to Uranus have not previously reached their potential within the soul history and are therefore being called to bust through any limitations to arrive at greater self-realization. There is great potential within the aspected planet, though it often takes years to mature and steady its function. Initially, it may seem out of reach, hard to understand or lack a clearly defined true purpose—especially in the formative years. When some life experience is gained, the planet aspected by Uranus becomes more consciously activated, but is prone to behave in erratic ways. This is part of the developmental process that leads to greater refinement of the planetary function. Ultimately, the goal is to use the Uranian energy rather than be used by it.

The following sections discuss Uranus in aspect to all the other planets. Many examples of famous people are provided to show the variety of ways that a planet can manifest in these pairings. Only major aspects will be explored, with the following orbs: 12 degrees for the conjunction, 10 for the opposition, 8 for the trine and square, and 4.5 for the sextile. The few examples that exceed these orbs are noted in parentheses.[2]

Uranus/Sun – Progressive Catalysts

The Sun vigorously animates the innovative and trailblazing spirit of Uranus. Individuals who carry this interchange are especially involved in the process of personal revolution, and many apply this sense of actualizing potentials into collective domains. In whatever fields these people enter, they serve the function of pushing the envelope, challenging the status quo to modernize. The fixed quality to Uranus often makes them insistent, rebellious and willing to take on outsider or maverick positions.

The life force itself (Sun) crackles with activity. Though they may be endlessly interesting, these people can also be irritating. When the impetus for catalyzing breakthroughs is poorly embodied, behavior becomes misdirected, and these individuals can alienate others or champion unwise aims. This wildness is not only witnessed in day-to-day living; the biographies of Uranus/Sun people are often marked by unpredictable turns, sudden re-orientations and decisions that seem confounding to others.

This highly dynamic pairing unequivocally calls for a strong alliance between the self and the higher self (or innate potential). We may speculate that in past life scenarios, the path of lesser resistance was taken and now greater gusto is required. Perhaps there was too much conformity, playing it safe or overly conservative thinking. The present life (Sun) is about unflinchingly embracing the personal truth. This self-allegiance not only equips Uranus/Sun individuals with a sense of knowing who they *really* are, but it also allows them access to understanding more global or transpersonal workings of Spirit.

These people have great potential to implement personally the next wave of collective progress. By taking the risk in following this venture through, they may face great opposition in personal and professional settings. This willingness to stick one's neck out allows Uranus/Sun people to inch ahead of others like a racehorse at the finish line. The exposed neck is also an attractive target for others who go for the jugular. Ultimately, the alignment with the transpersonal supersedes any personal issues that may arise.

Sun/Uranus figures are found in the "founding fathers" of the United States, who zealously toppled a regime; George Washington, Thomas Jefferson, and Benjamin Franklin are some of the more famous examples. Another form of revolutionary leader is seen in Oliver Cromwell, who helped transform Great Britain. The anti-establishment quality is seen in Guy Fawkes, who tried to blow up the British Parliament. Helen Keller brought awareness to the potentials of the disabled through her iconic story. Huey Long was a rabble-rousing populist politician, a symbol of reform during the Great Depression. Rosa Parks remains the dominant symbol of the modern Civil Rights movement by virtue of her disobedience. Elie Wiesel has made himself a symbol of raising Holocaust awareness through his activism and inspiring story.

Other examples of particularly Uranian people include Neil Armstrong (first to walk on the Moon) and John Glenn (first to orbit the Earth). Hillary Clinton reinvented the role of women in Presidential politics while Barack Obama (13 degree conjunction, Sun rules Uranus in Leo) has done the same for minorities. Dr. Jack Kevorkian blatantly challenged the establishment, all the way to prison, with his euthanasia practices. Thurgood Marshall was the first African-American to serve on the U.S. Supreme Court. Timothy Leary's advocacy of illegal substances was rebellious and challenged his adherents to find their own truth away from societal rules. Ram Dass is a celebrated spiritual icon—his famous book *Be Here Now*, captures the essence of being in the present (Sun). Jerry Rubin co-founded the anti-establishment Yippie Party in the 1960s.

In a variety of fields, Uranus/Sun people have transformed and modernized their craft while also attaining symbolic or iconographic status. Examples in literature include Arthur Conan Doyle, Henrik Ibsen, Ernest Hemingway, Lewis Carroll, Aldous Huxley, William S. Burroughs, Maya Angelou, and Stephen King. Examples in art include Jackson Pollack, Marc Chagall, Andy Warhol, and Frida Kahlo. Examples in philosophy include Emmanuel Kant, John Locke, Baruch Spinoza, and George Santayana. Examples in psychology include Sigmund Freud, Carl Jung, Abraham Maslow, and Karen Horney. Examples in astrology include Isabel Hickey, Marc Edmond Jones, C.E.O. Carter, Alan Leo, Grant Lewi, Howard Sasportas, Phillip Sedgwick, and Richard Tarnas (Bill Streett and Kelly Lee Phipps are part of the next wave). Examples in athletics include Michael Jordan, Michael Johnson, Babe Ruth, Lawrence Taylor, Muhammad Ali, Sugar Ray Leonard, and Rocky Marciano.

In addition to being giants in their sports, some Uranus/Sun athletes have also impacted society at large, such as Billie Jean King through feminism and Lou Gehrig with his battle with disability. Sandy Koufax refused to pitch in the playoffs in observance of Jewish holidays. Magic Johnson brought forth public awareness of AIDS. Tiger Woods is a highly accomplished golfer and a visible celebrity of mixed races. Danica Patrick was the first female to win an Indy 500 race, and is the most successful modern woman driver in the sport. Predictably, she has faced sexism—her autobiography is titled *Danica: Crossing the Line*, a most Uranian sentiment.

Many leading scientists, particularly those who have made significant discoveries or breakthroughs, have Uranus/Sun including Isaac Newton, Nicolaus Copernicus, Johannes Kepler, Galileo Galilei, Marie Curie, Linus Pauling, Werner Heisenberg, and Stephen Hawking. Robert Oppenheimer was instrumental in developing the atomic bomb—an innovation that changed the course of history. DNA decoders James Watson and Francis Crick have Uranus/Sun, as well as Jonas Salk, who discovered the polio vaccine. Fritjof Capra has been on the leading edge of integrating physics with spirituality, a new kind of science that bridges cultures and paradigms. Science fiction author Arthur C. Clark (*2001: A Space Odyssey*) and Stanley Kubrick, who directed the movie, also have it. Lisa Randall is a scientist currently doing cutting-edge and influential work in physics, breaking gender barriers and attracting significant interest in her work. All of these people introduced new ways for us to conceive of our place in the world.

In the realm of entertainment, Walt Disney brought animation and amusement to the masses. Jack Nicholson, Meryl Streep, Anthony Hopkins, Faye Dunaway, and Dustin Hoffman are titanic actors who have been nominated for many Academy Awards and will forever be associated with modernizing the craft. Earlier legends with Uranus/Sun include Judy Garland, Bette Davis, Jerry Lewis, Rock Hudson, Rudolph Valentino, Vincent Price, and Liza Minnelli. Howard Hughes was a larger-than-life entertainment mogul and eccentric. Contemporary entertainment personalities Dennis Rodman, Howard Stern, Sean Penn, Jennifer Lopez, Mary J. Blige, Paris Hilton, and Britney Spears have attained iconographic status through their iconoclastic ways. They have used their personalities (Sun) to shake up perspectives (Uranus) and have stirred a debate regarding socially acceptable behaviors. Photographer Annie Leibovitz is a Uranus/Sun figure whose work symbolically captures celebrities and personalities, while Barbara Walters spent her time interviewing them.

Progressive musicians with this combination not only have stretched musical boundaries, but also have made *message* an integral part of their art. Many have used the self as a vehicle for social change, including early pioneers Buddy Holly, Little Richard, Ritchie Valens, Miles Davis, John Coltrane, B.B. King, and Muddy Waters. 1960s revolutionaries Bob Dylan, Joan Baez, Jerry Garcia, Janis Joplin, George Harrison, Jimi Hendrix, and Jim Morrison are Uranus/Sun people, as well as John and Michelle Phillips and Cass Elliot from the Mamas and the Papas. Bob Marley not only brought reggae to the globe, he was an active champion of civil rights. Alice Cooper spent a career trying to shock us and added to the discussion of what is or isn't acceptable in our culture.

Bruce Springsteen has become increasingly more politically active in his career, particularly as a voice for the underprivileged. Bob Geldof organized the Live Aid and Live 8 festivals. Peter Gabriel has been a leading contributor to progressive rock, and his famous song "Biko," which details the struggle of the activist Stephen Biko (another Uranus/Sun figure), is explicitly Uranian. Bono not only leads U2, but has become an international champion of progressive causes. Natalie Maines, lead singer of the Dixie Chicks, provoked great controversy by opposing George W. Bush and the Iraq invasion. Madonna has been making headlines for over 20 years as a catalyst for change in a variety of ways, and Eminem is a more recent example of a wave-maker. Sting, Ani DiFranco and Dave Matthews have also been socially active.

Some Uranus/Sun musicians do choose to limit their inventiveness to music and have been responsible for catalyzing movements, blending genres, and bringing about major shifts in sound; Roy Orbison, Cab Calloway, Dizzy Gillespie, Charlie Parker, Louis Armstrong, Loretta Lynn, Roger Daltrey, Eric Clapton, James Taylor, Robert Plant, Roger Waters, David Gilmour, and Eddie Van Halen are some examples.

Film speaks to audiences through metaphor, motifs and symbols. Many innovative movie directors have Sun/Uranus contacts. In addition to Kubrick, Orson Welles, Steven Spielberg, Oliver Stone, Roman Polanski, Ang Lee, Martin Scorsese, Brian De Palma, Terry Gilliam, Spike Lee, James L. Brooks, George Clooney, Paul Thomas Anderson, and Paul Haggis have all challenged audiences to examine social norms and assumptions about life. They have taken on controversial projects and have adhered strongly to their truth.

Perhaps more than any other figure, Bill Gates launched the computer revolution. With his massive wealth he is now a leading humanitarian. Donald Trump is another iconic figure whose entrepreneurial prowess has shaped the world. Rudy Giuliani became a symbol as "America's Mayor" after the 9/11 attacks. Walter Cronkite embodied the archetype of the newsman and was the most trusted anchor in the twentieth century. Leading feminists Simone de Beauvoir and Susan B. Anthony influenced public opinion through challenging the dominant social structure. Terri Schiavo catalyzed discussion about euthanasia and the reach of congressional intervention in her debilitated state. Ellen DeGeneres is one of the most visible women in entertainment to have declared her homosexuality.

The maverick, anti-establishment quality of Uranus is vividly seen in these people: militant civil rights leader Malcolm X, cult-leader David Koresh, former Iraqi dictator Saddam Hussein, Iranian President Mahmoud Ahmadinejad, Venezuelan President Hugo Chávez, South Korean dictator Kim Jong-il, Adolph Hitler (11 degree opposition), as well as legendary outlaw Billy the Kid. Each of them has made the self a symbol for larger causes. Black Panther co-founders Bobby Seale and

Huey Newton, as well as Honorary Prime Minister Eldridge Cleaver, are Uranus/Sun individuals. Steve McQueen donned an anti-hero persona and was dubbed "The King of Cool." Social commentator, comedian and former host of *Politically Incorrect* Bill Maher is another Sun/Uranus figure. Professional boxer Rubin "Hurricane" Carter was falsely imprisoned and became a symbol of liberation. Salman Rushdie stirred a firestorm of conflict in the Muslim community with his *Satanic Verses*, prompting calls for his death

Circus founders P.T. Barnum, James Anthony Bailey and Philip Astley ("father of the modern circus"), as well as Joseph Grimaldi, the most famous English clown in history, have Uranus/Sun aspects. Steve Irwin was active with environmental and animal advocacy, showing the humanitarian Uranian impulse. Dennis Kucinich has run long-shot Presidential campaigns based on progressive principles. Zeng Jinlian, the tallest woman in history at 8'2", certainly stood out. Perhaps the best example of Uranus/Sun in recent times is Sacha Baron Cohen, whose portrayal of *Borat* is shocking and anti-establishment, and exposed underlying prejudices within society.

Uranus/Moon – Emotional Liberation

The Moon concerns the emotional unconscious within the soul, what has been absorbed and assimilated through the spiritual journey. It relates to fundamental needs and how the soul has been nurtured, and is tenacious about attaining security. Whereas the Moon is soft and vulnerable, Uranus is startling and edgy. Those with the Moon in major aspect to Uranus have likely experienced jolts to the emotional system, or have a profound inner need for progressive individuation.

The Moon is unconscious and resides in darkness, and triggers instinctual, often irrational responses. The Moon draws us back to the past, to how we have been impacted by our experiences. With Uranus/Moon contacts, the spiritual history has been marked by Uranian themes, including trauma or other jarring events, a lack of having strong familial roots as seen in divorce and estrangements, or a difficulty attaining continuity with nurturance. There could be emotional alienation or isolation, themes of being out of touch with the basic structure of primal needs. The severity of such conditions is modified by house and sign placements and the nature of the aspect connecting Uranus to the Moon.

Within the context of the present lifetime, the Uranus/Moon person often exhibits a heightened attunement to emotional connection. Functioning well, this leads to breakthroughs that help repair the buried emotional fragmentation. Then, the Uranus/Moon individual can transform the Uranian power absorbed and channel it for both personal and collectively-oriented progress. Without the healing of emotional bonds, the Uranus/Moon individual is prone to ungrounded, frantic, sometimes socially unacceptable behavior driven by the emotional disorganization. Forming successful attachments is of primary concern for Uranus/Moon people.

An example of the Uranus/Moon complex is seen with Princess Diana, who battled an eating disorder, substantial emotional turmoil and a vacant marriage that resulted in divorce—all on her path toward finding her truth. She became an advocate for healing trauma with her charitable work, as seen in her campaign to assist landmine victims. She also brought progressive change to the English Monarchy, challenging the orthodoxy and conventions of royal protocol. Diana died in a shocking way and left a legacy of being an emotional awakener to those she touched.

Other Uranus/Moon women have become symbols of the progressive feminine. Examples in politics include Golda Meir, Hillary Clinton, Geraldine Ferraro, Nancy Pelosi, and Condoleezza Rice. Benazir Bhutto of Pakistan was the first woman to lead an Islamic state. Sirimavo Bandaranaike of Sri Lanka was the world's first female Prime Minister, while Ellen Johnson-Sirleaf of Liberia was the first African female to be a head of state. Examples in entertainment include Mae West, Debbie Allen, Geena Davis, Helen Mirren, and Candice Bergen. Examples in art include Mary Cassatt and Grandma Moses.

Examples in music include Ella Fitzgerald, Patti Smith, Tracy Chapman, k.d. lang, Aimee Mann, Beth Orton, and Alanis Morissette. Examples in poetry include Maya Angelou and Emily Dickinson. Examples in journalism include Lesley Stahl and Katie Couric. Examples in feminist activism include Robin Morgan and Margaret Sanger. An example in psychology is Elisabeth Kubler-Ross, while Marie Curie is a scientific example. Examples in astrology include Liz Greene, Tracy Marks, and Demetra George. Valentina Tereshkova was the first woman to fly in space. Gertrude Ederle was the first woman to swim the English Channel. Rosa Parks refused to accept discrimination and helped launch the Civil Rights movement. Mother Teresa has healed many hearts as the world's greatest humanitarian. All of these women have been awakeners who challenge their chosen fields to incorporate greater sensitivity and depth by aligning with their inner truth.

Uranus/Moon contacts sometimes correlate with precociousness and childhood brilliance. Wolfgang Mozart began composing music at a very early age and is considered an eccentric for his wild behaviors. Shirley Temple had an active career by the age of five. Many of her early films had the Uranus/Moon storyline of her losing one or both of her parents. She was also the first major celebrity to reveal she had breast cancer (Uranus/Moon) to the public. Actress Jodie Foster's prolific career began with childhood fame. Her early biography has the Uranus/Moon theme of emotional estrangement because her father left the family before she was born. Ron Howard is another child star (*The Andy Griffith Show, Happy Days*) with a Uranus/Moon aspect, and went on to direct several movies consistent with this combination (*Splash, Parenthood, Ransom, A Beautiful Mind, The Missing*). JK Rowling has this contact, and her *Harry Potter* is a childhood (Moon) prodigy (Uranus). Daniel Radcliffe, who portrays Harry in the movies, shares it as well. Neil Patrick Harris played a child doctor in the TV show *Doogie Howser, M.D.* Jamie Lee Curtis has written children's books (Moon) that contain messages of tolerating differences (Uranus), while Jim Henson's *Muppets* brought endless wonder to children.

Jean Piaget was a precocious child before becoming a world-renowned expert on childhood cognition. John Stuart Mill was a brilliant young scholar pushed to a nervous breakdown by the age of 21. He later wrote that he didn't get to experience normal emotional development; his most notable academic contribution has to do with the idea of liberty. Figure skating champion Michelle Kwan began skating at age five, and her family sold their house (Uranus/Moon) to pay for rink time. Venus Williams became a famous tennis player at 14, pushed by her controversial father who wanted a better life for his daughter. As a youngster, tennis champion Roger Federer was very emotional on the court and allegedly threw many tantrums. He grew to have composure, but does emote substantially after winning big matches. Martina Navratilova attained success as a teenager, defected from her homeland (the former Czechoslovakia) at age 18, faced rejection from her parents because of her sexual orientation, and went on to be a champion for children's causes. John McEnroe was notorious for outrageous tantrums on the court. Tracy Austin also reached tennis superstardom at an early age.

Many child stars with emotionally unstable biographies have Uranus/Moon aspects. At age 10, Tatum O'Neal became the youngest person ever to win an Oscar. There was divorce and sexual and emotional abuse in her childhood, as well as inappropriate exposure to illegal drugs. She married the emotionally volatile John McEnroe, which also ended in divorce. Dana Plato (*Diff'rent Strokes*) never adjusted to adulthood after her childhood stardom. She had many personal problems and run-ins with the law and died of a drug overdose in her early thirties. Danny Bonaduce (*The Partridge Family*) describes his upbringing as dysfunctional, with physical and emotional abuse from his father. He went through periods of homelessness and drug addiction, and was arrested for beating up a transvestite prostitute. Maureen McCormick (*The Brady Bunch*) disclosed an eating disorder and addiction to cocaine.

Loretta Lynn grew up poor with a house full of siblings. She got married at 13, had four children by age 17, and was a grandmother at 29. Her marriage was abusive, and her husband Doolittle even left her while she was giving birth (Uranus/Moon). Famous Uranus/Moon songs she has penned are about divorce, losing virginity at a young age, and the liberation women experience through use of the birth control pill. Sissy Spacek, who portrayed Lynn in *The Coal Miner's Daughter,* also has a Uranus/Moon aspect. Another manifestation of Uranus/Moon is a bizarre fascination with childhood themes, as seen with John Mark Karr, who falsely claimed to have murdered JonBenet Ramsey, and Paul Reubens, who plays *Pee Wee Herman* and was arrested for public masturbation. Record producer and rapper R. Kelly has been implicated in child pornography and sex with minors.

Carl Jung and Fritz Perls used their Uranus/Moon contacts to be liberators of the unconscious. Deepak Chopra and astrologer Dane Rudhyar directed their Uranus/Moon combinations toward understanding the transpersonal and thereby finding emotional breakthroughs. Masaru Emoto's work addresses the connection between water and emotional energy, bringing a new understanding (Uranus) to feeling states (Moon). Nelson Mandela and The Dalai Lama had to deal with great instability (Uranus) in their respective homelands (Moon) and became agents for emotional change.

Milos Forman faced extreme early-childhood turbulence as an orphan when his parents died at Auschwitz. He later directed *One Flew Over the Cuckoo's Nest,* which also portrays great emotional disorganization and alienation. Dustin Hoffman has played characters who confront emotional obstacles (*Rain Main, Midnight Cowboy*) and also showed his feminine side in *Tootsie*. Surrealistic artist Salvador Dali was a world-class eccentric who likely suffered from mental illness. He portrayed the unconscious (Moon) in shocking ways (Uranus) through his art. Ray Charles, James Brown, John Lennon, Carlos Santana, Syd Barrett, Richie Havens, Tom Waits, Frank Zappa, Eminem, and Elliot Smith are other Uranus/Moon musicians who struggled with adverse situations in the early home life, or emotional turmoil or trauma. LeBron James dealt with a fatherless childhood and poor conditions and grew to super-stardom in basketball. Comedian Chris Rock created a TV show called *Everybody Hates Chris* about the challenges of his upbringing.

Other celebrities and notorious people with this combination include Evel Knievel, with his rebellious need for danger, and Timothy Leary, who promoted excessive drug use. Serial killers Charles Manson, Ted Bundy, and Aileen Wuornos have Uranus/Moon contacts, as well as Amy Fisher, the "Long Island Lolita," who shot her lover's wife. O.J. Simpson and Mike Tyson have extremely turbulent emotional sides filled with jealousy and rage, which have led to criminal behavior. Glenn Close portrayed such a character in *Fatal Attraction*. John Wilkes Booth and Lee Harvey Oswald assassinated Presidents (Lincoln and Kennedy respectively) and John Hinckley gave President Reagan his best shot and missed his heart by millimeters. Timothy McVeigh attacked his homeland in the Oklahoma City bombing of 1995. Hermann Göring was a top Nazi official who was convicted for crimes against humanity and committed suicide.

Charles Lindbergh is famous for having his child (Moon) abducted (Uranus). John F. Kennedy Jr. and John Belushi had traumatic (Uranus) early (Moon) deaths. Barack Obama comes from a mixed race upbringing without being firmly rooted to one place. He experimented with drugs, delinquency and had an absentee father. All of the Uranus/Moon people mentioned have an urge to reinvent the self and find emotional liberation, or have struggled mightily in finding satisfaction.

Uranus/Mercury – Intellectual Ingenuity

More than any other planet, Uranus has an affinity with Mercury because both are objective and mental energies. The difference between the two is that Mercury relates to the individual mind, while Uranus concerns the collective or universal mind. When these planets are in aspect, an individual's thought processes are wired into the progressive intelligence of nature. At best, this manifests in a spokesperson for evolutionary advancement—downloading futuristic ideas that challenge humanity to grow. A less optimal response results in erratic cognition, absurd ideas and intellectual estrangement from others. In this case, Uranus is distorted by personal struggles, and may contribute to instability.

Within the spiritual history, the soul that carries Uranus/Mercury may not have actualized intellectual talents, and realizing breakthroughs are relevant now. There may have been intellectual conformity, appeasement, laziness or the condition of being prone to brainwashing of some form. Another situation is the soul who has been an original thinker, though misguided or endlessly ruminative. The Uranus/Mercury individual is learning to (re)align with his or her own thought processes in novel ways and thereby teach others about phenomenal and inspired cognitive territory.

Uranus/Mercury is as quick as lightning in receiving information. The bolts of cognitive stimulation are so exciting that some with this combination are seen as "mad scientists." The Doc Brown character in the *Back to the Future* film series is an example of this archetype. (Incidentally, Christopher Lloyd, who depicts the character, does have this planetary combination). There is a risk of becoming addicted to this electrifying process, whereby sleep, normal socialization and other concerns of the mundane world are not attended to. The Uranus/Mercury individual may become isolated in his or her own intellectual world. Nevertheless, the evolutionary intent of having this aspect is realizing genius and assisting the forward movement of humanity.

Uranus takes on lively trickster energy when paired with Mercury. Some manifestations are the use of puns, paradox, striking words, invented languages, satire, double meanings, metaphors, and associations that are perplexing. This linguistic dexterity is matched by wild cognition. Uranus/Mercury finds ways to bend logic and discover the interconnections of the world's phenomena—for example, by linking astrology to physics, or weather patterns to psychology. These strange or unheard of associations often seem like a waste of time to more conventional thinkers, but the Uranus/Mercury individual is continually reinforced by the freshness of such mental excursions. In a world where there is "nothing new under the Sun," Uranus/Mercury is thrilled by its original thinking.

Uranus/Mercury is classically liberal—it shakes up traditional or conservative paradigms with its insistence on advancement. Some of its virtues are holism, inclusion, vision, freedom, and liberty. Some with this combination are James Madison ("Father of the Constitution"), Thomas Jefferson (author of the *Declaration of Independence*), Benjamin Franklin, Abraham Lincoln, Charles Darwin, Eleanor Roosevelt, John F. Kennedy, Lyndon Johnson, Thurgood Marshall, and Al Gore. Patrick Henry said it best with his famous words, "Give me liberty or give me death." Some modern commentators and figures with this combination are Al Franken, Jon Stewart, Phil Donahue, Steven Colbert, and Bill Maher (Mercury in Aquarius, widely opposed Uranus—just over 10 degrees). Progressive politician Ann Richards once quipped that George H.W. Bush was born with a "silver foot in his mouth," which illustrates her views and knack for wordplay. Al Sharpton is another outspoken politician known for colorful quotes.

Examples of comedic and improvisational use of Uranus/Mercury (often with an emphasis on language) are seen in Charlie Chaplin, George Burns, Gracie Allen, George Carlin, Mel Brooks, Howard Stern, Don Imus, Buck Henry, Lily Tomlin, Richard Pryor, Rodney Dangerfield, Dennis Miller, Howie Mandel, Billy Crystal, Martin Short, Jane Curtain, Jerry Seinfeld (8.5 degree square), Sam Kinison, Whoopi Goldberg, Nick DiPaolo, Joan Rivers, Rich Hall, David Letterman, Kevin Nealon, Phil Hartman, Jon Lovitz, Adam Sandler, Molly Shannon, Paula Poundstone, Kathy Griffin, Janeane Garofalo, Wanda Sykes, Dane Cook, *Saturday Night Live* creator Lorne Michaels, creator of *The Simpsons* Matt Groening, offbeat theatrical screenwriter Joel Coen, and parody singer Weird Al Yankovic. Five out of six Monty Python comedy troupe members—John Cleese, Graham Chapman, Eric Idle, Terry Jones, and Michael Palin—have Uranus/Mercury aspects. As for the Marx Brothers, Zeppo, Gummo and Chico Marx have Uranus/Mercury contacts. Harpo never spoke during the performances but frequently interrupted with physical comedy (Uranus/Mars) while Groucho was the creative visionary (Uranus/Jupiter).

Some examples of innovative and influential writers are Niccolò Machiavelli, James Fennimore Cooper, Robert Southey, Agatha Christie, George Sand, Johann Wolfgang von Goethe, Mark Twain, Charles Dickens, George Eliot (Mary Ann Evans), Jane Austen, Rudyard Kipling, Samuel Beckett, Franz Kafka, Marcel Proust, John Steinbeck, T.S. Eliot, Hunter S. Thompson, Gabriel García Márquez, Toni Morrison, Chaim Potok, Truman Capote, Kurt Vonnegut, Anthony Burgess, e.e. cummings, William Faulkner, Jean-Paul Sartre, Oscar Wilde, Antoine de Saint-Exupéry, and Sinclair Lewis who said, "When fascism comes to America, it will be wrapped in the flag and carrying a cross." Science-fiction writers Ursula LeGuin, Stanley G. Weinbaum, Hugo Gernsback, and Douglas Adams have Uranus/Mercury contacts, as well as Abraham Heschel, Kahlil Gibran, Paulo Coelho, Jane Roberts, Neale Donald Walsch, and Rabbi Zalman Schachter-Shalomi, who are noted for bridging the personal mind (Mercury) with a larger overview of spiritual phenomena (Uranus). The following songwriters all have Uranus/Mercury aspects: Stephen Foster, Smokey Robinson, Harry Belafonte, Neil Young, Roger Waters, Jim Croce, Patti Smith, Don McLean, Jimmy Buffet, Joan Armatrading, Todd Rundgren, Willie Nelson, James Taylor, Carole King, Randy Newman, Bonnie Raitt, Emmylou Harris, Suzanne Vega, Norah Jones, Beth Orton, and Ryan Adams.

Uranus/Mercury is associated with ground-breaking journalism and investigative reporting. H.L. Mencken, Edward R. Murrow, Howard K. Smith, Frank Reynolds, John Chancellor, Robert Trout, Bob Woodward, Carl Bernstein, Ben Bradlee, Mike Wallace, Robert MacNeil, Ted Koppel, Diane Sawyer, Tom Brokaw, Brian Williams, Chris Matthews, Mark Shields, Clarence Page, Maureen Dowd, Gwen Ifill, and Fareed Zakaria all have these planets in major aspect. Michael Moore has been an outspoken critic, author and documentary filmmaker stirring the ire of many conservative institutions. Joseph Wilson questioned the Bush Administration's rationale for invading Iraq, which led to his wife (Valerie Plame) being outed as a CIA operative. Mark "Deep Throat" Felt leaked confidential information to reporters, which helped bring about the Watergate scandal and the eventual resignation of President Nixon. Journalist Tariq Ali is outspoken against imperialistic regimes and the abuses of tyranny. Ward Churchill ignited a firestorm when he declared that 9/11 victims were "little Eichmanns."

Intellectual trailblazers and geniuses with Uranus/Mercury aspects found in the field of science include Galileo Galilei, Max Planck, Niels Bohr, Johannes Kepler, Stephen Hawking, Linus Pauling, James Lovelock, Carl Sagan, and Leonard Susskind. Examples in mathematics include Leonhard Euler, David Hilbert, and Srinivasa Ramanujan. Examples in philosophy include Noam Chomsky, Thomas Kuhn, David Hume, Bertrand Russell, Georg Hegel, Friedrich Nietzsche, and Jürgen Habermas. Examples in economics include Adam Smith, David Ricardo, John Maynard Keynes, Carl Menger, Arthur Cecil Pigou, Robert Lucas Jr., and Alan Greenspan. Examples in psychology include Sigmund Freud, Otto Rank, Wilhelm Reich, Hans Eysenck, Fritz Perls, James Hillman, William James, Virginia Satir, and Stanislav Grof. Examples in astrology include C.E.O. Carter, Isabel Hickey, Reinhold Ebertin, Jeff Mayo, Bruno Huber, Evangeline Adams, Noel Tyl, Stephen Arroyo, Ray Merriman, Gloria Star, Glenn Perry, and Robert Blaschke. Chess champions with this combination include Tigran Petrosian, Bobby Fischer, Anatoly Karpov, Garry Kasparov, Veselin Topalov, and Viswanathan Anand.

Uranus/Mercury is able to integrate the larger collective intelligence into smaller projects, details and finite ideas. It correlates with original inventions that bring the future to the present. Some examples of inventors with this combination are John Logie Baird (television), Donát Bánki (carburetor), Trevor Baylis (wind-up radio), Karl Benz (gas-powered automobile),

Ladislao José Biro (ballpoint pen), Wallace Carothers (nylon), Christopher Cockerell (hovercraft), Jacques-Yves Cousteau (aqualung and the Nikonos underwater camera), Nicolas-Joseph Cugnot (automobile), Georges Claude (neon lamp), George Eastman (film-roll), Douglas Engelbart (computer mouse), Ole Evinrude (outboard motor), James Fergason (liquid crystal display), Reginald Fessenden (two-way radio), Benjamin Franklin (pointed lightning rod conductor and bifocal glasses), William Friese-Greene (cinematography), Michael Faraday (rubber balloon and electric transformer), Christiaan Huygens (pendulum clock), Karl Jatho (aeroplane), Dean Kamen (*Segway* scooter), Willem Kolff (kidney hemodialysis machine), Sergei Lebedev (synthetic rubber), René Laënnec (stethoscope), Guglielmo Marconi (radio), Narcís Monturiol i Estarriol (submarine), Garrett Morgan (gas mask and traffic signal), William Murdoch (gas lighting), Yoshiro Nakamatsu (Floppy disk and a world-record claim of over 3000 inventions), Joseph Nicephore Niépce (photography), George Pullman (sleep wagon), Wilhelm Conrad Röntgen (X-ray machine), Charles Richter (Richter magnitude scale), Hassan Kamel Al-Sabbah (solar power and cathode ray tube), Adolphe Sax (Saxophone), David Schwarz (rigid ship, later called the Zeppelin), William Shockley (co-inventor of transistor), Joseph Swan (incandescent light bulb), Marc Seguin (wire-cable suspension bridge and the tubular steam-engine boiler), Percy Spencer (microwave oven), George Stephenson (steam locomotive), Edward Teller (hydrogen bomb), Kálmán Tihanyi (cathode ray tube and iconoscope), Robert Watson-Watt (first workable radar system), Eli Whitney (cotton gin), and Paul Winchell (artificial heart).

Allesandro Volta, who developed the electric battery, has Uranus conjoined Mercury in electric Aquarius! Also note that inventor Thomas Edison and intellectual visionary Jules Verne both had Mercury in Aquarius, so Uranus was the ruler. John Hadley invented the sextant, which enables the user to figure out the elevation of celestial objects in relation to the horizon. This breakthrough paved the way for significant advances in astrological understanding. “Rube Goldberg machines” are humorous, complicated, hi-tech devices designed to perform routine or simple tasks. Goldberg has Uranus/Mercury, as well as Nick Park, who hilariously incorporates such machines in his *Wallace & Gromit* cartoon franchise.

Other notable Uranus/Mercury people include witty political cartoonist Herb Block, actor Leonard Nimoy—famous for his cool brilliance as *Star Trek's* "Spock," *Jeopardy* quizmaster Alex Trebek, and the show's creator, Merv Griffin. Hugh Hefner published *Playboy,* which broke the social conventions of the day and began the era of printed pornography. Simone de Beauvoir spoke out for women's rights. Joseph Campbell is considered the foremost expert and commentator on mythology. Alfred Hitchcock's movies are famous for clever plot twists and surprises. Arthur Koestler is a multidisciplinary thinker. His career included several novels, some of which employ Uranian devices such as satire; he wrote about science, psychology and human development, philosophy, politics, mysticism, and the paranormal, and he was multilingual.

Uranus/Venus – Liberated Arts and Lifestyles

Venus concerns artistic and social endeavors. It is engaging with an eye towards sophistication. The paring of Uranus with Venus is wild, at times outrageous. The irreverent and untamed quality of Uranus mixes with Venus to produce extremely creative and often offbeat works of personal expression. Whether in artistic or social realms, this combination tends to be brightly colored and highly original.

From an evolutionary perspective, souls with Uranus in aspect to Venus have likely not been able to express their truth regarding style, artistry or sensuality, or within relationships. Further growth is achieved by aligning with who they really are, even if society or other forces disapprove. Having these planets in aspect does not predict that an individual will have an alternative relationship or lifestyle. Many times one's authentic truth is *not* erratic. However, since there is so much experimental energy with Uranus, there is potential to try out differing ways of relating (Venus) in order to learn of oneself through the synergy of personal connections. When functioning poorly, Uranus/Venus is responsible for some of the wildest fetishes and proclivities imaginable.

Many with Uranus/Venus contacts do insist upon unconventional relationships. Any pairing that is counter to societal norms qualifies: significant age or cultural differences between the partners, "open" relationships, homosexuality, and polygamy are some examples. Uranus infuses Venus with the spirit of awakening. Not only do the members of such pairings learn much through these associations, society itself is challenged to grow and redefine what it means to connect intimately. Uranus/Venus is also present for those with many marriages, divorces, and other unexpected occurrences with a partner.

Ellen DeGeneres led the way for greater tolerance of homosexuality by "coming out" on her television program. This echoed Billie Jean King's disclosure a couple of decades earlier. Elizabeth Taylor, Joan Crawford and Judy Garland are famous for their many marriages, and Warren Beatty is known as an A-list womanizer. Freddie Mercury practiced bisexuality and polyamory. Actor and politician Fred Thompson married a woman 25 years his junior. Star running back Travis Henry has nine children, all from different mothers. In her diary, Anaïs Nin detailed her colorful relationship history and intimate longings for unconventional practices. Jesse Jackson was implicated in adultery, and Woody Allen chose his teenage step-daughter to have an affair with. Both Gary Hart and Donna Rice have Uranus in aspect to Venus. Their rule-breaking relationship behavior sabotaged his Presidential candidacy. Congressman Mark Foley illegally pursued underage men.

Other Uranus/Venus behavior is witnessed in J. Edgar Hoover, with his notorious cross-dressing. Sharon Stone became a controversial figure for her famous "leg-crossing" scene in *Basic Instinct*. Senator Larry Craig pled guilty to lewd conduct in a men's restroom, allegedly soliciting strangers for sex. Eddie Murphy was caught with a transvestite, and Jeffrey Dahmer took his eccentric pedophiliac preferences into dark and criminal territory. Mark David Chapman was obsessed with John Lennon, another Uranus/Venus individual, who also had an unconventional relationship history. Linda Lovelace is an example in pornography. Dr. Ruth Westheimer challenges couples to break through to new levels of togetherness. Andy Kauffman took on perplexing comedic personas, and it was difficult to distinguish when he was in character. Mel Blanc was "The Man of a Thousand Voices"—he brought life to many cartoon characters that have become icons in American culture.

Venus in aspect to Uranus becomes amped-up. The potential with this contact is to be a wizard of artistic skill and technique, and to use the arts as a vehicle for social reform. Many of the ground-breaking figures in music have this aspect accentuated. Guitar innovators Les Paul and Leo Fender both have this aspect, as well as virtuosos T-Bone Walker, Andres Segovia, Chet Atkins, John Mayall, Jimmy Page, Steve Howe, Alex Lifeson, Robert Fripp, Ry Cooder, Leo Kottke, and Stevie Ray Vaughan. Keith Moon and Neil Peart revolutionized the drums, while Keith Emerson did the same for keyboards. Prince and Steve Winwood are famous for their proficiency at many instruments, and David Byrne was the leader of the Talking Heads' innovative sound. Stevie Wonder is considered a musical genius, one who revolutionized sound and recording technique. Frank Zappa is considered a brilliant musician and iconoclastic (Uranus) social (Venus) commentator. Legendary disc jockey Alan Freed, who coined the term "rock and roll," also has a Uranus/Venus aspect.

Jimi Hendrix is widely considered the most ingenious guitarist in rock history. His music also blended many genres, which brought a diversity of people together. Elvis Presley also bridged genres and peoples—his controversial hip thrusting challenged the accepted social norms of his day. Chubby Checker healed racial divides by getting everyone to "Twist," while Jerry Lee Lewis did his part to help liberate puritanical repression through his infectious energy. (He also did have a controversial relationship with his very young cousin.) Louis Armstrong and Duke Ellington helped bring jazz to a wide audience and contributed to the developing improvisational nature of the genre. Johnny Cash, Patsy Cline and Merle Haggard brought country to a wider audience—and Aretha Franklin did the same for gospel, Sade for soul, Harry Belafonte for calypso and Placido Domingo for opera.

Paul Simon led the folk rock sound of the 1960s and is lauded for his musical purity. Brian Wilson is the foremost innovator of surf music. Kurt Cobain led the "grunge rock" revolution in the 1990s. This movement aimed to get back to the substance of music in reaction to the stylistic excesses of the previous decades. Bonnie Raitt, Tori Amos, Sarah McLachlan, Amy Ray, Joan Osborne, and Jewel are talented musicians who also embody artistic (Venus) authenticity (Uranus), and became representative of modern feminine empowerment. Melissa Etheridge is a progressive artist who used her fame to help bring acceptance to homosexuality. Cat Stevens, Michael Franti, Ben Harper, and Billy Bragg sing their messages of freedom, peace and social inclusiveness—picking up where Uranus/Venus musical trailblazer John Lennon left off. Cyndi Lauper, Christina Aguilera, and Alanis Morissette are noted for their eccentricity or challenging "in-your-face" style. Mick Jagger and Cher embody many facets of Uranus/Venus—a progressive musical presence, colorful relationship history and provocative demeanor. Wavy Gravy, the "official clown of the Grateful Dead," embodies the wild, irreverent potentials of this combination.

Another facet of Uranus/Venus is style. Grace Slick's hypnotic presence is symbolic of the 1960s. In the 1970s, Gene Simmons became unrecognizable in his wild make-up in KISS, which promoted style and pyrotechnics as much as music. Annie Lennox and Adam Ant incorporated androgyny to their style, and are representative of the experimentation in the 1980s. Michael Jackson is a breakthrough figure in music and is notorious for the dramatic changes (Uranus) in his appearance (Venus). Joan Rivers is also famous for undergoing plastic surgery.

Venus is associated with beauty, what we find to be most pleasing. It has prominence in models and celebrities who have initiated new trends. In the 1950s, Bettie Page brought the pin-up to the masses, while portraying bondage with a smile. This brought controversy and congressional hearings. Jayne Mansfield helped usher in the age of the sex symbol as a pioneering "blonde bombshell," and her look helped define the decade. Twiggy and Edie Sedgwick are emblematic of the 1960s, Lynda Carter and Farrah Fawcett of the 1970s, Elle Macpherson, Heather Locklear, and Iman of the 1980s, while Naomi Campbell, Tyra Banks, Heidi Klum, Kate Moss (Uranus in Libra widely square Venus in Aquarius—10 degrees and in mutual reception), Uma Thurman, Angelina Jolie, and Lindsay Lohan encapsulate trends in the 1990s and today.

In the visual arts, Venus/Uranus figures have been at the forefront of movements. Leonardo da Vinci, Rembrandt van Rijn, Claude Monet, Caravaggio, Francisco de Goya, J.M.W. Turner, Auguste Rodin, Mark Rothko, Salvador Dali, Henri de Toulouse-Lautrec, and Georgia O'Keefe all have this combination, as well as photographer Ansel Adams. Hermann Rorschach developed a psychological tool using inkblots—an artistic innovation (Venus) designed to trigger awakening (Uranus). Modern environmental artists Christo and Jean-Claude both have Uranus/Venus. They use the Earth as their canvas and have generated much controversy for their boundary-breaking projects. Alex Grey is a contemporary artist with a transpersonal focus who blends many genres with his "syncretic" art. Eve Ensler created the *Vagina Monologues*, which promotes the beauty (Venus) of an area usually "out of bounds" (Uranus).

Comic strips blend visual art (Venus) with wit, satire, wry observations, and unusual comic situations that often take place in made-up worlds or with talking animals (Uranus). Many of the leading comic strips have been created by Uranus/Venus individuals: Jim Davis (*Garfield*), Gary Larson (*The Far Side*), Bill Watterson (*Calvin & Hobbes*), Garry Trudeau (*Doonesbury*), Bob Montana (*Archie Comics*), Mort Walker (*Beatle Bailey* and *Hi and Lois*), Johnny Hart (*B.C.* and *The Wizard of Id*), Al Capp (*Li'l Abner*), and Chic Young (*Blondie*). Charles Schulz (*Peanuts*) has a Uranus/Venus square of 8.5 degrees.

Uranus/Venus aims to bring people together and transcend cultural, racial, economic, or other differences. The famous abolitionist Frederick Douglass has this combination, as well as Booker T. Washington, who advocated harmony and collaboration among the races. W. E. B. Du Bois was a leading educator, activist and civil rights leader in the early part of the twentieth century. Marcus Garvey founded the Universal Negro Improvement Association and African Communities League. Nelson Mandela was imprisoned for his race, then later presided over shifting race relations in South Africa. Arthur Ashe was instrumental in bridging race relations in athletics and also became a leading advocate of AIDS research and awareness. Medgar Evers worked for racial integration for the NAACP. Jackie Robinson broke the color line in baseball, forever changing race relations in athletics, and Thurgood Marshall broke the color line of the Supreme Court. Rosa Parks was pivotal in launching the modern Civil Rights movement, and the murder of Emmett Till galvanized momentum for the cause. Paul Rusesabagina (the hotel manager portrayed in *Hotel Rwanda*) brought people together and helped heal ethnic tensions during conditions of genocide. Mahatma Gandhi sought to liberate his people from oppression and was a leading voice of non-violent togetherness. Jane Goodall helped bridge the gap between humans and other primates through her groundbreaking work on animal social relations.

Venus does have associations with money, and Uranus/Venus aspects do appear in some notable financial pioneers, including billionaires Warren Buffet, Ross Perot, and Lee Iacocca. Sam Walton is the co-founder of Wal-Mart and patriarch of the richest family in the world. His widow, Helen, also has a Uranus/Venus aspect, and is still among the richest people on the planet. Joe Girard holds the Guinness record (Uranus) for sales (Venus). Uranus/Venus can also break financial rules. Criminal investors Ivan Boesky and Michael Milken, and corporate criminals Dennis Kozlowski (Tyco), Jeffrey Skilling (Enron), and Bernard Ebbers (WorldCom) share this combination. Televangelist Jim Bakker was implicated in both a sex scandal and accounting fraud. Rapper MC Hammer amassed millions then squandered his money and filed for bankruptcy.

Other Uranus/Venus individuals include Robert Redford, a creative actor and director willing to take on progressive projects. He founded the Sundance Festival, which promotes independent (Uranus) art (Venus), and he's also a symbol of an attractive ideal to many. Tim Burton and Ethan Coen make wacky, original films, while Darren Aronofsky and M. Knight Shyamalan also display remarkable theatrical creativity in their works, which often include the transpersonal. The literary works of Stephen King and JK Rowling are highly original. They bring the extraordinary to vivid animation and depict situations and characters that exist out of the mainstream—often outside the boundary of what we think is possible. Linda Blair famously portrayed a possessed girl in *The Exorcist*—a movie that has become legendary in the horror genre.

Bessie Smith, Milton Berle, Gracie Allen, Buster Keaton, Red Skelton, Kate Smith, and Henny Youngman are all entertainment personalities who got their start in vaudeville, and Lucille Ball and Jackie Gleason brought a similar spirit to television. Circus founders Charles Ringling, P.T. Barnum and James Anthony Bailey (8 degree 15 minute trine) brought together a most diverse assemblage of characters. Josephine Baker, nicknamed "The Black Venus," was involved with dance, singing, acting, civil rights, and was married six times. Liberace embodies many facets of Uranus/Venus. He was flamboyant and musically eclectic, and wore his alternative lifestyle with pride.

Uranus/Mars – Empowered Behavior

Mars is behavioral—how we assert our free will and act in accordance with our passions. Whereas the Sun is one's essence, Mars directs energy outwards. It is necessarily selfish as it champions survival and ensures that needs get met. Its hot-blooded nature is seen within competitive athletics or in sexual desire. The appetites of Mars are primal, and its behavior is often unrefined.

Uranus in aspect to Mars indicates that progressive individuation is linked to this planet of desire and self-alignment. Both of these planets want to be true to the self. In the soul's past may be the condition where behavior didn't or couldn't realize self-alignment. Trauma, bodily disability or the surrendering of freedom are a few examples. Those who fall in line with societal norms or family expectations, or who blindly follow a religious/philosophical doctrine may not be truly living a life on their terms. In this case, having Uranus in aspect to Mars positions the soul to grow into its passions. The soul may also have experienced involvement with unexpected or shocking (Uranus) aggressive or sexual (Mars) circumstances, which removed the Martial function from conscious usage.

Since Mars is so immediate and behavioral, those with this aspect behave in noticeably Uranian ways. Their bodily movements and the decisions they make can be impulsive and ungrounded. Through the process of maturation, they can refine and craft their behavior to be exciting, awakening and even comedic. All of the Three Stooges (Larry, Moe and Curley) have these planets in aspect, as well as Harpo Marx, Marcel Marceau, Jerry Lewis, Peter Sellers, Steve Martin, Michael Richards (Kramer on *Seinfeld*), Robin Williams, Martin Short, Ben Stiller, Tracey Ullman, Roberto Benigni, and Mike Myers—all geniuses at physical comedy. Harry Houdini's ability to defy the laws (Uranus) of physical restraint and amaze through his dexterity is legendary. Fred Astaire's dance innovation broke new ground in movement. Debbie Allen is a leading dance choreographer. The erratic quality of Uranus could also manifest as physical problems, as seen in Michael J. Fox's battle with Parkinson's Disease.

Many athletes, particularly those who break (Uranus) records, have Uranus and Mars in major aspect. Jackie Robinson, Bruce Jenner, Carl Lewis, Wilt Chamberlain, Eric Heiden, Pete Sampras, Andre Agassi, Rod Laver, Babe Ruth, Reggie Jackson, Willie Mays, Goose Gossage, Joe Louis, Joe Frazier, and Lance

Armstrong all possess extraordinary talent and seem to have bursts of energy that propel them to victory. Roger Bannister was the first to run a four-minute mile. The first conquerors of Mount Everest, Edmund Hillary and Tenzing Norgay, both have this combination. Nadia Comaneci was the first gymnast to receive a perfect "10" for her performance. With his proficiency at many sports, Jim Thorpe is considered by many to be the greatest athlete who has ever lived.

Herschel Walker is an exceptionally talented athlete who also displayed remarkable courage in disclosing his mental illness. David Eckstein, 5'7" baseball player, surmounted long odds in making it to the major leagues, then became the MVP of a World Series. Glenn Burke was the first openly gay Major League baseball player, and is credited as the first to give a "high-five," an innovation (Uranus) that changed athletics (Mars). Billie Jean King is another record-setting athlete who also challenged organized sports to be tolerant of sexual (Mars) differences. Her publicized triumph of Bobby Riggs, in the "battle of the sexes," also fits this archetypal combination. Andre the Giant is literally and figuratively a massive figure in the world of wrestling. The iconoclastic sports announcer Howard Cosell is also a Uranus/Mars person.

Arnold Schwarzenegger and Jesse Ventura are ultra-masculine figures with leadership in bodybuilding (Schwarzenegger), wrestling (Ventura), entertainment, and politics—both became unlikely Governors. Uranus/Mars may break the rules (by doping, for instance) for competitive advantage. Schwarzenegger and Ventura have acknowledged using steroids, and the following athletes have similarly admitted to or have been caught doping in some form: baseball players Jose Canseco, Andy Pettitte, Miguel Tejada, Kevin Brown, Gary Sheffield, Jose Guillen, Paul Lo Duca, John Rocker, Jay Gibbons, Benito Santiago, Glenallen Hill, Guillermo Mota, Ryan Franklin, and Félix Heredia; track star Marion Jones; sprinters Ben Johnson, Tim Montgomery and Dennis Mitchell; cyclists Floyd Landis, Ivan Basso, Jan Ullrich, and Stefano Garzelli; discus thrower Natalya Sadova; and shot putters Georg Andersen, Lars

Arvid Nilsen, Mike Stulce, and Larisa Peleshenko. Carl Myerscough and his wife Melissa are both professional track and field competitors who were caught doping and suspended. Sammy Sosa is a record-breaking slugger who was caught using a corked bat and is widely suspected of using steroids.

Military leaders with this combination include Napoleon Bonaparte; Geronimo, with his defiant freedom fighting; George Marshall, who commanded Allied Forces in World War II; Che Guevara, with his revolutionary guerrilla tactics; and decorated Russian military leader Nikolai Gusev. Other Martial leadership is noted with mob bosses "Lucky" Luciano, Vito Genevese and Anthony Corallo. Benito Mussolini was a Fascist dictator obsessed with power. David Duke was a Grand Wizard of the Ku Klux Klan. Angela Davis is a black feminist leader who was most active in the 1960s. Oprah Winfrey conquered mass media and rose to be one of the most powerful people on the planet. Shirley MacLaine is known for her leadership in advocating spirituality, as well as for a feisty rebelliousness. Sidney Poitier is a breakthrough African-American leading actor, the first to win an Academy Award. John Wayne embodies masculine toughness and assertion, the championing of the individual in relation to larger forces.

Other Uranus/Mars leaders in civil rights include Mahatma Gandhi and Frederick Douglass. Examples in music include Eric Clapton, Paul McCartney, Keith Richards, and Jim Morrison. Examples in film direction include Federico Fellini and Francis Ford Coppola. An example in politics is Ann Richards. Entertainment figures include Marlon Brando and Bill Cosby. Examples in literature include J.R.R. Tolkein, Langston Hughes and Shel Silverstein. An example in science is Galileo Galilei, while Henri Matisse is an example in art. Transpersonal psychologist and philosopher Ken Wilber has a Uranus/Mars aspect, as do astrologers Jeffrey Wolf Green, Demetra George, and Liz Greene. Alexander Graham Bell is credited with inventing the telephone. All are considered pioneers in their respective fields.

Katharine Hepburn has won the Academy Award for Best Actress a record four times. The American Film Institute ranked her the number one female on its Greatest American Screen Legends list, and she is known for her ardent independence (Mars). Jack Kerouac led the Beat movement with the message of overthrowing the conventions of the 1950s. His most famous work is titled *On the Road*, which encapsulates the perpetual movement of Uranus/Mars—and his Mars is in traveling Sagittarius. John Jay was the first Chief Justice of the U.S. Supreme Court, and Hattie Caraway was the first woman elected to the U.S. Senate. Billy Graham is the foremost leader of the Christian Evangelical movement in the twentieth century.

Mars is associated with violence. British revolutionary Guy Fawkes attempted to blow up Parliament. Wes Craven's movies portray violence in shocking (Uranus) ways, and Chuck Norris embodies the renegade warrior persona. Ozzy Osbourne is notorious for biting off a dove's head, Pete Townshend began a revolution by suddenly smashing his guitar, and comedian Gallagher is famous for smashing watermelons. Others involved in bizarre, unexpected or wild violent scenarios include Princess Diana and Sam Kinison (fatal car accidents), Hank Williams and Edie Sedgwick (fatal drug overdoses), Dennis Wilson and Jeff Buckley (fatal drownings), Antoine de Saint-Exupéry, Ritchie Valens, John Denver, and Paul Wellstone (fatal aviation accidents), Mahatma Gandhi, Yitzhak Rabin and Huey Long (assassinations), Tonya Harding (conspiracy to harm an athletic opponent), Rodney King (infamous beating by police), and Jimmy Hoffa (mysterious homicide). Jack Ruby suddenly decided to kill Lee Harvey Oswald to avenge the assassination of President Kennedy—all three have Uranus in aspect to Mars (Oswald's square is 9 degrees though his Mars is in Uranus-ruled Aquarius).

Native American Leonard Peltier was implicated in a violent shootout with the U.S. government. John McCain experienced torture in Vietnam. Todd Beamer was on Flight 93 on September 11th, 2001, and lost his life helping to avert further terrorism. His words "Let's Roll!" capture the Uranus/Mars spirit of rising (Mars) in togetherness as a group (Uranus). John Walker has been dubbed by the media as the "American Taliban" for his involvement with terrorism, and Oklahoma City bombing accomplice Terry Nichols also has a Uranus/Mars aspect. Vladimir Arutinian attempted to assassinate President George W. Bush with a hand grenade. Slave rebellion leader Nat Turner aggressively (Mars) defied (Uranus) his imprisoners. Tennis champion Monica Seles is a relentless, record-setting athlete who was also the victim of an unexpected stabbing. Michael Vick, a quarterback famous for jaw-dropping plays, was indicted for arranging ultra-violent dog fighting. Manfred von Richthofen, also known as the "Red Baron," was the most successful fighter pilot in World War I.

Serial killers Ted Bundy, John Wayne Gacy, Luis Garavito (who had over 300 victims), Henry Lee Lucas, John Wesley Hardin, Andrei Chikatilo (known as the "Butcher of Rostov"), Joseph Paul Franklin, Thor Nis Christiansen, Rosemary West, Ian Brady, and Chester Turner all have Uranus/Mars aspects. Albert DeSalvo confessed to being the "Boston Strangler." Scott Petersen was found guilty of killing his pregnant wife. Josef Mengele (known as the "Angel of Death"), who performed grizzly experimental (Uranus) surgeries (Mars) on Holocaust victims, has a Uranus/Mars aspect, as do notorious Nazis Rudolph Hess, Heinrich Himmler and Adolf Eichmann. John Demjanjuk was identified as "Ivan the Terrible," the SS official who committed savage atrocities at the Treblinka death camp. Cult leader Jim Jones led over 900 people to their death by murder/suicide. Arthur Leigh Allen was the prime suspect believed to be the "Zodiac Killer"—and though never convicted, he did have a record as a sex offender. Other sexual predators and pedophiles with Uranus/Mars include Paul Shanley, Bruce Ritter, Donald Kimball, Caryl Chessman, Westley Allan Dodd, Brandon Hedrick, and Andrew Luster.

The correlation between Mars and sexual expression is well-founded. Many drawn to countercultural or alternative sexual trends—including homosexuality, promiscuity, infidelity, and unabashed showiness—have Uranus in aspect to Mars. Lou

Reed, Freddie Mercury, Elton John, George Michael, and Boy George are famous for flamboyant sexual histories. The sex industry (Mars) is countercultural (Uranus)—and true to expectations, the prominence of this interchange is widespread throughout the field. Some of the more famous examples include Traci Lords, Jenna Jameson, John Holmes, Anna Nicole Smith, and *Penthouse* founder Bob Guccione, as well as Marilyn Monroe, the first centerfold in *Playboy*. Audrey Munson was the first woman to appear nude on film. George William Crump is the first recorded streaker (1803), while Mark Roberts is a modern-day example who has allegedly streaked over 380 times. Madonna has been sexually provocative on stage, in magazines, and in the public's face. Janet Jackson is a leader in entertainment, and infamously experienced a "wardrobe malfunction" during a Super Bowl halftime show that exposed her breast. Dr. Ruth Westheimer is a trailblazing figure in sexual education and health. Tom Cruise, Julia Roberts, Uma Thurman, and Brad Pitt are leading actors as well as sex symbols.

In addition to being a record-setting athlete, Wilt Chamberlain claimed to have bedded thousands of women. Jimmy Swaggart's and Bob Packwood's sexual indiscretions became media circuses. Jessica Hahn claimed to be raped by Jim Bakker, then went on to pose nude for *Playboy*. Monica Lewinsky's rule-breaking sexual behavior contributed to the impeachment of President Clinton, while Gennifer Flowers almost derailed his Presidential aspirations with her participation in infidelity. Clinton consultant Dick Morris was caught in a sex scandal just before the 1996 Presidential election. He has Uranus in aspect to both Mars and Venus, as does Congressman and gay spokesman Barney Frank. Camille Paglia, the challenging social commentator on sexual behavior, describes herself as "a feminist bisexual egomaniac." Allen Ginsberg was a leader of the Beat Generation and pioneering poet, and made no secret of his homosexuality, including his desires for young men. Sean "P Diddy" Combs is a leading entertainment performer and executive with involvement in assault and incidents of gunfire—he also has sired children with several women. Boxer Mike

Tyson is a record-breaking athlete in a violent sport and has a criminal record for both aggressive and sexual infractions.

Uranus/Jupiter – Unlimited Ceilings

Jupiter and Uranus are both idealistic and expansive energies. The main difference is that Jupiter functions within the Saturnian orbit—it deals with belief systems and ideas of how to approach life as part of the social/collective fabric. Uranus is outside the Saturnian orbit and relates to the overarching metaphysical structure that is not bound by the limitations of time, gravity and matter. When Jupiter is integrated with Uranus, the philosophy that governs a life path is informed by the greater collective intelligence. The result is a progressive and inspiring world view, a boundless optimism about our human potentials.

Jupiter seeks adventure while Uranus wants to break the rules. This combination can lead to the most uplifting peak experiences or misguided and reckless behaviors. Checks and balances, which would temper enthusiasm with realism, are lacking. Therefore, this combination may come across as zealously threatening to order and reason. However, if used intentionally and with clarity, Jupiter/Uranus understands that there are always greater frontiers to explore.

Some with this aspect have a soul condition in which they were unable to claim this uplifting potential in prior lives. As Jupiter/Uranus has a social and collective scope, these people can have great influence into broader trends of progress. When Uranus is in aspect to the inner planets, the extension of personal breakthrough *may* enter collective scenarios. With Uranus in aspect to the social planets (Jupiter and Saturn), impacting the world is the purpose. The individual becomes a vessel of larger forces.

Political arenas are a primary area where Uranus/Jupiter finds an outlet. Many progressive politicians and public figures hold this combination, including James Monroe, Alexander Hamilton, Franklin Roosevelt, Harry Truman, Adlai Stevenson, Mahatma Gandhi, Mikhail Gorbachev, Golda Meir, Nelson

Mandela, Jimmy Carter, Walter Mondale, The Dalai Lama, Gary Hart, Bill Clinton, and Ralph Nader. Amazingly, John F. Kennedy, Robert F. Kennedy and Edward Kennedy all have these planets very tightly in major aspect. Oftentimes, Jupiter manifests with a dominant purpose. Al Gore's crusade to deal with global warming seeks to change our approach to life (Jupiter) in order to align with a larger vision of evolution (Uranus). Outspoken liberal strategists Howard Dean, James Carville, and Donna Brazile have a Uranus/Jupiter aspect, as well as commentators Jon Stewart and Al Franken.

Many notable Jupiter/Uranus people do not hold or seek positions of influence but instead advocate a progressive agenda in other ways. Bob Dylan's music is filled with political themes, and he is considered a philosophical voice of his generation. Dylan Thomas, whose transcendent poetry inspired a young Robert Zimmerman to use the name Bob Dylan, also has it. Stevie Wonder has advocated civil rights, as well as other humanitarian causes. 1960s countercultural icon Abbie Hoffman, feminist leader Gloria Steinem and black activist Malcolm X have all zealously promoted their philosophies in revolutionary ways. George Soros is a leading philanthropist and advocate for progressive politicians. The plight of Leonard Peltier has been symbolic of the fight for freedom from tyranny. Current ACLU President, vocal feminist and supporter of legalizing marijuana, Nadine Strossen also has this interchange. Rosie O'Donnell has been a visible celebrity promoting homosexual rights and other liberal causes. Musicians Eddie Vedder, Michael Stipe and Sting are leading proponents of environmental awareness and civic action, while Julia Butterfly Hill is an environmental activist who lived in a tree for over two years to protect it from loggers.

Hermann Hesse infused his works with a progressive philosophy and helped bring eastern ideas to a western audience through such works as *Siddhartha* and *The Glass Bead Game*. Virginia Woolf's feminist (she preferred the term "humanist") philosophy runs through her writing. Norman Mailer is another literary figure whose liberal philosophy informs his work. He did end up writing specifically on politics, and ran for office at one time. James Redfield authored *The Celestine Prophecy* series, which combines adventure (Jupiter) with learning about metaphysical (Uranus) understandings. Ram Dass and Eckhart Tolle are spiritual teachers who travel the world with their messages of living in the moment and spiritual liberation.

Many philosophers have this interchange. Sri Aurobindo's works detail a philosophy (Jupiter) of progressive evolution (Uranus). Confucius is a major figure whose philosophy revolutionized an entire epoch of civilization. Rene Descartes, Bertrand Russell, John Locke, David Hume, Pierre Teilhard de Chardin, Friedrich Nietzsche, Søren Kierkegaard, Émile Durkheim, Erich Fromm, Richard Rorty, Paul Feyerabend, Karl Popper, Susan B. Anthony, Francisco Varela, and spiritual philosopher Meher Baba all have Uranus in major aspect with Jupiter. Immanuel Kant is a gigantic figure in philosophy and his work is called "transcendental idealism," perfectly encapsulating this dynamic. He has Jupiter square Uranus just over 8 degrees, but his Jupiter is in Aquarius, so Uranus serves as its ruler.

We lack accurate birth information for most of the great explorers of the middle centuries of the second millennium—only the year is available. The prominence of Uranus/Jupiter in all of these explorers is speculative. Given a window of a couple of months for their birthdates, both Marco Polo and Christopher Columbus would have this aspect. In more recent times, Reinhold Messner is known as the greatest mountain climber of all time. He made the first solo ascents of Mount Everest without supplemental oxygen and was the first to ascend all 14 peaks above 8000 meters. Alexander von Humboldt explored (Jupiter) South and Central America and was the first to describe it from a scientific point of view (Uranus). Andrew Croft once held the record for the longest self-sustaining journey, and is the inspiration for the James Bond character. Roald Amundsen led the first successful expedition to the South Pole. Matthew Webb was the first to swim the English Channel. Martin Strel is a world-record marathon swimmer who conquered the Mississippi, Yangtze, Danube, and mighty Amazon River, which involved negotiating piranhas and sharks.

Uranus/Jupiter is prominent in famous space pioneers. Yuri Gagarin was the first man in space, Svetlana Savitskaya, the second woman in space and Sally Ride, the first American woman in space; all have it. Vladimír Remek (Czechoslovakia) was the first person from a country other than the U.S. or U.S.S.R. to enter space. Other significant astronauts with Uranus/Jupiter include Neil Armstrong, Buzz Aldrin, John Glenn, Edgar Mitchell, Scott Carpenter, Deke Slayton, Jim Lovell, Frank Borman, Wally Schirra, Thomas Patten Stafford, and John Watts Young. Theodore von Kármán and Jack Parsons are scientists whose efforts contributed substantially to making space travel a reality—both have a Uranus/Jupiter aspect.

The adventuresome spirit of taking off (Jupiter) into the unknown (Uranus) is seen with aviation pioneers Orville and Wilbur Wright. Joseph Michel Montgolfier invented the hot air balloon, the first craft to bring humans into the sky. Clément Ader was the first to fly in a powered, heavier-than-air craft for a significant distance. Otto Lilienthal is credited with inventing the first controllable glider. Ferdinand von Zeppelin founded the famous airship company that bears his name. Louis Blériot took the first flight over a large body of water in a heavier-than-air craft. Frank Whittle patented the jet engine, and Chuck Yeager was the first to break the sound barrier. Bertrand Piccard was the first to circle the Earth in a balloon. Antoine de Saint-Exupéry was both an accomplished pilot and a philosopher who, in *The Little Prince,* commented upon the ideals and the truths that people forget. Richard Branson, who is attempting to bring space travel to common people, also has this inspiring planetary mixture. Not everyone with this combination will channel it clearly, however. Cult leader Marshall Applewhite persuaded his followers to commit suicide in order to join a passing comet—showing a most unstable (Uranus) philosophy (Jupiter), and unrealistic (Uranus) travel (Jupiter) aspirations.

Superheroes come to mind at the mention of unlimited ceilings, boundless exploration, and the sense of being fueled by a mission or moral imperative. Sure enough, *Superman* creators Jerry Siegel and Joe Shuster have Uranus/Jupiter aspects, as does

Richard Donner, who directed *Superman*—the first modern superhero film that was instrumental in shaping the fantasy genre. Actors George Reeves, Christopher Reeve and Dean Cain all have portrayed the superhero, and "Lois Lane" actresses Margot Kidder and Teri Hatcher also have this aspect. Tobey Maguire brought *Spider Man* to the silver screen, and Steve Ditko, creator of the arachnid hero, also have Uranus/Jupiter aspects. *Wonder Woman* creator William Moulton Marston and actress Lynda Carter, the most recognizable face of the heroine, both have Uranus/Jupiter aspects as well. *Batman* co-creator Bill Finger; Frank Miller, who created the comic revival of the character in *Batman: The Dark Knight Returns;* and actor Michael Keaton, who played Batman in the movies all have Uranus/Jupiter aspects. In addition, Bill Bixby and Lou Ferrigno (8.5 degree square) who portrayed *The Incredible Hulk* on TV have it, while Eric Bana (who played the Hulk in the movies) has the planets in the same sign, though not classically in a conjunction. Other heroes with Uranus/Jupiter aspects include Clayton Moore (title character from *The Lone Ranger*), Mark Hamill ("Luke Skywalker" in *Star Wars*), Henry Winkler ("The Fonz" on *Happy Days*), Robin Williams ("Mork" on *Mork and Mindy*), Kate Jackson and Cheryl Ladd (*Charlie's Angels*), Richard Dean Anderson (title character of *MacGyver*), and David Hasselhoff ("Michael Knight" on *Knight Rider*). John Wayne played heroic figures in the movies, while former concentration camp prisoner Simon Wiesenthal dedicated his life to hunting down Nazis—a true real-life hero on a mission.

Uranus/Jupiter also correlates with superhuman height. Robert Pershing Wadlow reached 8'11", the tallest person on record. Apparently, when he was dying (at age 35) he was still growing, reaching upward toward the heavens (Jupiter) and breaking records (Uranus)! Manute Bol, Yao Ming, Sandy Allen, and Jane Bunford are some other examples of people who have reached 7'6" and gained notoriety for their height. Andre the Giant is another enormous figure, and like Wadlow, he also suffered from pituitary problems.

Ingmar Bergman is widely considered the foremost visionary of modern cinema. Alexander Pushkin is the founder of modern Russian literature and is also considered a visionary. One of the greatest visionaries is Albert Einstein, whose philosophical (Jupiter) and scientific breakthroughs (Uranus) have made many advances and explorations possible. Some inventors who similarly brought a leap (Jupiter) in progress (Uranus) through inventions that enable greater expansion include Thomas Edison (light bulb, phonograph and projector) and Alexander Graham Bell (telephone); Tim Berners-Lee is credited with inventing the World Wide Web. Dennis Gabor invented holography, which brings perception (Jupiter) to non-tangible territory (Uranus). Buckminster Fuller is credited with many inventions, most notably the geodesic dome; he also put forth philosophical ideas (Jupiter) regarding the implications of technological advancement (Uranus). Giovanni Luppis invented the torpedo, which delivers long-range (Jupiter) explosion (Uranus). Louis de Broglie pioneered wave mechanics, uniting the physics of light and matter—a major advancement in our understanding of nature. János Bolyai discovered non-Euclidian geometry and said, "Out of nothing I have created another, new universe," Jupiter/Uranus words par excellence.

Uranus/Saturn – Inside-outers

Uranus/Saturn is a clash of the titans. Saturn is the solidity of the status quo that Uranus wants to reform, if not obliterate. As depicted in the myth, Saturn castrates Uranus and renders him inaccessible. Saturn holds fast to the order created, often fearfully, for he knows that lurking in the distance is continual change. This pairing concerns the tension between conservative and liberal, physical and metaphysical, form and abstraction, time and timelessness, the ordinary and the extraordinary, resistance to change and revolution. Those with this aspectual combination are learning how to ground progressive agendas into workable solutions.

Uranus always points to the cutting edge of future potentials, individuation and the claiming of new attributes and skills. Successful evolution involves being completely true to the self (Uranus) in one's public contribution (Saturn). We can surmise that many with this combination have a soul history in which they were unable or unwilling to forge a career completely on their own terms. Now they are finishing this work, and by so doing, they implement the next wave of evolution in concrete ways. Saturn draws the line between the visible world (inner and social planets) and the world of unseen potentials (outer planets). These individuals bridge the two worlds and serve as "inside-outers"—those who catalyze far-reaching change in society from insider or recognizable positions.

It is often the case that these individuals take on both mainstream and maverick tendencies—being insiders and outsiders at the same time. Jesse Jackson's political career is a leading example. He has run as a mainstream candidate, as well as functioned as a maverick progressive force. Muhammad Ali was the heavyweight champion of the world and also a visible opponent of the Vietnam War. Chief Joseph was a Native American leader in the nineteenth century who negotiated the freedom of his people (Uranus) against pressure from the U.S. government (Saturn). Dr. Martin Luther King (8.5 degree square) led the Civil Rights movement (Uranus) that pressured the dominant social structure (Saturn) to be more inclusive.

Other examples of Saturn/Uranus integration include Aleister Crowley, who made a career out of esoteric interests. Thich Nhat Hanh has been instrumental in creating schools and institutions (Saturn) designed for spiritual awakening (Uranus). Rupert Sheldrake is a leading biologist who posits a metaphysical understanding of nature. Stanislav Grof is a leading psychologist whose work incorporates the transpersonal, including astrology and controversial (that is, illegal) drug therapies. Marie Tussaud is noted for her wax figures that preserve (Saturn) the image (Uranus) of celebrities with shocking realism. Woody Allen is a megastar movie director (Saturn) who stays away (Uranus) from Hollywood as much as possible. Roseanne was able to rise to the top of mainstream success in television and entertainment while mocking, if not displaying outright hostility to, the establishment, and even her audience. Bob Saget has worked the Saturn/Uranus complex by conforming to a traditional television role in the sitcom *Full House*, but also being an irreverent and vulgar stand-up comedian. Tennis star Bjorn Borg amassed great success then shunned the limelight by suddenly retiring at the age of 26. Hugh Hefner and Larry Flynt became successful publishers (Saturn) that revolutionized social change (Uranus).

Helen Thomas, Bob Woodward, Ed Bradley, Morley Safer, Charlie Rose, Lesley Stahl, Dan Rather, Andy Rooney, John Chancellor, Robert MacNeil, Jim Lehrer, David Brinkley, Eric Sevareid, Bill Moyers, Sam Donaldson, Art Buchwald, Anna Quindlen, Thomas Friedman, and Maureen Dowd are all mainstream journalists who expose the truth (Uranus) of how things are run (Saturn). They serve as necessary checks and balances to governmental and institutional operations. Valerie Plame was part of the CIA (Saturn) before suddenly getting outed (Uranus), due to her husband's criticism of the Bush Administration.

Many authors with Saturn in aspect to Uranus have used the pen as a sword—their works tend to stir controversy. Ken Kesey's anti-establishment literary works are matched by his behavior as a "Merry Prankster." Tom Wolfe penned the *Electric Kool-Aid Acid Test* and is similarly a countercultural icon. Native American writer Sherman Alexie has given voice to the oppressed, and his works challenge the assumptions of the dominant power structure, while Amy Tan has brought cross-cultural and gender-inequity awareness though her writings. Dan Brown's wildly popular *Da Vinci Code* challenges orthodox Christianity. Carlos Castaneda brought alternative understandings of spirituality and sorcery to the Western mainstream. J.D. Salinger's *Catcher in the Rye* portrays a continual battle between being authentic with oneself (Uranus) and conforming to the expectations of the establishment (Saturn). L. Ron Hubbard's books launched the Scientology movement, an unconventional (Uranus) religion that has attracted many visible celebrities

(Saturn). Literary figures William Butler Yeats and D.H. Lawrence inspired and gave ideas to the New Age movement (Uranus/Saturn) in the twentieth century.

Musicians with this exchange similarly push the envelope while being widely embraced. Woody Guthrie changed American music and was the central player in the folk movement in the Depression era. Elvis Presley and Chuck Berry helped launch rock and roll in the 1950s. Otis Redding, Aretha Franklin and Miles Davis were leaders in soul and jazz music and furthered acceptance of African-American artists by the mainstream. Paul McCartney, Bob Dylan, Jerry Garcia, Jimi Hendrix, and Janis Joplin pushed rock and roll from being anti-establishment to being the dominant musical culture in the 1960s. Punk rock pioneers Joe Strummer and Johnny Rotten led the anti-establishment movement in the 1970s. Michael Jackson and Madonna sculpted the pop sound in the 1980s, and Kurt Cobain was the central figure for grunge music in the 1990s.

Other "inside-outers" in the world of entertainment include Barbra Streisand, who has enjoyed soaring popularity while being an outspoken progressive force. Andy Warhol amassed great success as a modern artist, largely through manipulating (Uranus) the media establishment (Saturn). Sinead O'Conner notoriously ripped up a picture of the Pope on mainstream television. Jackie Robinson, who broke the color barrier in baseball, also has Uranus/Saturn. Conan O'Brien has been able to find success with a quirky style on a show broadcast at an unconventional time that pokes fun at celebrities while welcoming them as guests. Steven Wright's comedic style is bizarre (Uranus) and dry (Saturn). He comments on the interface between the absurd (Uranus) and the commonplace (Saturn). Paul Reubens portrays "Pee Wee Herman," with ingenuity at marketing (Saturn) the eccentric (Uranus). "Dr. Demento" (Barret Hansen) has created an unconventional radio franchise based on parody and silliness.

James Dean brought the Uranian attitudes of recklessness, countercultural "hipness" and rebellion to the mainstream. Clint Eastwood's famous line, "Go ahead, make my day," illustrates the rugged flavor of taking the law in one's own hands. Mr. T has been a wildly popular celebrity as an outlaw persona wearing a scowl and a mohawk. Johnny Depp chooses outrageous and eccentric characters to portray, and his career is a study of balancing success (Saturn) with artistic purity (Uranus). Robert Altman and Mike Nichols are innovative movie makers who are socially conscious and often considered "ahead of their times." Some of their films have themes of exposing broken systems or taboos in society. Baseball player Barry Bonds expresses a rebellious, if not rule-breaking, attitude in his career. Hank Greenberg was a Jewish ball player who challenged the hallowed homerun records and was subsequently antagonized by mainstream currents in society. Mark Gastineau took steroids and had run-ins with the law but was one of the most popular football players of his day. Martha Stewart, who made up her own rules when it came to stock trading, is another celebrity widely embraced by the masses. NBA referee Tim Donaghy was caught for betting on games he officiated.

Winston Churchill has Saturn in aspect to Uranus, and his life typifies the struggle and reconciliation of conservative and progressive impulses. As a theologian, Albert Schweitzer advocated making the immediate world (Saturn) a reflection of our divine connection (Uranus). He established a medical infrastructure (Saturn) for people in the third world (Uranus). Paul Newman has used his celebrity status (Saturn) as a vehicle for his humanitarian (Uranus) work. John Sinclair, jailed for marijuana possession, became a protest symbol (Uranus) against the government (Saturn), with top musicians writing songs in his name.

Susan B. Anthony, Elizabeth Cady Stanton and Gloria Allred challenged the status quo with their feminist agenda. Isabel Martínez de Perón of Argentina was the first woman to preside over a country. Sandra Day O'Connor was the first female Supreme Court justice and forever changed the institution. Mae Jemison was the first African-American woman in space. Amelia Earhart, another figure championed by feminists, is most famous for disappearing (Uranus) while testing the limits

(Saturn) of aviation in her World Flight of 1937. Douglas Wilder of Virginia was the first African-American to be elected governor of a state. Harry Houdini not only had an unconventional career as stunt performer, but he also sought to debunk (Saturn) spiritualists and was an impassioned skeptic of the metaphysical. Cyril Fagan was instrumental in bringing sidereal astrology to the west. Robert Hand has helped bridge ancient (Saturn) and modern (Uranus) branches within the field. Moses Siregar has organized (Saturn) astrology (Uranus) conferences and is also involved with integrating older and newer forms of astrology. Shelley Ackerman is a popular astrologer who appears in mainstream media outlets to comment on current events.

James Lovelock posited the Gaia Hypothesis, which claims that the physical Earth (Saturn) is an interconnected and aware organism (Uranus). Ravi Shankar helped bring innovative sounds to the west and holds the Guinness record for the longest international musical career. David Geffen is a music executive (Saturn) and outspoken political activist (Uranus). Theodore Kaczynski, the “Unabomber”, shunned society (Saturn) and attacked it with explosives (Uranus). Jeanne Calment lived to be 122 years old, the oldest person documented. She defied (Uranus) the limits of aging (Saturn) and extended our understanding of what is possible. With Uranian gusto she quipped, "I've only got one wrinkle, and I'm sitting on it."

Uranus/Neptune – Imagining the Future

Uranus and Neptune combine to create the most inspired vision of evolutionary advancement. Whereas Uranus correlates to the intelligence of nature, Neptune is the divine love that makes this life blessed. People with this combination may potentially *feel* a part of Spirit and become compelled to act in accordance. If Uranus/Neptune does not form aspects to any of the personal or social planets, this pairing would be more “generational” in nature, to use the popular label. These transpersonal planets would function in the background of, but still inform, the psyche.

A soul that incarnates with this aspectual combination is interested in learning more about dreaming, or in imagining possibilities. Individuation is furthered through inspiration, creativity and handling advanced states of consciousness with aplomb. Some people with Uranus/Neptune may have a soul history in which they have felt lost or confused within the enormity of consciousness. Now they are learning that there are entire worlds available through spiritual practice. Through this development, they ready themselves to contribute an inspirational message to the collective. Oftentimes, their work takes an archetypal or symbolic form that triggers shifts in consciousness for the members of their audience.

Sacrifice, surrender and selflessness are a part of Neptune. Some with Uranus/Neptune aspects tirelessly serve the collective without any recognition. They are the unsung heroes in soup kitchens or assisting a disease-infected country. Highly attuned to feeling connected to humanity, they exhibit compassion that heals on both collective and personal levels, and their individual growth is furthered by such acts. Some notable individuals with Uranus/Neptune aspects include Mother Teresa, Clara Barton, Florence Nightingale, Harriet Tubman, Frederick Douglass, Mahatma Gandhi, Ammachi, and The Dalai Lama. None of these individuals sought fame—each was motivated by transpersonal forces that flowed through him or her.

Other individuals who have infused their works with this combination include child poet Mattie Stepanek, who demonstrated a remarkable spiritual vision in his short life. *Course of Miracles* author Helen Schucman, as well as Marianne Williamson who popularized the course for a modern audience, have helped awaken (Uranus) many to Spirit (Neptune). Neale Donald Walsch did the same with *Conversations with God*. Dr. Wayne Dyer's message of individuation (Uranus) through developing compassion (Neptune) has touched many hearts. Chögyam Trungpa helped bring Buddhism to the west and is known for wild and even eccentric methods (dubbed "Crazy Wisdom") to arouse others to Spirit. Joseph Campbell's breakthrough works on mythology have stimulated leagues of people to consider the archetypal realm. Byron Katie's program called "The Work" aims to strip away the personal story to find the authentic (Uranus) spiritual (Neptune) self. Abraham Maslow is considered the father of humanistic psychology and put forth a model of reaching self-actualization. Oprah Winfrey has increasingly become an advocate for individuation in a spiritual direction. Maimonides and Martin Buber were both progressive religious figures advocating a mystical understanding of God.

The visionary capacities may become substantial in these individuals. The creative imagination teams with futuristic ideas to produce unique and compelling works that are highly attuned to archetypal or imaginal realms. Michelangelo, Raphael, William Shakespeare, Pablo Picasso, Henri Matisse, and Jules Verne are some examples. Arthur Schopenhauer espoused a philosophy of salvation and escape (Uranus) from suffering (Neptune). Jean-Jacques Rousseau posited that we find our true individuality (Uranus) within nature (Neptune) and was a great influence on Romanticism. Other figures of the Romantic movement with this combination include François-René de Chateaubriand (known as the "Father of French Romanticism"), Marquis de Sade, Alfred de Vigny, Novalis, Samuel Taylor Coleridge, William Wordsworth, Lord Byron, John Keats, Mary Shelley, Henry David Thoreau, Oscar Wilde, Walt Whitman, Washington Irving, Walter Scott, Sergei Rachmaninoff, Franz Schubert, Niccolò Paganini, Ludwig van Beethoven, and Eugene Delacroix—all of them brought attention to the universal themes of nature and beauty, and idealism about how life can ultimately be. The photography of Ansel Adams also captures this sentiment.

The existentialist movement encapsulates the paradoxes and questioning of this pairing. How can we break through (Uranus) and find meaningful experiences (Neptune) in such a crazed world around us? Or is spiritual redemption and meaning (Neptune) forever out-of-bounds (Uranus)? Subsequently, there is an emergence of feeling part of an absurd (Uranus) and unreal (Neptune) existence. Fyodor Dostoyevsky is mentioned as a forerunner to the existentialist movement, and his works are filled with these themes. Jean-Paul Sartre, Albert Camus, Franz Kafka, Simone de Beauvoir, Karl Jaspers, Samuel Beckett, and Eugène Ionesco all have Uranus/Neptune aspects, as well as the artists Jackson Pollock, Willem de Kooning and Arshille Gorky, whose works are often construed in an existentialist way.

James A. Michener is a visionary writer of far-reaching proportions, frequently writing about the seas and epic spiritual quests. The works of Dr. Seuss portray wild fantasy landscapes, other worlds of the imagination that often are quite advanced. Robert Heinlein wrote *Stranger in a Strange Land,* which animates fantasy (Neptune) combined with technology (Uranus). H.G. Wells penned *The Time Machine*, a story about transcendence (Neptune) through technological advancement (Uranus). Virginia Woolf was a creative innovator with her experimentation in "stream of consciousness" writing, and Anaïs Nin and Alice Walker are writers who address issues of liberation (Uranus) through developing one's vision (Neptune).

George Washington and John Adams helped envision the direction of a new country, and Francis Scott Key (who wrote "The Star Spangled Banner") helped form the soundtrack for it. Franklin Roosevelt sought to align his Presidency with this ideal and is a noted humanitarian. Susan B. Anthony is another progressive figure who put forth a vision of inclusiveness. Karl Marx's philosophy seeks to diminish personal concerns for the greater collective.

The twentieth century saw the emergence of Integral thought—which aims to unify global understanding (Uranus) into an overarching spiritual (Neptune) philosophy. Pierre Teilhard de Chardin developed the concepts of the Noosphere ("the sphere of human thought") and the Omega Point (point of convergence of unified consciousness). Sri Aurobindo developed a sophisticated spiritual model of the development of consciousness. Others with Uranus/Neptune aspects who are associated with this movement include Edward Haskell, Arthur M. Young, Clare Graves, Jean Gebser, William Irvin Thompson, and Rupert Sheldrake.

Woody Guthrie sang his vision of how life might be during the drudgery of the Great Depression. George Harrison organized a benefit concert for Bangladesh, and Bob Geldof is largely responsible for Live Aid—examples of putting humanitarian intentions into action. Bob Marley and Marvin Gaye are other revolutionary figures who carried a message of universal love, freedom and environmental awareness. Many of the musicians who came of age in the 1960s were born around 1940 when Uranus and Neptune were in trine. The optimistic and uplifting spirit of their works is obvious. A few examples are John Lennon, Joni Mitchell, Bob Dylan, and Joan Baez.

George Lucas, creator of the *Star Wars* series, is known for his epic storytelling. His works resonate so deeply because his characters embody mythic or archetypal themes. Another franchise that endures because of its strong archetypal resonance is *The Wizard of Oz*. Originally written by L. Frank Baum, the movie was directed by Victor Fleming, and Noel Langley was the screenwriter. All three of them have Uranus in aspect to Neptune. This story endures largely because of its universal themes of finding one's true self (Uranus) through the imagination (Neptune) and envisioning new possibilities. Even the song, "Somewhere Over the Rainbow," captures this dynamic perfectly. The movie was released in 1939 when Uranus was in trine to Neptune by less than 1 degree.

Oskar Schindler was motivated by an altruistic love of humanity in his efforts to help save Jews in the Holocaust. Cindy Sheehan is a renowned anti-war activist (Uranus) who is steadfast with her message of healing (Neptune). Amelia Earhart imagined boundless flight, which she may have been ill-prepared for—one of the hazards of these two transpersonal planets. Albert Einstein went on trailblazing (Uranus) explorations through consciousness (Neptune) to arrive at his theories. Alice Bailey was an influential and controversial (Uranus) voice for esoteric spiritual studies (Neptune) in the early twentieth century. Rachel Carson brought environmental awareness and advocated greater love of the Earth. Galileo Galilei and Nikola Tesla were visionary scientists, while Jacques Cousteau was a pioneer (Uranus) in oceanography (Neptune). Ferdinand Magellan was the first explorer to navigate the oceans (Neptune) all the way around the globe. Albert

Hoffman was the creator of LSD, and Franz Mesmer is widely considered the foremost innovator (Uranus) of hypnosis (Neptune).

Uranus/Pluto – Unlocking the Vault

Pluto brings urgency and psychological complexity, the underlying power of evolutionary momentum, to the progressive agenda of Uranus. As discussed with Neptune, Pluto emotionalizes Uranus. Instead of injecting compassion and yearning, the contribution of Pluto is raw, intense and unconcerned with pleasantries. Uranus/Pluto correlates to the regenerative power of nature—to emerge forcefully, at times uncompromisingly, in the direction of natural law. This combination is explosive and even harrowing—aligned with the truth of our collective consciousness, the limitations and potentials.

Those with Uranus/Pluto contacts carry the necessity of realizing the dormant power of the subconscious and using it intentionally. Like a coiled snake asleep in an underground well, once awakened it assumes a mysterious and alluring intensity. For many possible reasons, the soul histories of people with Uranus/Pluto have collections of deeply buried psychic energy in need of resolution through intentional dispersal. Some reasons why such soul imprints exist are extreme cases of violation, subjugation, condemnation—involvement in darker scenarios that are unacceptable to the psyche and therefore banished away to the recesses of the mind.

Many with this combination were caught up in larger forces that required the personal will to carry forth some agenda contrary to what it would otherwise have chosen. War, propaganda, manipulations, being sworn to secrecy, cult associations, and other forms of being a pawn to an empire (real or perceived) are possible scenarios. Individuation is furthered when one takes back control and lives a life rooted to the gifts that this power bestows. Without acknowledgment, and without a revolution (Uranus) of deep feeling (Pluto), these individuals are prone to relive and embody the insidious and chaotic potentials of such traumatic (Uranus) soul wounding (Pluto). With optimal growth, these souls become the strongest agents for growth. They potentially catalyze collective evolution through their wisdom and their insistence on what they understand as "right action."

The biographies of Uranus/Pluto individuals are often marked by confrontations with issues of force, power and extreme psychological dynamics. These people tend to face grave tests and may have great impact on evolutionary direction. Napoleon Bonaparte's global military exploits, and assassinated Israeli Prime Minister Yitzhak Rabin or Charles Manson's murderous manipulation of his followers are some vivid examples. Many caught up in the atrocities of Nazi Germany, including perpetrators (Heinrich Himmler), victims (Anne Frank), and survivors (Roman Polanski), have this combination. George S. Patton, "Old Blood and Guts," was an exceptional military commander of historical import. Timothy McVeigh was responsible for the Oklahoma City bombing in 1995, while Eric Rudolph engineered an attack at an Olympic Park the very next year, followed by Andrew Cunanan's killing spree that took Versace's life. Theodore Kaczynski is the notorious "Unabomber," and Yasser Arafat was known to have a plethora of terrorist connections. Donald Rumsfeld's overseeing of the dire conditions of the Iraq War, including torture at Abu Ghraib, is a current example. Actor Robert Blake is suspected of covertly arranging the murder of his wife.

Cult leader Jim Jones manipulated his followers into a mass murder/suicide which killed over 900 people. Nathan Bedford Forrest was the principal founder of the Ku Klux Klan in the nineteenth century. Byron De La Beckwith is the white supremacist guilty of killing NAACP organizer Medgar Evers. Robert Hanssen was a CIA operative caught up in a dangerous game of treason. Dan Ellsberg also defied the government by leaking top secret information regarding U.S. foreign policy to the press in the famous "Pentagon Papers." Rupert Murdoch controls mass media as much as any individual in history.

Many artists and writers with this planetary exchange infuse their works with a rawness that captures the most compelling dramas, often in graphic ways. Edgar Allen Poe's forays into shock and horror, Herman Melville's epic confrontation with the relentless *Moby Dick,* and Quentin Tarantino's theater of the macabre are some examples. Little Richard infused early rock and roll with primal urgency. In classical music, Wolfgang Mozart and Ludwig van Beethoven captured the epic and cataclysmic nature of this aspect in sound. Although classical composers cannot be pigeonholed into one category, there is a preponderance of them with Uranus/Pluto aspects, particularly those who have defined their times; Wagner, Vivaldi, Chopin, Liszt, Verdi, Offenbach, Rossini, and Schumann are some examples.

Artists Vincent van Gogh and Paul Gauguin both have this aspectual interchange. Though aesthetically pleasing, their works contain many undertones of grave psychological disturbance and revolt from societal norms. These men had a confrontational friendship. Van Gogh infamously cut off his earlobe, and Gauguin sought refuge in Tahiti. John Steinbeck wrote about the struggle for independence and individuality (Uranus) in lieu of powerful forces (Pluto). Isaac Asimov's work addresses the psychological and humanizing implications (Pluto) of scientific/technological breakthroughs (Uranus). Fyodor Dostoevsky's novels address the individual's psychological reaction to trying political, social and spiritual conditions. George Orwell wrote about extreme governmental control in *1984*. Jack Kerouac headed the countercultural Beat generation, which sought to powerfully align the self with its truth.

Hank Aaron faced an onslaught of racism as he broke Babe Ruth's homerun record, the most glorified in all of sports. Don King is notorious as a ruthless, corrupt and controlling boxing promoter. James Dean personified the iconoclastic, smug and dangerous Uranus/Pluto archetype on film, and lived his life in similar fashion. Alex Haley documented the psychological struggle of African-Americans in his landmark *Roots* series.

Organized crime, with its themes of control, murder and underhanded business operations, is classic Uranus/Pluto at its darkest. Bernardo Provenzano was the head of the Sicilian Mafia until his capture in 2006. He ran the crime empire in hiding (Pluto) for over four decades. Calogero Vizzini was a highly influential mob pioneer in the early decades of the twentieth century and was dubbed the "boss of the bosses" by the media. Legendary mob boss Carlo Gambino, notorious gangster Al Capone, mobster-turned-informant Sammy "The Bull" Gravano, as well as *Godfather* author Mario Puzo, have this combination. Agent Eliot Ness led "The Untouchables" against the forces of organized crime, and Rudy Giuliani became a celebrated mob prosecutor who landed several big names behind bars. Each of these figures brought a significant turn of events (Uranus) to the crime (Pluto) world. Actor Robert DeNiro has portrayed many such characters in film.

Other Uranus/Pluto figures are feminists Gloria Steinem, Betty Friedan, Lucy Burns, and Alice Paul; political and spiritual leader Eva Perón of Argentina; influential former First Lady Eleanor Roosevelt; and Supreme Court Justice Ruth Bader Ginsburg. Mikhail Gorbachev helped change the power structure of the Soviet Union, and Yuri Gagarin, the first astronaut in space, later met a sudden (Uranus) death (Pluto). Star Trek creator Gene Roddenberry filled his show with dramatic confrontations (Pluto) and innovative technologies (Uranus) taking place at the outer regions of the universe. David Lynch's movies are surrealistic ventures into the underside of the American psyche. Psychologists Stanislav Grof and Carl Rogers are trailblazers into the depths of the unconscious, revealing hidden truths about our most essential needs. Edgar Cayce sank deeply into the unconscious mind to assist people with medical and health issues. Influential artist and poet William Blake uttered the words, "If the doors of perception were cleansed, every thing would appear to man as it is, infinite." We notice a theme of approaching transpersonal truth, devoid of the distortions of the physical world.

Since Uranus and Pluto were in conjunction for most of the 1960s, millions of people carry this interchange. It has a multitude of meanings and manifestations. Some of the more graphic examples follow. Terri Schiavo suffered severe brain trauma and became the symbol of a national debate on euthanasia—the liberation (Uranus) from suffering through death (Pluto). This debate exposed (Uranus) the underlying agendas (Pluto) of politicians. Robert Downey Jr. has played out his descent (Pluto) into drug addiction, and breakthroughs (Uranus) to sobriety, publicly. Kurt Cobain captured the intensity of this combination through his rebellious, screaming, suicidal rock-star persona. Billy Corgan of Smashing Pumpkins similarly evokes psychological disturbance and rebellion. Mike Tyson's career and biography is a study of the extreme dynamics of control, violence and brutality. Anna Nicole Smith's life was marked by issues of power, sexuality, and control of money, and ultimately a shocking (Uranus) death (Pluto).

The Beginning of the Nuclear Age

The specter of nuclear devastation is Uranus/Pluto at its most menacing. While conducting research for the Uranus/Pluto section, the correlations I found regarding the beginning of the nuclear age and Uranus/Pluto were so prominent, an additional section became necessary. Here, we'll review the storyline and central players at the start of the nuclear age. Warheads are particularly Martial, so Mars will also be a part of this analysis.

During the 1930s, Uranus and Pluto were square. This correlates with the rise of Hitler and Mussolini, the extreme conditions of the Great Depression, and also the development of the technologies that could be used to make nuclear weapons. In 1932 John Cockroft (Sun/Pluto conjunction, Sun sextile Mars, Uranus/Saturn in Scorpio) and Ernest Walton (Uranus/Mars conjunction opposite Pluto) split the atom. Frédéric Joliot-Curie (Uranus/Mars/Pluto T-square) and Enrico Fermi (Uranus/Pluto opposition, Mars in Scorpio) were instrumental in further research and development of nuclear fission. In Germany, Otto

Hahn (Uranus square Pluto, Pluto trine Mars), Fritz Strassmann (Uranus/Mars/Pluto T-Square) and Lise Meitner (Sun in Scorpio opposed Pluto, Uranus sextile Mars) were the first to publish research on the nuclear fission of Uranium. Niels Bohr (Uranus/Pluto trine), George Placzek (Uranus/Mars conjunction opposite Pluto) and John Wheeler (Uranus square Mars, Pluto sextile Mars) helped work out the science of harnessing the energy into a bomb.

In the United States, three Jewish refugee physicists—Leó Szilárd (Uranus/Pluto opposition, Uranus sextile Mars), Eugene Wigner (Uranus/Pluto/Mars T-Square) and Edward Teller (Uranus/Sun conjunction, Pluto/Moon conjunction)—were worried about the Germans using recent advancements in nuclear technology for weaponry. Szilárd and Albert Einstein (Uranus square Pluto, Pluto trine Mars) wrote to President Franklin Roosevelt to alert him of the potential danger. Roosevelt set up a Uranium Committee led by Lyman Briggs (Sun/Pluto conjunction, Uranus sextile Mars) on which Phillip Abelson (Pluto square Mars, Uranus trine Sun) was a leading physicist.

Meanwhile in England, Otto Robert Frisch (Uranus/Pluto opposition, Uranus trine Mars) and Rudolf Peierls (Uranus/Mars conjunction, Sun/Pluto conjunction) made significant strides in the mechanics of bomb detonation. They reported to Henry Tizard (Uranus/Pluto trine), who decided that the British government should proceed further. Britain shared its research with the United States, which remained passive because it was not actively a part of World War II at this time. Englishman Mark Oliphant (Uranus/Pluto opposition) flew to the U.S. to gather information. Oliphant knew of the potential ramifications of the Frisch-Peierls research and contacted Ernest Lawrence (Uranus/Pluto opposition, Uranus sextile Mars, Pluto trine Mars), James Bryant Conant (in possession of what can only be described as a "Nuclear Yod": Sun in Aries sextile Pluto in Gemini [with Mars in late Taurus in conjunction with Pluto], Sun/Pluto quincunx Uranus in Scorpio!) and Fermi to motivate them to take action. In the fall of 1941, the United States decided to build nuclear weapons. The first meeting for a new Top Policy

Group was held on December 6, 1941, the day before Japan bombed Pearl Harbor. On the attack of December 7th in Hawaii, Uranus was sextile Moon/Pluto, and Mars was trine the Sun.

Some scientists involved in the Top Policy Group were Gregory Breit (Uranus/Pluto 11.5 degree opposition, Pluto square Mars), John Manley (Uranus/Mars conjunction, Pluto square Saturn), Hans Bethe (Sun/Mars conjunction opposite Uranus, Pluto square Saturn), John Van Vleck (Uranus/Pluto opposition, Sun trine Mars), Felix Bloch (Uranus/Mars conjunction, Uranus sextile Sun, Pluto trine Sun), and Richard C. Tolman (Uranus opposite Sun, Pluto sextile Mercury, Moon square Mars). Plutonium, which had been discovered by Glenn Seaborg (Uranus square Sun, Pluto/Mars conjunction) in February 1941, was still largely unknown. The program became "The Manhattan Project." Robert Oppenheimer (Uranus/Pluto 10.5 degree opposition, Sun/Mars conjunction trine Uranus) was the scientific director of the operation, and Leslie Groves (Uranus square Sun, Pluto/Mars conjunction) was the military administrator.

Franz Simon (Uranus/Sun opposition, Pluto/Mars conjunction of 13 degrees) and Nicholas Kurti (Uranus trine Sun, Pluto/Mars conjunction) worked on the Uranium bomb that would eventually devastate Hiroshima. Emilio Segrè (Sun trine Pluto, Sun square Mars, Uranus/Moon conjunction) was a leading scientist working with Plutonium, and with the bomb that would eventually destroy Nagasaki. The first nuclear test occurred on July 16, 1945 (Sun sextile Mars, Pluto sextile Venus/Uranus), under the supervision of Thomas Farrell (Sun/Pluto opposition, Uranus/Mars conjunction).

President Harry S. Truman (Sun square Mars, Mars trine Pluto) ordered the Enola Gay to drop the bomb on Hiroshima. Commander Paul Tibbets (Sun trine Pluto, Uranus/Mars conjunction) was in charge of the Enola Gay crew. Major Thomas Ferebee (Uranus square Sun, Pluto/Mars opposition) was the bombardier, William Sterling Parsons (Uranus/Pluto opposition) was the weaponeer, and Morris R. Jeppson (Mars/Pluto trine Uranus) served as his assistant. On the fateful day of August 6, 1945, Uranus was in conjunction with Mars and sextile a Sun/Pluto conjunction. Three days later on August 9, 1945, the other bomb was dropped over Nagasaki. The sextile between Pluto/Sun and Uranus/Mars was even tighter that day.

Meanwhile, the Soviet Union began its nuclear program. Joseph Stalin (Uranus trine Sun, Pluto/Mars opposition) put Igor Kurchatov (Uranus/Pluto opposition, Pluto trine Mars) in charge of the Soviet atomic bomb project. The U.S.S.R. received much of its nuclear information from spy Klaus Fuchs (Sun/Pluto opposition, Uranus trine Mars) and Theodore Hall (Uranus trine Pluto). Vyacheslav Molotov (Uranus/Moon conjunction, Pluto/Mars opposition) played a central role in the Soviet government during this time.

In 1962, Linus Pauling (Uranus/Sun/Pluto T-Square, Sun/Mars opposition) was awarded the Nobel Peace Prize for his efforts against above-ground nuclear testing. During the Uranus/Pluto conjunction of the 1960s, millions engaged in anti-nuclear demonstrations. Nevertheless, the United States and Soviet Union were engaged in a decades-long nuclear standoff during the Cold War. Some of the central heads-of-state during this era include Dwight D. Eisenhower (Sun/Uranus conjunction, Sun square Mars, Pluto square Saturn), Nikita Khrushchev (Uranus square Mars, Pluto trine Mars), John F. Kennedy (Uranus square Mars, Pluto exact semisquare Mars), Leonid Brezhnev (Sun/Pluto opposition, Sun/Uranus conjunction, Mars in Scorpio), Ronald Reagan (Pluto/Mars opposition, Sun in Aquarius), and Mikhail Gorbachev (Uranus square Pluto, Pluto/Mars conjunction, Pluto trine Sun).

Chapter 3
Uranus in the Signs

The following descriptions are of Uranus in the 12 signs of the zodiac These essays will be intentionally broad since the personal expression of Uranus is colored by the totality of other factors in the chart that together form a cohesive psyche. Like a spinning mirror ball, we all have a variety of reflectors unique in themselves, but that join to make something greater than the parts. The sign that Uranus occupies is but one piece of information. To get the most specific account of one's attunement to the planet, a thorough understanding of the aspects, house position and the chart's inherent message are necessary.

When considering how Uranus interacts with the styles and evolutionary processes of the signs, there are a few points to be mindful of:

- In most cases, the chart owner has a turbulent relationship with the sign that Uranus is in. There is likely to be some form of disruption that needs attention in order to restore the sign's healthy functioning.

- From an evolutionary perspective, qualities of the sign may have been poorly integrated in the soul in past lives. The estrangement from the nature of the sign has led to some degree of unfamiliarity with its promise.

- As Uranus often pertains to forces that are sudden or shocking, the sign Uranus is located in may suggest the nature of stress or trauma in the soul.

- Ultimately, greater individuation is achieved with a more secure partnering with the sign. When a person becomes aligned with his or her truth and attempts a personal breakthrough, the sign Uranus falls in portrays enhancing qualities that are novel and exciting.

- The sign also conveys how a person can fashion his or her skills and focus attention on humanitarian or collective ideals.

- It's important to note that there is a wide spectrum of evolutionary growth. Some souls are further developed than others and less prone to the shortcomings or pitfalls mentioned in the following descriptions. Always, there is further territory to be claimed, so greater mastery of the processes of the sign Uranus is in is possible.

Uranus in Aries

As a cardinal fire sign, Aries involves courage, decisive action, and moving forward unimpeded towards a sought-after goal. The Ram is driven, aligned with the will, and is embroiled in the "fight or flight" drama of survival. Primal and instinctual, Aries is aware that if you don't attempt to be the predator, you may become the prey. With so many running around asserting the self in this dog-eat-dog competition, some are bound to lose or become injured. Aries has much to do with war and conflict—its opposite sign, Libra, concerns diplomacy and peace.

With Uranus occupying this initiatory sign, several themes may be evident in the soul, including detachment or removal from the fire within, trauma due to fighting, or a general lack of potency. Uranus in Aries may be the loner on his own deserted island, be it literal or figurative. It might be the soul unable to exercise free will due to imprisonment, to following rigid codes of behavior, or to just never trusting that its power might find liberation (Uranus) through personal acts of valor. With successful individuation, the self becomes one's hero. This may sound selfish, and those with this placement must guard against overcompensating in this direction. Finding a balance between healthy self-centeredness and being able to work well with others and the world at large is the goal.

Another facet of Aries is desire, which includes sexuality as well as other personal hungers. Uranus placed here may suggest a soul that has been estranged from the primitive heat of passion. Being a member of a repressive society or community, suffering bodily harm, or experiencing celibacy (voluntary or imposed) renders in the soul a state of disconnection, a severing from the blood rush of excitement. Further growth and integration (Uranus) is achieved through an active engagement (Aries) with such processes.

With Uranus in Aries, it is appropriate to take charge, trust in oneself, maximize potency, and grow into the warrior or leader. Conquest may take many forms, but the common denominator is that at the end of the day, those who navigate this placement well declare their personal independence and meet life on their own terms.

The rugged individual or hero quality of Uranus in Aries is seen in Clint Eastwood, Sean Connery, James Dean, Steve McQueen, Jesse James, Buffalo Bill Cody, and Wyatt Earp. Those who have been pioneers and courageously aligned themselves with their will include Neil Armstrong, Yuri Gagarin, Dr. Martin Luther King Jr., Sandra Day O'Connor, Mikhail Gorbachev, Ram Dass, Ralph Nader, Maya Angelou, Ray Charles, Elvis Presley, and Gloria Steinem. Examples of erratic use of Uranus in Aries or overcompensation are seen in Charles Manson, Yasser Arafat, Donald Rumsfeld, Jimmy Swaggart, and James Earl Ray. Other notable Uranus-in-Aries figures include Elizabeth Taylor, Thomas Edison, Friedrich Nietzsche, Yoko Ono, Anne Frank, Shirley MacLaine, Barbara Walters, Elie Wiesel, and George Steinbrenner.

Uranus in Taurus

Taurus the Bull is interested in calmness, inner peace, sensuality, artistry, self-esteem, and confidence. All forms of security—physical, emotional and spiritual—pertain to this earthy, fixed and resourceful sign. When the Taurus process is not functioning smoothly, there could be a lack of self-reliance, inner disquiet, a headstrong disposition, exaggerated materialist tendencies, overindulgence, or insecurity. This sign concerns the attainment of serenity—Uranus placed here suggests that the soul is striving to secure this promise.

The spiritual history of a soul with Uranus in Taurus may include significant involvement with themes and events that were personally unsettling, leading to a current difficulty in finding relaxation. Some possibilities include self-loathing, a lack of trusting oneself, Post-Traumatic Stress Disorder, or even a predilection for gambling or squandering one's resources. There could be a lack of pleasure, abundance or the material necessities needed to feel viable. Uranus introduces a restless component to the otherwise quiet Taurus temperament. The soul is learning to find comfort.

Taurus relates to the body itself, issues of self-care, sensuality and feeling content in one's skin. Eating disorders, poor hygiene, disconnect from pleasure, or other issues regarding self-soothing are possible with Uranus in Taurus. The path to transforming these issues is to develop one's grasp of the physical and then use it as an asset. Bolstering self-worth through greater physical accomplishment, channeling the restlessness into a creative endeavor or even enjoying sensuality shows a newfound relationship with the beautiful. Some of our greatest painters, singers and celebrities have utilized the archetype of Taurus to allow us to feel safe and show us that the world has bountiful gifts.

Those with Uranus in this sign have spiritual license to enjoy and to feel content in life. They must guard against the tendency to overcompensate through unnecessary personal fortification and indulgence. Ultimately, they may find solace and use this gift to hammer a contribution that allows others to similarly feel at ease. When functioning well, Uranus in Taurus is like a firm handshake coming from a place of confidence and self-alignment.

Famous people with Uranus in Taurus noted for their sensuality or artistry include Rembrandt van Rijn, Vincent van Gogh, Ludwig van Beethoven, Johann Sebastian Bach, John Lennon, Bob Dylan, Sophia Loren, Raquel Welch, Jack Nicholson, Jane Fonda, Natalie Wood, Barbara Streisand, Robert

Redford, and Brigitte Bardot. Celebrities who seem uncomfortable in their skin, who suffer from bodily disability or who are individuating into greater calmness include Stephen Hawking, Roy Orbison, Muhammad Ali, Saddam Hussein, Woody Allen, Tina Turner, Lee Harvey Oswald, Calamity Jane, Napoleon Bonaparte, Wes Craven, Ghengis Khan, and Dick Cheney. Notable people who have overcompensated or broken rules with finances include Jim Bakker, Pete Rose, Ted Turner, and Martha Stewart.

Uranus in Gemini

The Twins are famous for their quick wit, continual dialogue and endless questioning. Gemini is a mutable air sign and concerns mental, rational, communicative, and linguistic functioning. This is the most curious and intellectually open-minded sign of all. Gemini wants to be dazzled and fascinated. Potential problems include poor decision-making, lack of emotion, restlessness, immaturity, scattered energy, and superficiality. Gemini is potentially a nice home for the airy planet Uranus. With successful spiritual development, this is a brilliant and innovative combination.

Reasons for having Uranus in this sign vary. At the top of the list is simply a need for intellectual individuation—to make up one's own mind and have autonomy regarding cognition. Some with this placement had prior-life indoctrination into belief systems that didn't serve the Gemini style of open-ended data accumulation. Therefore, evolutionary progress involves breakthroughs (Uranus) in thought processes (Gemini). The communicative function could also be compromised in some way. Aligning the voice with one's authentic truth is often discouraged in many cultures. To speak out confidently using unconventional or unpopular words often carries a price. The work with Uranus in Gemini is to take risks in communicating from the most genuine place.

Gemini is intellectually dexterous, but it also has correlates to physical movement. Ideally, the process involves perception and variety, so one needs to have freedom to move about the world to see such diversity. Uranus in this sign could point to the need to seek a wider breadth of experiences—to open the mind further through greater stimulation.

Those with Uranus in Gemini may develop virtuoso minds. They must guard against overcompensation through unstable or erratic communication that alienates rather than inspires. They may take their freedom into unnecessary displays of intellectual rebellion. Nevertheless, if a person with this placement extends effort toward claiming the brilliance available here, there is no endpoint to discovery. It is the birthright of those holding Uranus in Gemini to stimulate our minds to open further.

Famous people with Uranus in Gemini noted for their creative intelligence are Rudolph Steiner, George Washington Carver, Rupert Sheldrake, Steven Spielberg, George Lucas, Deepak Chopra, Liz Greene, Steven Forrest, Andy Kauffman, David Letterman, George Santayana, and Newt Gingrich. Those noted for messages of freedom, progress or rebellion include Theodore Roosevelt, Bob Marley, Jim Morrison, Salman Rushdie, Billie Jean King, Larry Flynt, Camille Paglia, and Hillary Clinton. Many breakthrough writers and songwriters have this placement, including Anton Chekhov, Stephen King, Anne Rice, Paulo Coelho, Paul McCartney, Janis Joplin, Joni Mitchell, Dolly Parton, and Thomas Moore.

Psychic Uri Gellar used his mind to bend spoons, challenging his audience to rethink the limits of what is possible. Alois Alzheimer made great strides in understanding cognitive pathology. Edvard Munch, in *The Scream*, portrays erratic vocalization. Jerry Springer is famous for hosting a television program largely defined by verbal outbursts and unpredictable communication. Many argue that George W. Bush would benefit by opening his mind to other perspectives and is famous for mangling the English language. Oliver North reached notoriety for lying to Congress, while Pete Townshend has described himself as a compulsive liar.

Uranus in Cancer

Cancer is a cardinal water sign and relates to the heart, inner life, family conditioning, roots, vulnerability, and emotional receptivity to others. The Crab is defensive and protective, interested in the survival of itself and its offspring. This is the sign of nurturance and home. As we apply the Uranian qualities of disruption, instability, detachment, and coolness to this realm, a picture of emotional disorganization emerges. This is in equal measure to the emotional breakthroughs and personal revolutions available with successful advancement.

Many with this placement do have unstable home lives with unpredictable events to adjust to. The spiritual history is likely to be marked by such turmoil, and any destabilizing experiences in the early years are necessary for maximal growth and advancement when this pattern is eventually reconciled. The family of origin or early home experiences may be Uranian in spirit, such as at a commune or other environment that is non-conventional. This may sound attractive to some, but a lack of order and structure could lead to erratic anchoring within the self. Membership in a tribe or clan (Cancer) that is relegated to the fringes of society (Uranus) undercuts the Cancer need to sink its claws in and find deep roots. One's familial membership may have led to jarring emotional experiences in society, including discrimination or ostracism. Finding one's true identity and integrating it proudly is the work. To jettison one's lineage and live someone else's life is the weaker response.

Perhaps the most common manifestation of Uranus in Cancer is the condition of emotional avoidance. The refusal to truly be with one's vulnerability is so widespread that most anyone could claim to use this strategy at times. In fact, western society promotes this defensive measure by championing stoicism, results and overt displays of strength. Those who carry this placement of Uranus are likely to distance themselves from upset, pain or the more unseemly dynamics of poor developmental influences. There is potentially a high degree of unconsciousness regarding such matters. Uranus in Cancer seeks to catalyze greater awareness, to find the buried self and fashion a new, more genuine relationship with the heart.

Those who are able to venture into the depths emerge with an impenetrable self-alliance. They also stimulate greater emotional awareness in others, and the work is completed by forming a new family system based on emotional truth and supportive individuation. The refusal to take on this work results in deeper emotional chaos, a failure to empathize with others, and the obliteration of feeling.

Notable people who have deepened into being heartfelt and emotionally responsive, often in resolution of emotional upset, include Ammachi, Oprah Winfrey, Stevie Wonder, Christopher Reeve, Ron Howard, Bob Geldof, and Richard Gere. Some who have publicly wrestled with poor emotional integration or mismanagement and display erratic emotional tendencies are Roseanne Barr, Mark David Chapman, David Berkowitz, Karen Carpenter, Howard Stern, Margot Kidder, Elvis Costello, and Paul Reubens (Pee Wee Herman).

Figures involved with disputes over homeland, security or tribal relations are Mahatma Gandhi, Gerry Adams, Benjamin Netanyahu, Ayman Al-Zawahiri, Tony Blair, and Condoleezza Rice. Michael Moore has sought to awaken his audience to how the homeland is being governed, while Ang Lee's films focus on liberating the inner landscape. Alfred Adler has been a leading psychologist of emotional development. The United States itself is named after Amerigo Vespucci.

Uranus in Leo

Leo roars a unique personality, creatively expressing itself to the world. A fixed fire sign, Leo is extraverted, commanding, warm, generous, engaging, charismatic, and even regal. It must guard against egocentricity, boasting, childishness, overindulgence, an inflated sense of importance, and the tendency to keep everything sunny. Uranus in Leo finds inclusion and validation by developing greater style, talent, or other means of being noticed.

How heartbreaking to give up on a dream. There are bills to pay, children to nurture, the grind of reality bursting the balloon of achieving greater visibility, perhaps even fame. Uranus (break) in Leo (heartfelt expression) conveys the spiritual circumstance in which a soul is picking up the pieces and molding creativity into a new, more wild gift that enthralls others. The transformation from the sidelines to center stage furthers growth and completes the intention.

Another strong possibility is the need to re-engage with fun. Many souls are worn-out and tired, involved in fixing crises or so wounded that life has lost its luster. Individuation (Uranus) moves toward reaching greater merriment and positivity (Leo). Some souls with this placement have been afraid, held back or just unaware that life can be endless pleasure. It is time to claim it!

Since Leo equates to personality, Uranus here produces a most compellingly unique and interesting temperament. These people naturally command attention and are learning to use this ability to inspire others, contribute artistically or entertain in some capacity. With this newfound spiritual liberation, the folly is to overcompensate by adapting a demanding, narcissistic style that turns others off. This would sabotage the efforts to attain more healthy visibility and acclaim.

The potential for generosity on a global scale is substantial. Ultimately, those with Uranus in Leo can spread good cheer and fortune to put smiles on many faces. Developing and zealously partnering with personal creativity is the cutting edge of growth. The failure to do so produces the lonely, wishful also-ran who never took the initiative in finding happiness. Life on the sidelines becomes increasingly unacceptable.

Larger-than-life personalities with Uranus in Leo include Madonna, Sean Penn, Tom Cruise, Magic Johnson, Princess Diana, Sarah Ferguson, Carl Jung, MC Hammer, and Benjamin Franklin. Those with an unusual or extraordinary talent include Michael Jackson, John McEnroe, Edgar Cayce, Harry Houdini, Prince, Jim Carrey, Martina Navratilova, Sergei Rachmaninoff, Michael Flatley, and Yo Yo Ma. Those noted for narcissistic tendencies include Dennis Rodman, Osama bin Laden, Jeffery Dahmer, David Koresh, and Simon Cowell. Other personalities who are individuating in the direction of Leo pursuits include George Clooney, Bill Gates, Bo Derek, Eddie Murphy, Geena Davis, Melissa Etheridge, Whoopi Goldberg, Tom Hanks, George Stephanopoulos, Kim Cattrall, Tracey Ullman, Denis Leary, Spike Lee, and Howie Mandel.

Uranus in Virgo

Virgo relates to industriousness, self-improvement, humility, competence, detail, functionality, and service. As a mutable earth sign, it entails the process of working on a project in the pursuit of greater precision, better health and the realization of a more refined state of being. Struggles of this sign include perfectionism, anxiety, repression, obsessions, and a tendency toward criticism of self and others. Ultimately, Virgo arrives at modesty and humility, feeling satisfied about the efforts extended in making a better world.

Uranus alludes to phenomena that lack successful integration in the soul. Therefore, the task of incarnation is to evolve and welcome in these attributes. Development for Uranus-in-Virgo people proceeds by crafting works, figuring things out, and honing skills. By bringing the innovative and brilliant qualities of Uranus into earthy manifestation and utility, great leaps of progress are realized. By so doing, the soul feels good about itself, proud of its efficacy.

One reason why Uranus appears in Virgo is the refusal to focus and concentrate. Think of the slacker, couch potato, or complacent millionaire. Many ease into a comfortable routine devoid of critical self-analysis, an assessment of how to further grow. It is incumbent upon these souls to roll up their sleeves and increase productivity. If not, there could be disruptions (Uranus) with health issues (Virgo), which would force them to become more resolute and practical in taking care of the self.

From another angle, Uranus in Virgo could pertain to the condition of not feeling very good about the self. This electric planet energizing the self-deprecating sign yields a heightened state of anxiety. "I can't do anything right!" might be the slogan. If one succumbs to self-pity and impotence, then this combination produces chaos (Uranus) in the process of achieving competence and satisfaction (Virgo). In the extreme, one gives up and pours another drink, opens another bag of potato chips or cuts another scar in the arm for punishment. The evolutionary task is to take measures to improve one's lot and reach greater alliance with the higher self. Then, the potentials for innovation are awakened, and fascinating creations both boost the sense of competence and contribute to the world.

In the grips of such potentials, overcompensation occurs with tunnel vision. Sure, many interesting inventions are made, but Virgo is prone to be less than well-rounded. If too much effort and focus are directed narrowly, problems in other areas of life will emerge. It's healthy to get on the treadmill, but it should not become a religion. Eating healthy is important, but knowing *all* of the nutritional information for every meal is unnecessary. Nevertheless, those with Uranus in Virgo are here to work on the self and to use that momentum to access spiritual insight (Uranus) and transform it into tangible contributions (Virgo) that further humankind.

Famous people with Uranus in Virgo include Alexander Fleming, who discovered Penicillin. Others who have made steadfast contributions through their diligence and critical thinking include Albert Einstein, Tycho Brahe, Franklin Roosevelt, Gary Kasparov, HL Mencken, Upton Sinclair, John Maynard Keynes, Jean-Jacques Rousseau, Baruch Spinoza, Auguste Comte, and John Keats. Some who have taken measures to liberate the poor, disempowered or oppressed include James Joyce, Virginia Woolf, Bono, Eleanor Roosevelt, Tracy Chapman, Salma Hayek, and Rodney King. Some celebrities who would clearly benefit from greater health practices, humility or accountability include Benito Mussolini, Kurt Cobain, Anna Nicole Smith, Charlie Sheen, Mike Tyson, Chris Farley, Heidi Fleiss, Timothy McVeigh, and John Wayne Bobbitt. Some who have reached personal liberation and fulfillment through perfecting their craft or being complete professionals are Steffi Graf, JK Rowling, Harry Connick Jr., Pablo Picasso, Eugene Delacroix, Reggie Miller, Johnny Depp, Jamie Foxx, Tori Amos, Halle Berry, Don Cheadle, and Jodie Foster.

Uranus in Libra

Libra, a cardinal air sign, involves concepts such as justice, civility, fairness, etiquette, and appreciation. It concerns relationships, aesthetics, socialization, diplomacy, and peaceful interactions. Balance and harmony are frequently used key words to describe this most pleasing, even charming sign. On the struggling side of Libra are the tendency to orbit around others, superficiality, placation, over-polished style, incessant fawning, obsession with fairness, poor decision-making, and lack of bravery. The disruptive nature of Uranus located here points to a soul in need of repairing the jolts that have thrown equilibrium out of balance. Individuation occurs by finding equality and concord with others.

Having equal partnerships is elusive. So many times one partner holds greater stature, skills, or charisma, or carries the self in a more dominant fashion. Entering roles that cement power differentials may lead to a workable relationship, but Libran qualities are left out of bounds. Many with Uranus here are learning to have successful egalitarian relationships based on mutual trust, sharing and seeing eye-to-eye. If this is not an aspiration, there is the potential to have turbulence (Uranus) in partnerships (Libra) based on an unconscious rejection of patterns that do not serve growth.

Many souls have experienced jarring events that rupture trust in others, or that have made them question if life is indeed fair. Uranus in Libra presents the opportunity to create a newfound connection with peace that inspires one to contribute artistically or socially to a more integrated world vision. Uranus, as a diplomat (Libra), enters into interpersonal scenarios that trigger greater awareness. This can be accomplished through the fields of counseling, politics, activism, or dealing with some form of negotiation.

An example of overcompensation would be militant animal or environmental activism where, in the name of fairness and justice, individuals create interpersonal turmoil, break the rules of civility and further their own sense of mistrust in life. Some with Uranus in Libra are so preoccupied with finding a just and harmonious relationship that their histories become marked by failure after failure from making poor choices. This just adds to the elusive (Uranus) situation of finding satisfying interpersonal engagement (Libra). These individuals also may be drawn to unconventional (Uranus) connections that do not deliver interdependence (Libra). It is the path of those with Uranus in Libra to bring balance into their lives and help the rest of humanity bring to greater fruition the ideal of an interconnected peaceful society. Members of this group are keenly aware that a more civilized existence is possible.

Famous people with Uranus in Libra who serve as examples of individuation through relationships (and their accompanying struggles) include Angelina Jolie, Jennifer Lopez, Ben Affleck, Andre Agassi, Monica Lewinsky, Alanis Morissette, Lance Armstrong, Renee Zellweger, Amy Fisher, and Soon-Yi Previn. Some figures who are growing into a greater sense of fairness or civility are King Louis XIV, Adolph Hitler, Machiavelli, Ho Chi Minh, and Chiang Kai-Shek. Some would benefit by adding grace, tact or consideration for rules and decorum: Eminem, Marilyn Manson, Allen Iverson, Winona Ryder, Snoop Dogg, and Sammy Sosa.

Breakthrough artists with Uranus in Libra include Marc Chagall, Georgia O'Keefe, Johann Strauss, Al Jolson, M. Knight Shyamalan, Hans Christian Andersen, Charlie Chaplin, and Sinclair Lewis. Some Uranus-in-Libra figures have become idealized symbols of beauty: Catherine Zeta-Jones, Leonardo DiCaprio, Naomi Campbell, Jude Law, Matthew McConaughey, Kate Moss, Charlize Theron, and Claudia Schiffer.

Uranus in Scorpio

This water and social sign concerns processing with others, the deep impact of our connections, the exchange of emotional truths, and the resolution of interpersonal hurts. Scorpio is a fixed sign and is famous for its intensity, probing, determination, and fascination with the dark, taboo and sexual. It must guard against being ruthless, domineering, antagonistic, suspicious, manipulative, and vengeful. Many of us have been wounded by complex psychological territory; abuse, betrayals and control dynamics are a part of its scope. Those with Uranus in Scorpio find individuation through making powerful and intimate soul contact entering this terrain and finding liberation.

Some of our greatest surprises (Uranus) are packaged in intimate relationships (Scorpio). As we engage in deeper and deeper ways, more of who we are emerges and connects with partners for better, and sometimes for worse. Ideally, we persevere and grow, heal, find greater truths and self-revelations. For whatever reason, those with Uranus in Scorpio have unfinished work in this regard and likely have a spiritual history of some trauma associated with its resolution.

Scorpio processes by their nature are hidden or unconscious. Uranus too deals with what is inaccessible or out-of-bounds. Many with this combination have deep (Scorpio) unconscious remnants of shocking (Uranus) material buried in the soul. Sudden death, suicide, sexual issues, or emotional violations are possible. The common defensive measures of repressing or dissociating from such material is understandable but also postpones the inevitable confrontation. With Uranus in Scorpio, the time to free these psychic artifacts has arrived. By doing such important soul-level work, a newfound engagement with power, a sense of conviction, and a desire to be an agent of radical transformation is born.

Those pursuing this path have considerable reserves of energy available to make drastic changes, not only in the self but also in the evolution of the world at large. Since we teach what we are learning and become experts at the very things that trouble us, people with Uranus in Scorpio may develop into our greatest informers of the mysteries of the unconscious. They can be alchemical spiritual healers, shamans or guides. They may cultivate an uncanny sense of mission, and relentlessly attempt to make an impact. Uranus in Scorpio promises intense awakenings.

Scorpio is compelling territory, and overcompensation with Uranus here leads to compulsions. Preoccupations with power, control, morbid fascinations, unconventional sexual interests and expressions, or overly shocking presentations that are designed to scare others are possible. This does not heal the relationship with Scorpio; rather, it exaggerates its style and renews an erratic (Uranus) connection with it. The path of personal freedom is a noble one, and those with this combination have substantial power at their disposal to be profound instruments of evolution if they choose to walk that path.

Alfred Kinsey is perhaps the central figure for the liberation of sexuality in the twentieth century. Lesser known is Wilhelm Reich, a psychologist who advocated "orgastic potency," and greater emotional health through aligning with sexuality. Jean Piaget, Fritz Perls and Anna Freud are other famous psychologists who have focused on freeing the unconscious. Indeed, freedom from controlling forces is a major theme in the works and lives of Abraham Lincoln, Charles Darwin, Harriet Beecher Stowe, Dane Rudhyar, Soren Kierkegaard, Emmanuel Kant, Amelia Earhart, Paramahansa Yogananda, Meher Baba, Krishnamurti, and Sir Francis Bacon, who declared that "knowledge is power." Erwin Rommell dealt with liberation from powerful forces by hatching a plot to overthrow Hitler. Some who have not found freedom from control act out the darker potentials of controlling others: Paul Joseph Goebbels, Rudolph Hess and other Nazi figures have Uranus in Scorpio, as does Chinese dictator Mao Tse Tung.

A fascination with the dark is evident in the writings of Edgar Allen Poe. In a much different way, the work of Charles Dickens exposed social truths that were often ignored. Louis Braille literally helped blind people out of darkness through the system of reading-by-touch that is named for him. J. Edgar

Hoover led the secretly investigative F.B.I. and was also involved with hidden sexual taboos. Heath Ledger portrayed a homosexual cowboy in *Brokeback Mountain,* while Maggie Gyllenhaal involved herself with sexual power ploys in *Secretary*. Hayden Christiansen took on the role of a young Darth Vader in the *Star Wars* prequels. Other modern figures known for an edgy, alluring or mysterious nature are Colin Farrell, Liv Tyler, Eva Longoria, Fiona Apple, Justin Timberlake, and Christina Aguilera.

Uranus in Sagittarius

Fiery and mutable Sagittarius is expansive, broad-minded, adventurous, philosophical, optimistic, political, and enthralled by the exotic and foreign. It is interested in spiritual direction, arriving at moral clarity and understanding larger questions. A less evolved expression results in dogmatism, closed-mindedness, nomadic sprawling, unwise risk-taking, and fanatical behavioral routines. Uranus in Sagittarius is one of the most exploratory and spacious combinations in all of astrology. With successful individuation, these souls understand, teach, and inspire new horizons of discovery.

Applying the often turbulent and erratic qualities of Uranus to this sign yields the lost soul. Feeling alienated (Uranus) regarding religion, belief systems and life direction (Sagittarius) is a central possibility. In the spiritual history could be a renunciation of faith in favor of an atheistic or even nihilistic world view. Individuation occurs upon embracing a new, more holistic or Uranian perspective that is inclusive, meaningful and quite possibly non-denominational. Uranus and Sagittarius combine to form a universal religion, one that includes all souls in the spirit of evolutionary advancement. Souls with Uranus in Sagittarius are hopping back on the horse that threw them and finding that they can indeed make it gallop with purpose.

Another possibility in the soul is the inaccessibility of risk, adventure and expansion; isolation, imprisonment, the trappings of routine, and the yielding to others' limiting expectations are some ways this might manifest. Souls that have been grounded are now ready to fly, and Uranus in Sagittarius promises high-octane travel.

Overcompensating behaviors include the complete dismissal of common sense and reason in favor of high-flying ideas and manic behavior. If one approaches religious territory in an unbalanced way, wild, unstable beliefs and practices may result. An individual may be under the illusion that he or she knows *the truth* and develop a messianic complex. Nevertheless, those with Uranus in Sagittarius may develop into our utopian philosophers, our teachers of what is possible, our great scientific discoverers and political pioneers. They will live life large like a Viking, cowboy or trailblazer, and inspire the rest of us to pursue our own ventures (Sagittarius) into the unknown (Uranus).

Famous people with Uranus in Sagittarius who have conceived new political or religious visions include George Washington, John Adams, Frederick Douglass, Karl Marx, and Martin Luther, while some artistic visionaries are Raphael, Alfred Hitchcock, William Shakespeare, George Orwell, Joseph Haydn, John Steinbeck, Vladimir Nabokov, Duke Ellington, MC Escher, and Walt Disney. Discoverers of larger truths include Galileo Galilei, Werner Heisenberg, Linus Pauling, Franz Mesmer, Benjamin Spock, Margaret Mead, and Robert Oppenheimer—each in very different ways. Florence Nightingale typifies the life lived by purpose, while Fred Astaire's connection with the archetype has more to do with freedom of movement. Some notable adventurers, free spirits, travelers, and outlaws are Ernest Hemingway, Walt Whitman, Anaïs Nin, Bob Hope, Humphrey Bogart, Cary Grant, Joan Crawford, Gary Cooper, Salvador Dali, Ansel Adams, Marlene Dietrich, Charles Lindbergh, Rene Lacoste, Al Capone, John Dillinger, and Louis Armstrong.

All living people with Uranus in Sagittarius are still young. We do notice a similar adventuresome and free-wheeling quality in such persons as Britney Spears, Prince William, Raphael Nadal, Lindsay Lohan, Scarlet Johansson, Andy Roddick, Paris Hilton, and Avril Lavigne.

Uranus in Capricorn

Capricorn is a cardinal earth sign and regards social structures, institutions and functioning within the parameters of the status quo. Personal attributes of the sign include fortitude, stature, endurance, ambition, integrity, reliability, and concern for creating a personal legacy. Some struggles are insensitivity, rigidity, fearfulness, exaggerated need for control, and the burden of carrying heavy responsibility. Having Uranus placed in this sign produces the evolutionary program of achieving breakthrough by means of public visibility and longevity. Becoming an elder or a dignified leader, or achieving career success is at the forefront of growth.

Many with Uranus in Capricorn feel alienated by the way society is run, by the tenor of governing frameworks, and can't relate to the status quo. The soul history may include themes of despair, oppression, estrangement, or the inability to control one's destiny. Individuation takes the form of entering social structures and implementing new operating procedures to procure innovative solutions. These people are attuned to how fixtures (Capricorn) are broken (Uranus) and are natural progressive (Uranus) leaders (Capricorn).

Some souls are unsure of how to rise from dire circumstances to attain success. Some give up trying and become rebels or antagonists to the mainstream reality. Others are opposed to slogging through the work necessary to see tangible changes in their lives. All of these conditions are indicative of Uranus in Capricorn. Spiritual advancement proceeds when one takes concrete measures to improve one's lot and reach toward greater rewards. Becoming the goat who climbs the mountain to the summit is very much the idea. By performing this task of stamina and working on one's aims, the authentic individuality (Uranus) may become an institution (Capricorn) in itself. The contributions of those with Uranus in Capricorn are memorable and enduring. These people potentially reshape whatever field they enter and become legendary contributors.

One way overcompensation may ensue is by injecting too much of a progressive agenda into one's work. This may cause rejection and antagonism leading to removal from conventional structures, and thus the cycle of alienation is repeated. Another pitfall to avoid is becoming too focused on material gain, which could lead to a hardened, stoic demeanor. This in itself becomes a source of disaffection or divisiveness from others. Uranus-in-Capricorn people may potentially change the world from the inside out. They aspire to positions where power is centralized and gradually implement advances that bring us closer to a new vision.

Famous people with Uranus in Capricorn who have held authoritative positions and instituted progressive changes include Thomas Jefferson, Julius Caesar, Mother Theresa, Claude Levi-Strauss, Bugsy Siegel, Howard Hughes, Oskar Schindler, and Arthur Koestler, the founder of the League Against Capital Punishment. Some who have solidified an enduring legacy through their inventiveness are Johannes Kepler, Jules Verne, Frida Kahlo, Django Reinhardt, Feodor Dostoyevsky, Jackson Pollock, Tennessee Williams, Ian Fleming, and Elia Kazan. Notable individuals who have secured a legacy of originality include Vincent Price, John Wayne, Lucille Ball, Roy Rogers, Josephine Baker, Jimmy Stewart, Katharine Hepburn, Milton Berle, Sir Laurence Olivier, and Bette Davis.

In *12 Angry Men*, Henry Fonda was able to work within the jury system as a progressive force. William Herschel discovered Uranus. Ayn Rand posited a philosophy championing rugged individualism (Uranus) as the pillar of society (Capricorn). Abraham Maslow's theory of development involves the attainment of self-respect and solidity (Capricorn) through self-actualization (Uranus). Daniel Radcliffe is a youngster with this combination. His most famous movie role to date, Harry Potter, is a character wrapped up in all sorts of unexpected mayhem (Uranus) at a revered institution noted for its protocol (Capricorn).

Uranus in Aquarius

Uranus is in its home in the fixed air sign of Aquarius, and shares the attributes of revolution, ingenuity, liberation, futuristic focus, wildness, and all-around brilliance. Personal attributes of Aquarius are self-allegiance, uniqueness, communal focus, and unpredictability. The lower vibration of Aquarius includes personal detachment, eccentricity, erratic behavior, rebellion, orneriness, and over-analysis. Aquarius has a transpersonal focus, so it's visionary about humanity's evolution and potential. Those with Uranus in Aquarius are developing into the innovators who push the progressive envelope in every conceivable way.

The most obvious hallmark of souls with Uranus in Aquarius is a spiritual history devoid of such breakthrough. Therefore, growth proceeds by staking individuality on this very process of personal liberation. Then, these individuals are able to fantastically contribute to our advancement. Souls that have conformed, adopted a complacent style, sought too much validation, been an anonymous face in the crowd, or been tied to family or career responsibilities often do not individuate into their own brilliant truth. They may incarnate with Uranus in Aquarius to perform this essential function.

The other major possibility is a condition of significant trauma, breakdown, impairment, or dissociation of some variety in the soul. There are many circumstances that can prevent someone from realizing who he or she really is. Someone who has both legs accidentally blown off may reincarnate with Uranus in Aquarius. There would be a particular sensitivity to the uniqueness of all people, and this would inform the evolutionary work to follow.

Another consideration is group-related karma. Some with Uranus in Aquarius have spiritual issues of rejection from a tribe or community. They find greater individuation by group inclusion and joining with others to make a difference. Still others have given up caring about the world and are completely let down and disaffected by the state of affairs on the sociological level. Their evolutionary work is to transform this energy into its positive manifestation, and to be an agent of change.

Modes of overcompensation include a preoccupation with individuality, which can lead to eccentricity and might repeat a pattern of detachment from others. Choosing to immerse the self in global causes may unwittingly prevent someone from aligning with personal truth. Being the unwise maverick or rebel may lead to rejection and estrangement. Ultimately, Uranus is in its clearest expression in Aquarius, and souls with this placement are called to take risks in discovering personal uniqueness. By so doing, they tap into the fantastic divine intelligence that holds the timeless answers that unlock the greatest riddles. These individuals bring the future to the present.

Individuals who have taken it upon themselves to be agents of sociological change are Nelson Mandela, Rosa Parks, Indira Gandhi, Menachem Begin, Jesse Owens, and Jackie Robinson. Some progressive thinkers or visionaries include John F. Kennedy, James Madison, Maharishi Mahesh Yogi, Alan Watts, and Lewis Carroll. Those who have put forth significant innovations in their respective fields include Jonas Salk, Peter Paul Rubens, Francisco de Goya, Federico Fellini, Ingrid Bergman, Orson Wells, Thor Heyerdahl, Karl Pribram, Mark Twain, Leonard Bernstein, Ella Fitzgerald, Helena Blavatsky, Henrik Ibsen, and Les Paul.

Albert Camus is noted for his ideas of the absurd, opposition to totalitarianism and devotion to human rights. JD Salinger shunned mainstream success, and the *Catcher in the Rye* championed individuality over conformity. Jimmy Hoffa and Mike Wallace became famous by challenging the status quo, and Richard Nixon refused to follow the rules while occupying office. Frank Sinatra captured the spirit of this combination when he sang about doing it "My Way." William Burroughs was a leader of the anti-establishment Beat Generation. Other highly individualistic personalities and breakthrough figures include Dylan Thomas, Zsa Zsa Gabor, Jackie Gleason, Joe DiMaggio, Dean Martin, and Billy Holliday. Pearl Bailey fits this description and also earned the Presidential Medal of Freedom.

Uranus in Pisces

Pisces is a mutable, watery, mystical sign that concerns the development of consciousness, the resolution of karma, and letting go. Its emotionality involves compassion, the universal love of humanity. Pisces has a dreamy, ethereal, often visionary or inspiring quality. The struggle is being wishy-washy, unreliable, ungrounded, gullible, impotent, and escapist. Those with Uranus in Pisces have a soul intention to find individuation through the transcendence of limitations, through contemplative practice and ultimately through being an instrument of a new spiritual vision.

Many in this spiritual group have soul histories of limitation, fear or mistrust that Spirit can actually be experienced. This leads to sadness, dejection, existential malaise, or crises. By adapting a new (Uranus) relationship with the divine (Pisces), they may find a most loving, inclusive set of validating spiritual experiences that personally connects them with the mystical workings of nature. This informs a humanitarian contribution aimed at catalyzing (Uranus) the collective consciousness (Pisces) to similarly download a progressive vision. The potential in this combination is to be nothing less than the compassionate nerve endings of Spirit that distribute love.

Another reason why someone may have Uranus in Pisces is to latch on to unbounded creative potential and inspire the collective to feel something transcendent. The soul history may include an unfulfilled dream, a longing to have a breakthrough (Uranus) in one's imagination (Pisces). This combination is similar to Dorothy's wish that somewhere over the rainbow there could be magic and fantasy—to find such wonder and ultimately nourishment.

Those who grasp that there really are other worlds to explore may overcompensate by obliterating their connection to this one. The reckless (Uranus) substance abuser (Pisces) or purveyor of ill-advised risks are faces of the darker version possible here. In the grips of Uranian potential, Pisces territory needs to be navigated consciously, or the dissolution of the self is possible. Managed well, this combination is perhaps the most uplifting and imaginative of collective progress in the entire astrological system. Those born with this combination are here to invite us to a new, more holistic and compassionate world.

The urge to find and make contact with new worlds is seen in the biographies of air and space pioneers John Glenn and Chuck Yeager, and *Twilight Zone* creator Rod Serling. Inspired and brilliant artists with this combination include Wolfgang Mozart, Claude Monet, Auguste Renoir, Paul Cezanne, Auguste Rodin, Kurt Vonnegut, Peter Tchaikovsky, Miles Davis, and Norman Mailer. Having a vision of collective togetherness, compassion and redemption is a theme dear to Chief Joseph, Thich Nhat Hanh, Jimmy Carter, Robert F. Kennedy, Ramakrishna, Pope John Paul II, Yitzhak Rabin, Harry Belafonte, Alex Haley, and Eva Peron. Elizabeth Kubler-Ross helped ready people for the transition of death, while Betty Friedan advocated coming together in the transcendence of gender differences. William James addressed the psychology of mystical experiences. John D. Rockefeller revolutionized philanthropy, and Paul Newman has exhibited Uranus in Pisces through his selfless establishment of charities. Some may argue that Fidel Castro and Malcolm X struggled with achieving the softness and perspective this combination welcomes. Their biographies nevertheless show an alignment with an ideal.

Some who have taken risky or self-destructive paths of transcendence are psychedelic advocate Timothy Leary and the literary creative minds of Truman Capote and Jack Kerouac, who succumbed to alcoholism, as did Judy Garland. Marilyn Monroe had difficulty coping with daily life and committed suicide through an overdose. Her life, more than most others, was dreamlike and strange to her. Claus von Bulow was caught up in alleged murder charges, also through administering an overdose. Beer mogul Alfred Heineken also has Uranus in Pisces. Nostradamus embodies the psychic potentials of this combination, as does the inspirational Romantic poet William Blake.

Note on Uranus in the Houses

The house placement of Uranus suggests a primary area for personal breakthrough to ideally unfold. Thematically aligned with the zodiac signs (Aries/1st House, Taurus/2nd House, etc.) there is some validity to the frequent practice seen in astrology literature to interchange sign and house. However, one should approach this with caution as houses are different than signs.

In my understanding, planets are energy (what), signs are processes (how) and houses are areas where the planetary energy (modified by sign) play out. Therefore, planets are primary, signs are secondary and houses are tertiary. The planets in aspect to a particular planet (in this case Uranus) *energetically* impact it and hold the dominant influence. Signs are the next step, to see what psycho-spiritual processes and lessons are coloring the energetic exchange, while the application to a house follows.

Through aspect and rulership every planet has relevance to several houses. In fact, a holistic view of the chart (as a single psyche) would yield the conclusion that every planet must influence every house—we simply carry all of who we are wherever we go. Given the complexity of how planets (in aspect and in rulership to other planets and involved with processes relevant to the signs) govern activity pertaining to houses, it would be too simplistic to offer rote explanations of Uranus in the 12 houses. For instance, Uranus in conjunction with Mars in Capricorn in the 1st House is vastly different from Uranus in Aquarius in the 1st House sextile Mercury in Aries in the 3rd.

It is beyond this author to provide catch-all paragraphs that honor this complexity. I have found the ordering of examining planet, sign then house to be a most useful method. The understanding that houses interrelate allows the planet in question not to be constricted to the confines of any one house. Its energetic process is dispersed in many ways. The many chart examples given later on will illustrate how Uranus plays out in houses.

Chapter 4
Uranian Individuals

Some individuals are particularly Uranian. They have catalyzed significant shifts in society through their willingness to align with their truth, vision or insistence on change. A selection of these progressive figures is detailed in this section. First, a brief biographical sketch is offered, followed by an astrological analysis of Uranian factors in the chart.[3]

Galileo Galilei

Galileo is cited as one of the most important scientists in history. He made significant discoveries and advances in astronomy, physics and technology. He laid the groundwork for many later breakthroughs, including Newton's laws and Einstein's theory of relativity. What makes him even more of a Uranian figure is his assertion that we shouldn't just blindly believe authorities, but rather question what we're told. This led to the split of science from the church and ultimately his recognition as the "father of science" in later generations. Galileo stood trial for heresy, had some of his work banned, and spent years under house arrest—"the crime was looking up the truth," as the Indigo Girls like to sing. Galileo continued to support the heliocentric view despite the consequences, and we can view him as a Uranian hero. Remember, he was an astrologer too!

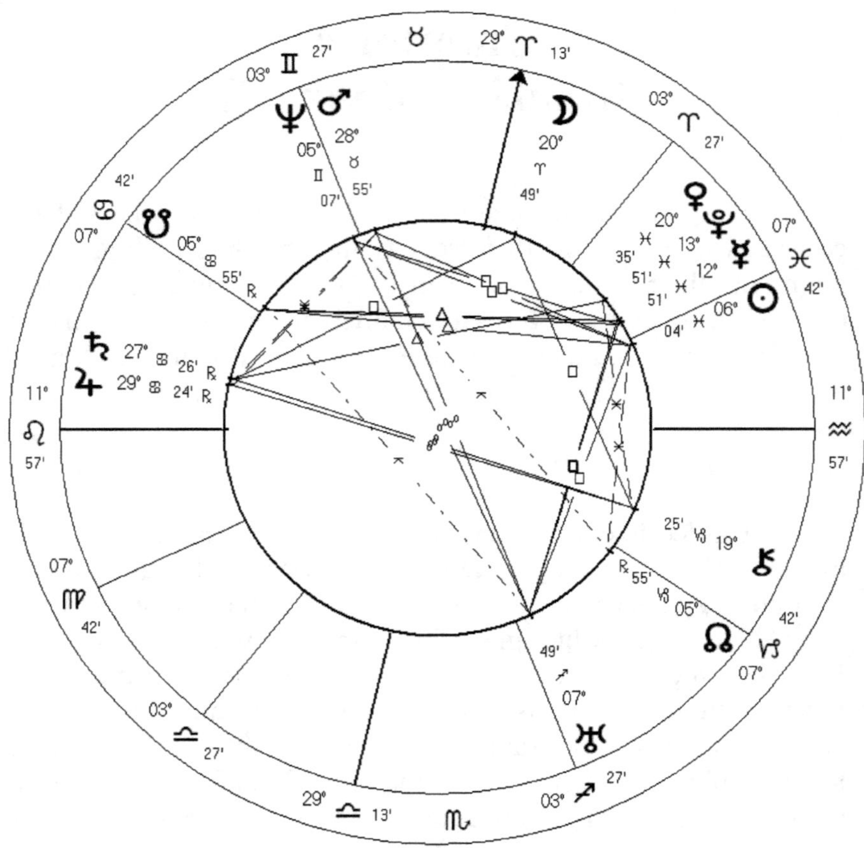

Uranian details: Galileo has Uranus in Sagittarius in the 5th House square his Sun in Pisces in the 7th House, and a Mercury/Pluto/Venus stellium in Pisces in the 8th House. Uranus is opposed Mars in Taurus and Neptune in Gemini on the 11th House cusp. Mercury is the ruler of his 11th House. He has Aquarius on the 7th House cusp.

Uranus in Sagittarius in the 5th House suggests breakthroughs in global understandings, far-reaching discoveries and reforming philosophical/religious assumptions. In the 5th House, the ability to express one's truth (Uranus) is being developed. The square to the 7th House Pisces Sun indicates that sharing his truth with others is going to be difficult. He is a visionary (Pisces) of an intellectual variety (Neptune in Gemini, also squaring the Sun). Ultimately, he becomes a teacher (Uranus in Sagittarius), and an inspiration (Sun in Pisces).

Uranus square Mercury is simply his brilliance. In the probing, investigative realm of the 8th House, the loftiness of his Piscean mind attains focus. Venus/Pluto indicates more of the interpersonal work he needed to address. Venus/Pluto in Pisces is prone to giving away its power to others, especially in the 8th House. Individuating into his truth (Uranus in Sagittarius), Galileo is better able to hold his ground. This allows Venus/Pluto to potentially transform into deep, collaborative exchanges. With Mercury involved, speaking up is the way forward.

Galileo has Neptune in Gemini and Mars in Taurus on the 11th House cusp. Here we see unbounded intellectual exploration grounded in earthy pragmatics. Neptune in the 11th House correlates with astronomy and the endless universe; Mars in Taurus investigates the physical world. There is a steadfast commitment (Mars in Taurus) to channel the will toward far-reaching intellectual pursuits. This conjunction is opposed his Uranus, quite fitting for philosophical advances in astronomy and physics.

With Gemini on the 11th House cusp, Mercury serves as the ruler of this house. Galileo's contribution to global progress (11th House) is scientific and intellectual in nature. Mercury in Pisces is the visionary, far-reaching quality he brought to his work, while the 8th House has much to do with death/rebirth—transforming our minds to consider new possibilities. Aquarius on the 7th House cusp echoes the theme of holding one's truth with others.

It wasn't until 1992 that the Catholic Church admitted to wrongdoing in the Galileo matter—pardoning him for adhering to the heliocentric view. Interestingly, at this time, transiting Saturn in Aquarius entered Galileo's 7th House. The establishment (Saturn) was able to modernize (Aquarius) and form a more equitable relationship (7th House) with him. Also, transiting Uranus was in conjunction with Neptune in the middle degrees of Capricorn, forming a sextile to Galileo's Mercury/Pluto/Venus stellium in Pisces. This too suggests that the traditional church (Capricorn) was modernizing (Uranus) and healing (Neptune) with Galileo's ideas (Mercury) and the prior conflict (Pluto/Venus).

Abraham Lincoln

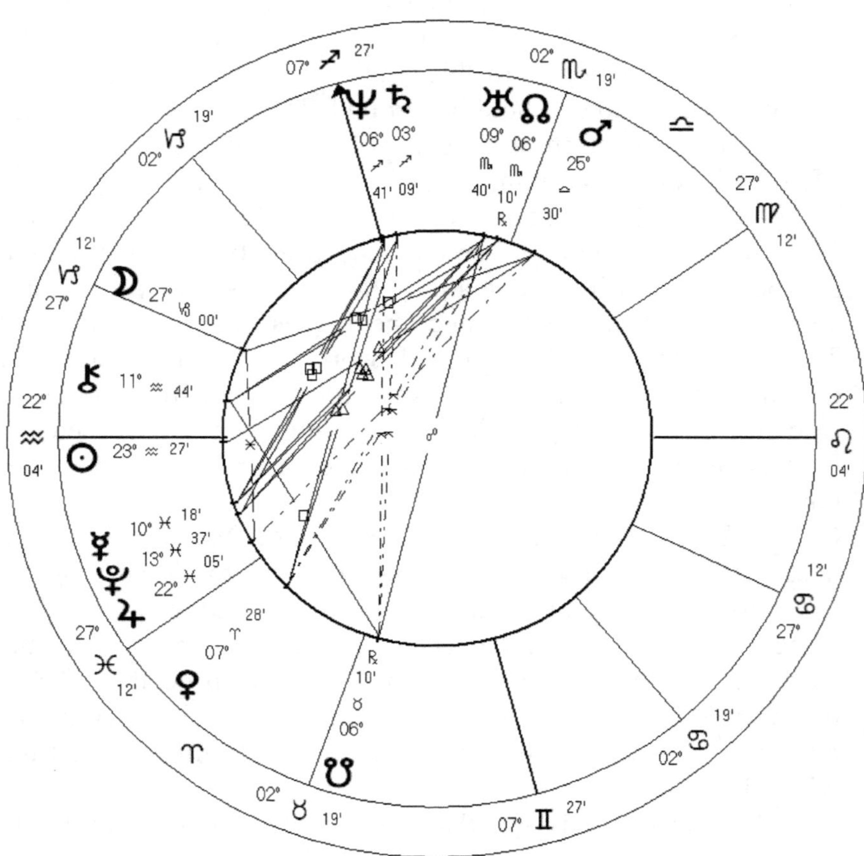

President Abraham Lincoln's *Emancipation Proclamation* is one of the most Uranian treatises in history. By ending slavery, Lincoln not only revolutionized government, he also opened a new chapter in race relations—one where all men could truly be seen as equals. (Women though, had to wait until the next century!) All great Uranian people and events, though, carry some risk. Lincoln was willing to forge ahead despite the threat of war, despite the antagonism to him personally. Of course we know the story. A most uncivil war ensued and Lincoln was murdered.

Uranian details: Lincoln has an Aquarius Sun sitting directly on his Aquarius Ascendant. The Sun is trine Mars in Libra in the 8th House. His Uranus is in Scorpio in the 9th House trine a Mercury/Pluto/Jupiter stellium in Pisces in his 1st House. Uranus is also square Chiron in Aquarius in the 12th House. Saturn rules his 11th House and resides in Sagittarius in the 9th House in conjunction with Neptune.

Having an Aquarius Sun directly on an Aquarius Ascendant means action. The decisions, behaviors and life force itself catalyze change. Lincoln was the embodiment of a vehicle for progress. The trine to Mars in the 8th House connects revolutionary intentions into arenas of working out business with others (8th House) by standing one's ground (Mars) and advocating equality and fairness (Libra).

Uranus in Scorpio in the 9th House indicates a world view or philosophy (9th House) of liberation (Uranus) from control, wounding and oppression (Scorpio). Lincoln is a progressive politician (Uranus in the 9th House) who is determined, passionate and understanding of deeper realities of human connection (Scorpio). Mercury/Pluto/Jupiter in Pisces in the 1st House is a contemplative intelligence musing on future possibilities—a voice of compassionate truth. In aspect to Uranus, Lincoln's overriding philosophy (9th House) takes on behavioral dimensions through his words (Mercury) and persona as a powerful politician (Jupiter/Pluto). The square from Uranus to Chiron in Aquarius in the 12th House shows a sensitivity to collective (12th House) suffering (Chiron)—to those who are marginalized and lack freedom (Aquarius in the 12th House).

Saturn in Sagittarius in the 9th House is the ruler of Lincoln's 11th House. Again, we notice the mark of a politician, statesman, clergyman, or philosophical leader of some kind. This authoritative position governs the collective (11th House)—his contribution (Saturn) to humanitarian progress (11th House) is in being a leader. Neptune in Sagittarius in conjunction with his Saturn adds the component of healing, oneness and the inspiration to reach a spiritual ideal. Also, Neptune close to the Midheaven does suggest that Lincoln is willing to be a martyr (Neptune) for his cause (Sagittarius). The Moon is at the very end of the 11th House, so its momentum is toward the 12th House. Here we see more evidence that Lincoln is emotionally attuned to collective rhythms, and feels a responsibility (Capricorn) to do something about what he feels.

Marie Curie

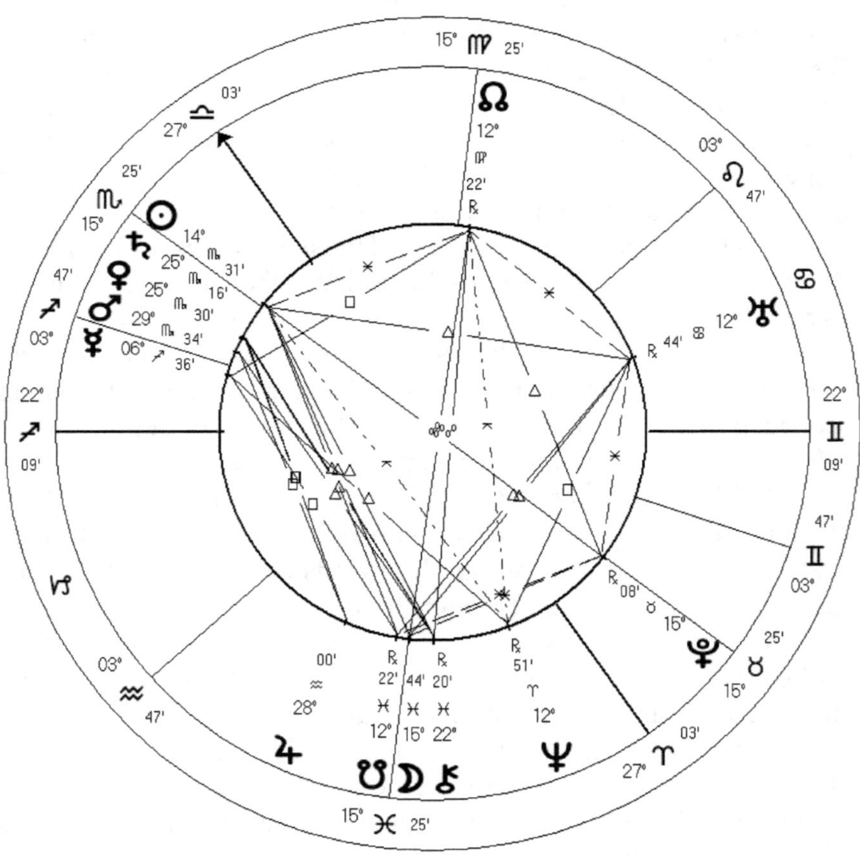

As a pioneering scientist, Marie Curie is a titanic figure. She was the first woman to be awarded a Nobel Prize. She ended up earning two Nobel Prizes, one each in chemistry and physics—the only individual to receive two in different scientific fields. She discovered two new chemical elements, polonium and radium, and was the foremost expert on radioactivity in the early part of the twentieth century. In fact, a unit of radioactivity, the "Curie," was named in her honor. She accomplished all of this in a male-dominated field. Her stature as a breakthrough woman is enhanced by her being the first female professor at the Sorbonne.

Uranian details: As we would expect, her chart is incredibly Uranian. She has Uranus in aspect to the Sun, the Moon, Pluto, Neptune, and the Nodal Axis. She has the Sun on the cusp of the 11th House, and Saturn, Venus and Mars within it. Curie also has Jupiter in Aquarius, which rules her Mercury in Sagittarius, and squares her Scorpio planets—most notably Saturn, the planet of career contribution.

As discussed previously, many women with Uranus in aspect to the Moon have risen to become trailblazers. The underground (Moon) need for breakthrough has propelled them to actively change their position in the world—and by extension, the world itself. Marie's Sun makes the Uranus/Moon trine into a rare Grand Trine. This provides a harmonious energy flow among the planets, and brings the inner Uranian need straight to her life force (Sun). The Scorpio Sun channels the progressive volts of Uranus into research—and radioactivity, with its dangers, is quintessential Scorpio. Indeed, lifetime exposure to her research materials is considered responsible for her death from aplastic anemia.

When used adeptly, those with active outer planets may reach historical significance. In addition to Uranus trine her Sun, Marie also has Pluto opposed her Sun, while Uranus is sextile Pluto. This aspectual configuration not only brings a concerted sense of mission, it elevates Curie to a worldly focus. Furthermore, Uranus square Neptune (in the 3rd House of learning, perception, mindset) illustrates an urgency (square) to become an intellectual leader (Neptune in Aries)—to assist in bringing about a more complete or holistic (Neptune) understanding of our world.

The worldly focus is echoed by the crowded 11th House. An air house, it is concerned with advancement, the environment and cosmos, science, and sociology—how we're all interconnected. Marie's Scorpio planets here further emphasize investigation into such matters and arriving at an understanding of the underlying laws of nature. Furthermore, all of the Scorpio planets are ruled by Pluto, which makes an aspect to Uranus. As noted before, Uranus is also trine the Sun, which sits right at the cusp of this house. This area of the chart is a natural outlet of energy.

Jupiter in Aquarius equates to a progressive philosophy, a mission to achieve breakthrough and discovery. With this uplifting and visionary energy, unbounded possibilities enthrall her imagination. With links to science (Aquarius), Marie receives reward and expansion (Jupiter) through such pursuits. Jupiter's square to Saturn connects this to the deep investigative work of Scorpio in the 11th House. As the ruler of her Mercury, Jupiter informs her mind to seek new frontiers, to continue to aim for breakthrough.

Anne Frank

Beginning as a 13-year-old, Anne Frank expressed in her diary thoughts and feelings about the Holocaust unfolding around her. Her words survived as a human voice of those times, what it was truly like to face the unspeakable. She continues to awaken legions of readers to reflect upon how we treat each other. She is, perhaps, the most famous victim of the Nazis. Though she died at only 15, she lives on in our collective memory.

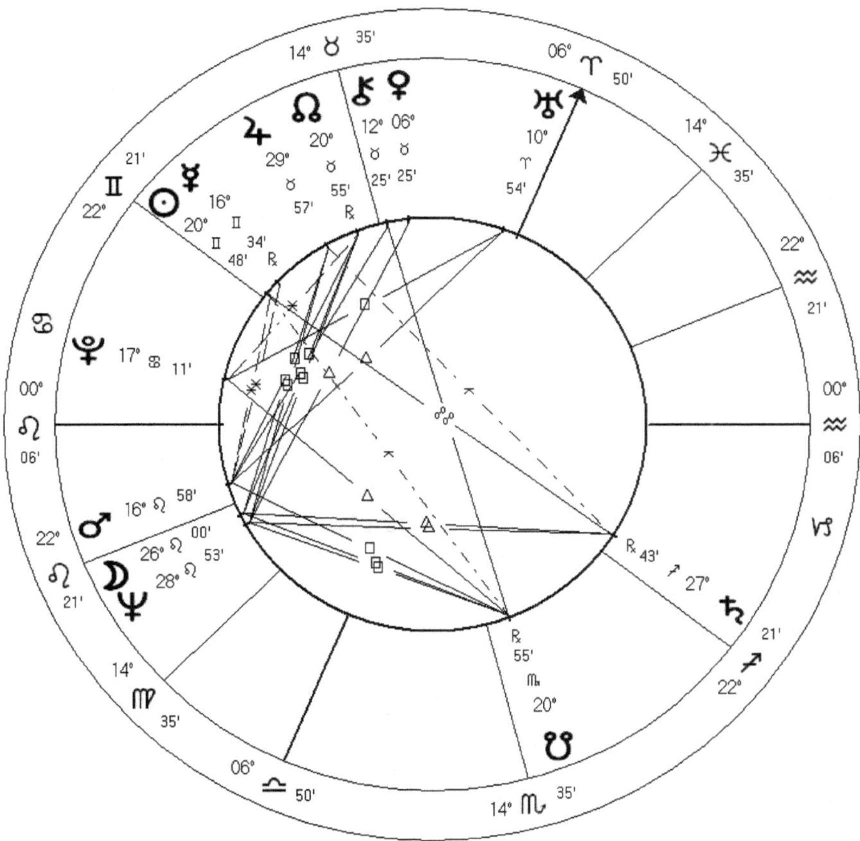

Uranian details: Uranus is located in the 10th House in Aries trine Mars in Leo in the 1st House, and square Pluto in Cancer in the 12th House. She has Jupiter/North Node in Taurus and Sun/Mercury in Gemini in the 11th House. Frank has Aquarius on the cusp of the 7th and 8th Houses.

Uranus in Aries in the 10th House involves the process of developing courage and modeling strength to others. She has the job (10th House) of awakening (Uranus) others to war (Aries). Mars in Leo in the 1st House is interested in squeezing out the goodness of life, in expressing the self colorfully and openly. Uranus in aspect to Mars speaks of unexpected aggression (which did happen to her) but also of the personal development of power in the face of surprise.

Uranus square Pluto illustrates the gravity of her predicament. Pluto in the 12th House suggests that her soul is caught up in collective forces that are extreme and hostile—genocide certainly fits here. Furthermore, Pluto in Cancer suggests that her family identity or roots are involved in the dynamics. The wounding touches her very deeply. In addition to grief, loss and undoing, the 12th House has associations with removal and hiding. Managing the lessons of the square between Uranus and Pluto equips Anne to use the power within the pain to emerge with force and as an agent for change.

Jupiter/North Node in Taurus in the 11th House is an intention to provide perspective and comfort to the masses. Through the reconciliation of wounding (Scorpio South Node), Anne then informs the world that there is indeed meaning (Jupiter) and we should take solace (Taurus) in knowing that the universe itself (11th House) is benevolent. Sun/Mercury in Gemini suggests that she is a writer or spokesperson for this message—wanting to spread it as widely as possible (11th House).

Aquarius on the 7th and 8th House cusps delivers her message personally to others. She is speaking to us (the collective) as if we're in a personal relationship with her. Her diary is most engaging (7th) and revealing (8th), and brings the worldly drama of the Holocaust to an interpersonal dialogue. Her growth towards courage (Uranus in Aries in the 10th) connects with others, and inspires them to similarly follow her example. Even children can become leaders.

Jackie Robinson

African-American baseball player who broke the color line, Jackie Robinson instigated societal change. He endured harassment from not only the public, but also from his own teammates. Nevertheless, he adhered to his sense of integrity and to his right to be a professional athlete. Racial tensions were quite pronounced in the 1940s, and he brought the dialogue into the national spotlight. His grace and professionalism exposed prejudices and helped create greater racial harmony. Jackie won the Rookie of the Year award in 1947 and later went on to become an MVP and frequent All-Star selection.

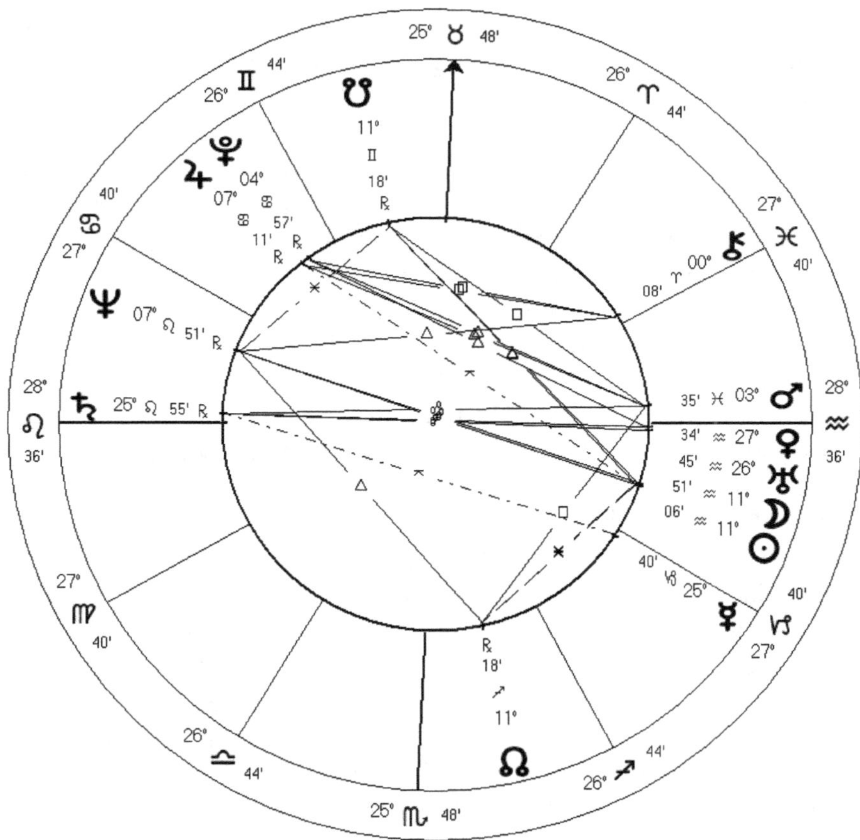

Uranian details: Uranus is in conjunction with Venus in Aquarius in the 6th House and Mars in Pisces in the 7th House. Uranus in Aquarius is opposed Saturn in Leo in the 12th House. Sun and Moon are in Aquarius. Pluto is in conjunction with Jupiter in the 11th House, and Gemini is on the cusp. Aquarius rules the 7th House.

As expected, Robinson's chart is extraordinarily Uranian. His Aquarius New Moon positioned in the house of work, service and self-improvement suggests the need to overcome obstacles in order to rise to a challenge. The New Moon is eager, full of forward-looking energy, and forges ahead. The 6th House is concerned with skill-development, specifically what he needed in order to make it to the big leagues. Traditionally the "House of Servants," the 6th House also concerns the dynamics of power differentials. With successful growth, the servant or apprentice later becomes the master or mentor. Robinson did become a role model after scratching and clawing his way to acceptance.

Uranus is the ruler of his Aquarius Sun and Moon. Uranus, too, is positioned in the 6th House and Aquarius, repeating the theme that individuation is furthered by busting through limitations by hard work and effort. Uranus is in conjunction with Venus in Aquarius, suggesting that attaining humanitarian and inclusive social relations is at the cutting edge of not only his growth, but of what he can offer to the world. Uranus/Venus is also in conjunction with Mars in the 7th House. Mars brings in the element of competition, especially in the "I-Thou" realm of the 7th House. His Uranus/Mars conjunction indicates that he has the potential to be a breakthrough figure in athletics, while Venus and the relational 6th and 7th Houses bring in social and interpersonal dimensions.

Robinson's Uranus is tightly opposed Saturn in Leo near the Ascendant, but still residing in the 12th House. Saturn in Leo suggests a career in entertainment or recreation, while the connection to his Aquarian Uranus brings in revolutionary, society-changing components. The 12th House does pertain to dissolution, and the electric volts from Uranus serve to change the structure of his chosen profession (Saturn). Integrating Uranus with Saturn reveals an intention to help conservative ways change and evolve at the collective level.

Robinson has Jupiter in conjunction with Pluto in Cancer in the 11th House. This indicates a wounding (Pluto) regarding group participation (11th House) that hits home (Cancer) very deeply. The inclusion of Jupiter brings in issues of worldviews and philosophy, underlying assumptions about life. The intention of this configuration is to powerfully align (Pluto) with his sense of mission (Jupiter) in order to change the hearts (Cancer) of the greater world family. This Jupiter/Pluto conjunction is connected to the Uranus/Venus/Mars stellium, described earlier, through the trine aspect. This 11th House emphasis equates to a global sensitivity to worldly issues. With these inner planets in connection to the Uranus/Aquarius archetype, Robinson assumes a personal role in such changes.

Robinson has Gemini ruling his 11th House, indicating that part of his progressive contribution is getting people to think—by bringing them new ways of seeing things. With Aquarius on his 7th House, Robinson's Uranus is naturally involved in dealing with and healing interpersonal dynamics.

Margaret Sanger

Margaret Sanger was the leading proponent of birth control in the twentieth century. As early as 1916 she opened a family planning clinic. That same year she published *What Every Girl Should Know*, which had important information about menstruation and adolescent sexual development. In 1921 she founded the American Birth Control League, which eventually became Planned Parenthood. She remained active for decades, faced censorship, was arrested eight times pursuing her freedom of speech, and even served time in prison. In the 1960s, she was actively promoting the newly available birth control pill. She died shortly after *Griswold vs. Connecticut* legalized birth control for married couples in 1966. There are parts of her biography that remain controversial across the political spectrum—Sanger is Uranian even to the left!

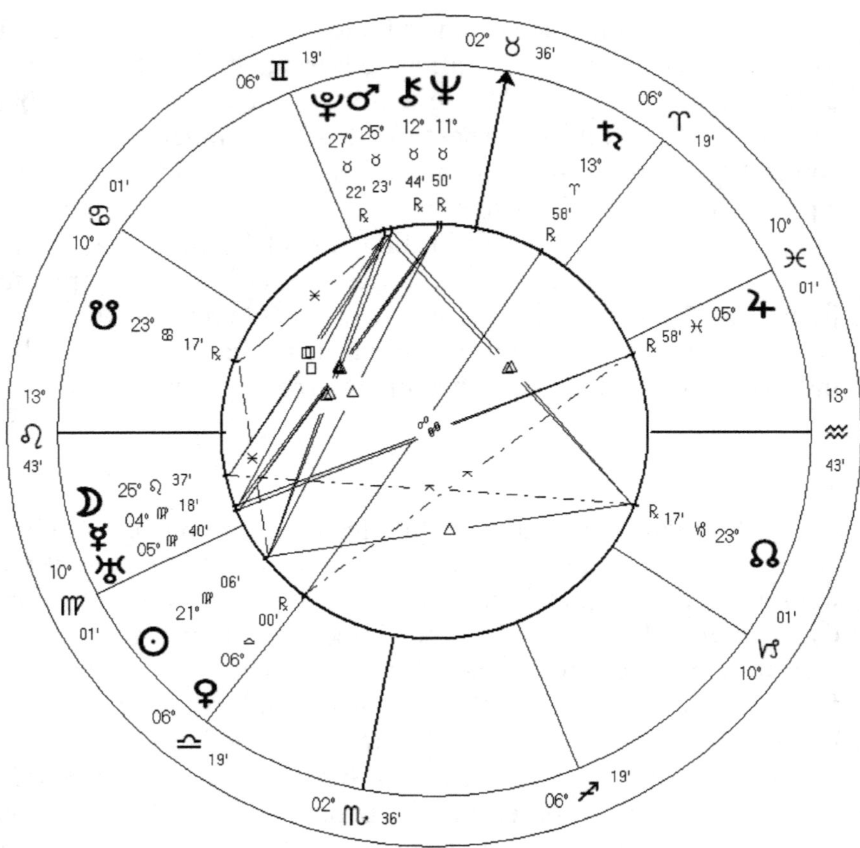

Uranian details: Uranus is situated in the 1st House in Virgo in conjunction with Mercury and the Moon (late Leo), and opposed Jupiter in Pisces in the 7th House. Uranus is trine Neptune/Chiron in Taurus in the 10th House. Sanger has Gemini on the 11th House cusp, and Aquarius rules her 7th House. Also note that Sanger's Sun shares the same sign as Uranus, though they are not classically in conjunction.

Uranus in the 1st House is behavioral in manifestation and may act in controversial ways. This Uranus is in conjunction with Mercury, and will use the voice and words as the means to direct change. Virgo relates to areas of health care, self-improvement and the practices of daily living. Having the Moon involved not only gives an emotional impetus to act in these ways, but it also has correlates to feminine and bodily issues, including birth. Jupiter in Pisces in the 7th House has a philosophy (Jupiter) about what it means to truly merge (Pisces) in equal relationships (7th House). Uranus/Jupiter is politically progressive—situated along the 1-7 axis, it pertains to the "I-Thou" dynamics of relating. Sanger's views on relationships (Jupiter in the 7th House) involve breakthroughs (Uranus) in feminine (Moon) empowerment (1st House).

Neptune/Chiron is in Taurus in the 10th House. Neptune shows a longing, and Taurus involves comfort, security and naturalness in one's body. Chiron suggests a wound in the attainment of this serene goal. Because Chiron is in the 10th House, Sanger's career involves being a visionary (Neptune trine Uranus) who helps others heal (Chiron) and find greater solace and pleasure (Taurus) in themselves. Birth control removes worry and may foster greater sensual (Taurus) togetherness (Neptune). Connected to her activist Uranus, this is what she is advocating through her leadership.

With Gemini on the 11th House cusp, her contribution to future trends has to do with education. She has mobilized groups (11th House) through her determined voice (1st House Mercury/Uranus ruling the 11th House). Sanger gets people (11th House) to think (Gemini). Aquarius rules the 7th House, so her Uranus naturally addresses issues of relationship, particularly of a one-to-one and equal nature.

Neil Armstrong

It's hard to get more Uranian than being the first person to set foot on a celestial sphere other than the Earth. Neil Armstrong will forever be remembered for his famed walk on the Moon. His iconic words, "One small step for man, one giant leap for mankind," are permanently archived in our collective memory. In addition to having this noteworthy accomplishment as an astronaut, Armstrong was also a Naval Aviator and test pilot. His entire biography is about venturing bravely into the unknown, and his astrology chart reflects the same.

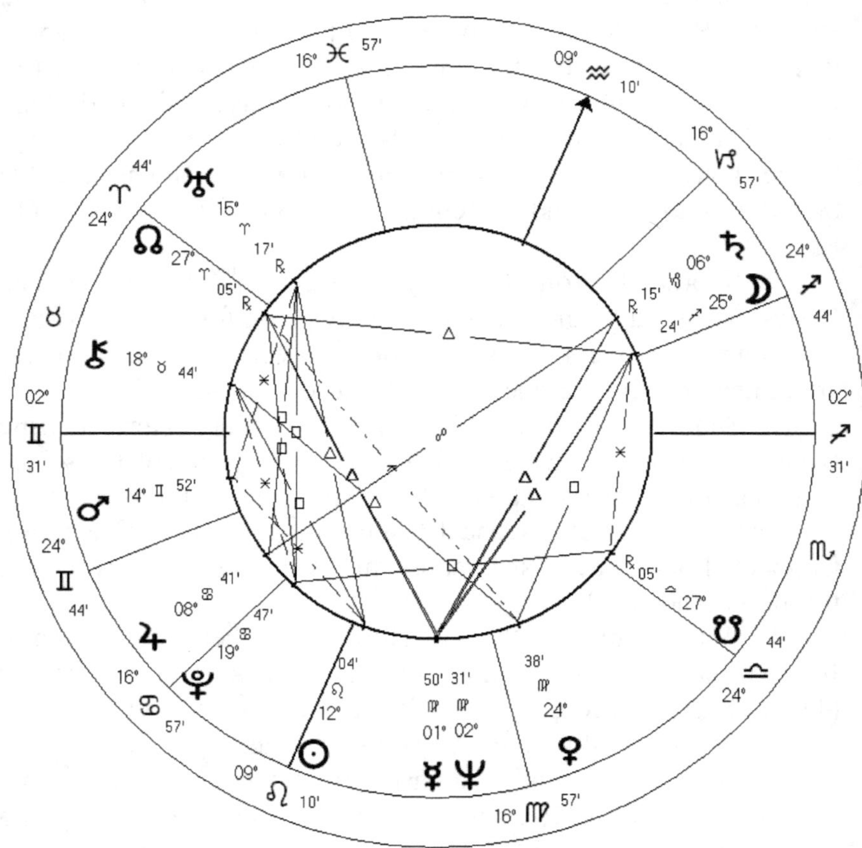

Uranian details: Armstrong has Uranus in Aries in the 11th House trine the Sun, square Pluto and Jupiter and sextile his Mars. He has Aquarius on the Midheaven, so Uranus rules his career-focused 10th House. Neptune is the ruler of his 11th House. Also of note: Jupiter in Cancer is in mutual reception with the Moon in Sagittarius.

Uranus is in its natural home in the 11th House. This strengthens its reach into areas of global advancement and connectedness. Armstrong has Uranus in Aries—his contribution is being a personally active leader and pioneer (Aries) in this airy realm. With Uranus trine his Leo Sun, his personality becomes equated with breakthrough. He embodies the boundless Uranian spirit through personal fame and celebrity (Leo). Since Uranus rules the 10th House, it becomes naturally dispersed through his career house.

Mars in Gemini in the 1st House plays a central role. In the 1st House, Mars is naturally driven and promises leadership abilities. In Gemini, it is directed toward movement, learning and communication. To become an astronaut, Armstrong had to be intellectually proficient, and the restlessness of Gemini fits well with his need for a variety of experiences involving motion. This Mars rules the Uranus while also being sextile to it. The scope of his travels (Mars in Gemini) is brought to the vastness of the 11th House. Mars is also sextile his Sun, making his personal energy crackling with excitement for experience.

Like many astronauts and explorers, Armstrong has Uranus in aspect to Jupiter. Jupiter provides lift-off, a sense of optimism and yearning for discovery. The square suggests that he feels pressure to burst through into new frontiers. Unlike the more flowing connections from Uranus to Mars and to his Sun, this aspect compels Armstrong to develop a mission. Uranus square Pluto indicates a sense of historical significance if he is able to manage the Uranus/Jupiter mission well.

Neptune rules his 11th House. Positioned in aspect to Mercury and Saturn in earth signs, this suggests that his yearnings (Neptune) into areas of breakthrough (11th House) are made possible through diligence, study and hard work towards his vision. All of the exploratory indicators are complemented by this earthy grounding.

It's interesting to note that Jupiter in Cancer and the Moon in Sagittarius are in mutual reception, while also not being too far from opposition. Also, the Moon's conjunction with Saturn plays a role in bridging these planets. The themes of exploration and discovery (Sagittarius) are connected with the Moon itself—and here that takes on literal dimensions.

David Kopay

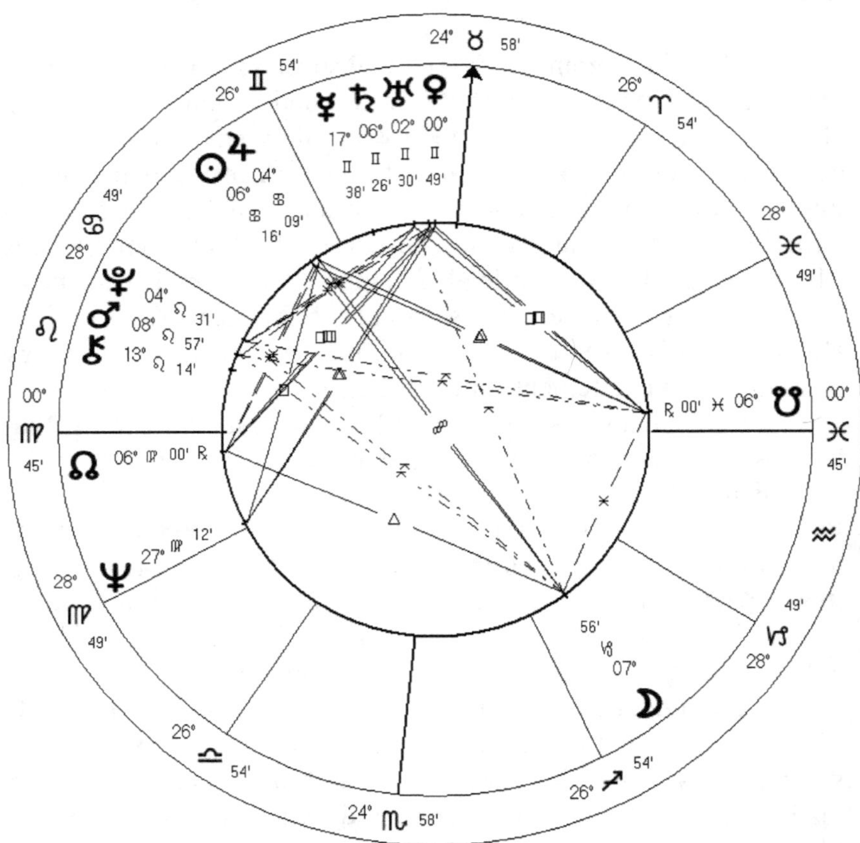

David Kopay was the first professional football player to publicly announce his homosexuality, and one of the first athletes in a major sport to do so. Since his disclosure, he has been unable to find a coaching position despite being considered a worthy candidate. He wrote a biography, *The David Kopay Story*, which details his experiences in the NFL as a gay man and sheds light on the sexual behaviors of football players. Kopay continues to be a leading advocate of gay rights, and also continues to have a fractious relationship with the NFL.

Uranian details: Kopay has Uranus in the 10th House in conjunction with Venus and Saturn in Gemini forming a stellium.

Together, the stellium sextiles a Pluto/Mars/Chiron stellium in Leo in the 12th House. Jupiter is in conjunction with the Sun in Cancer in the 11th House, with Mercury serving as the ruler of this area. Aquarius is intercepted in the 6th House.

Uranus in the 10th House immediately attunes Kopay's public life to catalyzing change. Uranus in conjunction with Venus suggests that interpersonal relations are emphasized, while Saturn has institutional correlates. All of these planets in Gemini are geared toward giving voice to his role in challenging the status quo to be more open about diversity. Pluto/Mars/Chiron in the 12th House illustrates his pent-up frustrations and wounding regarding sexuality. His joy and exuberance (Leo) are trapped in the closeted 12th House. The sextile brings this to the most visible area (10th House), in order to have transparency and to induce societal change. Kopay is able to relax and have fun (Leo) when he can publicly be himself.

Sun/Jupiter in the 11th House in Cancer indicates a philosophy (Jupiter) of living one's life (Sun) in touch with what is inside (Cancer). He naturally networks and builds community (11th House) as an inspiration (Jupiter) to others. His life force (Sun) gravitates to progressive causes (11th House) stemming from a very personal (Cancer) investment. Mercury rules the 11th House, indicating that he is a spokesperson for such matters. Because Mercury is connected to the Venus/Uranus/Saturn stellium in the 10th House, his experiences in his career are what informs his message.

Aquarius is intercepted in the 6th House and doesn't easily inject its energy there. While actively playing football, Kopay chose to stay in the closet for fear of recrimination from those he worked with (6th House). It was after he paid his dues (6th House) that he ascended to the height (Uranus in the 10th House) of his activist public role.

Jerry Rubin

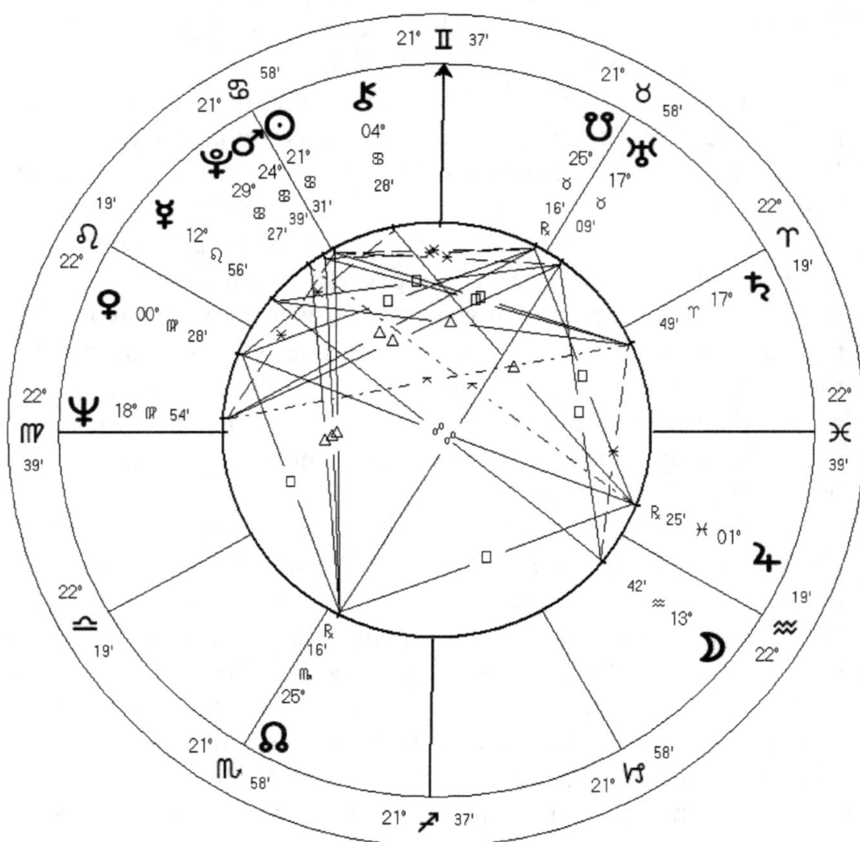

Jerry Rubin co-founded the social activist, anti-establishment Yippie party with Abbie Hoffman in the 1960s. Rubin led many types of demonstrations, culminating in his anti-war activism at the 1968 Democrat Convention. He was part of the "Chicago Seven," and was put on trial for inciting a riot. He was famous for employing outrageous tactics and showmanship to make his points. At a hearing for the House Committee on Un-American Activities, Rubin made appearances as a guerrilla rebel holding a plastic rifle, Santa Claus, and a Revolutionary War soldier who reminded Congress that George Washington grew and smoked pot. Rubin was active with the human potential movement of the 1970s before reinventing himself as an entrepreneur in the 1980s. His most Uranian period was his younger days. He once said, "A young person without an arrest record has been living his life in a closet."

Uranian details: Rubin has Uranus in Taurus in the 8th House square his Aquarius Moon in the 5th House, square Mercury in Leo in the 11th House, sextile his Cancer Sun on the 11th House cusp and trine Neptune in Virgo in the 12th. His Aquarius Moon rules the 11th House, and the Sun, Mars, Pluto, and Mercury reside within it. Aquarius rules his 6th House.

Rubin's Uranus shows a disturbance in arriving at peace and security (Taurus) in crisis scenarios with others (8th House). Uranus square his Aquarius Moon suggests an unwillingness to emotionally settle down to truly receive another. He has a pronounced need (Moon) to express (5th House) his rebellious nature (Aquarius). This square reeks of interpersonal antagonism. His soul is attempting to find comfort (Taurus) by developing the skills necessary to peaceably be in the psychological cauldron (8th House).

Uranus square Mercury in Leo in the 11th House indicates that his mind is on the big picture, larger causes, the forming of alliances. He naturally speaks in colorful (Leo) ways and has a flair for humor. The Uranus/Mercury square can be expressed as a restless mind with many inventive ideas, but it also may express itself impulsively, and from an egocentric place, in Leo. Together, Mercury, Uranus and Moon form a T-Square—his interpersonal challenges connect with his ideas (Mercury) about social activism (11th House).

Uranus is sextile the Cancer Sun, which sits on the 11th House cusp. His life force naturally gravitates to finding his group or allies who might make the world a better place. Cancer here indicates that Rubin is motivated by his inner desire for change—his need to be a nurturer of the future and its promise. Cancer can also be prickly, defensive and reactive—especially with his stellium of Sun/Mars/Pluto, in that sign. He is a powerful (Pluto) leader (Mars) driven by his emotions and uncompromising about his vision. Pluto/Mars in the 11th House suggests the need to resolve power dynamics regarding his relationship with the broader world. These planets are fierce and convey a very public life, particularly in his role as an agent for change since Uranus itself is sextile the Sun (which connects to Mars/Pluto). The Aquarius Moon rules the 11th House, further bringing Uranian influence to this area, and also echoing how his progressive needs (Moon) find outlet on the larger stage.

The trine between Neptune in Virgo and Uranus illustrates what he is fighting for. Neptune in the 12th House shows a longing for a new vision, compassion for the planet, and a need to contact greater benevolence. In Virgo, this Neptune is practical and humble, quite aware that we are small within the vastness of Spirit. It is willing to perform hands-on works to improve our collective lot. Uranus trine Neptune wants to awaken this yearning and specifically connect it to the other planets with which Uranus forms aspects. It invites Neptune out of the 12th House removal and into the rhythm of everyday life.

Aquarius rules the 6th House, an area associated with the downtrodden, the servant or the commoner. It relates to the Virgo theme of improvement through discipline and attaining concrete results. Rubin's Uranus naturally spreads its energy here, meaning that much of his daily regimen and working space (6th House) involve his prominent Uranian attunement and its interpersonal and worldly challenges.

Andy Warhol

Andy Warhol is a world-class eccentric, multi-media creator, and pioneer of Pop Art. He assembled a cadre of bohemian personalities at "The Factory" and is one of the first major American artists to openly embrace his homosexuality. Warhol was initially dismissed by the mainstream, then redefined the modern art era as its central figure. Warhol was a deeply religious person who attended Mass on an almost-daily basis. He was also fascinated with death and disaster, which were frequent subjects of his work. His persona was devoid of affect, which challenged his audience to form their own opinions of his work and of him. Warhol used urine, nudity and gay culture in his art, but also made some of the most commercial and accessible pieces that have since become icons.

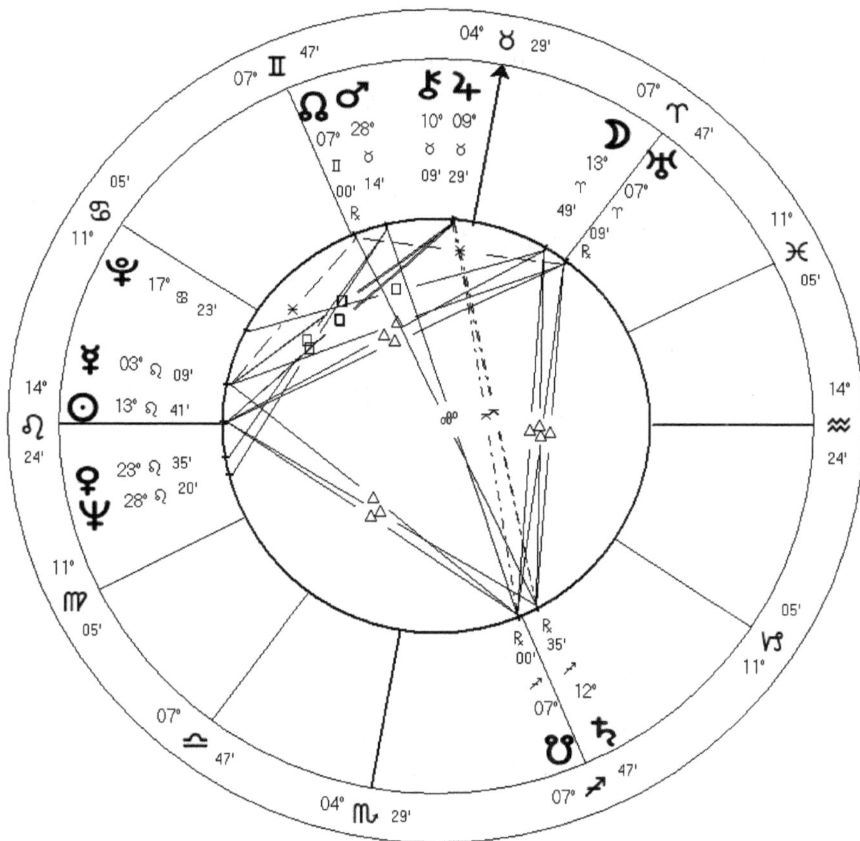

Uranian details: Warhol has Uranus on the cusp of the 9th House in Aries in conjunction with his Moon, trine Saturn in Sagittarius in the 5th House and trine Sun/Mercury in Leo in the 12th House. He has Gemini on the 11th House cusp, and Aquarius rules his 7th House.

Uranus in Aries is developing leadership capabilities through risk and alignment with one's truth. Aries, because it's ruled by Mars, also involves desire and sexual dimensions. In the

9th House this may indicate the need to find a world philosophy that is broad enough to allow him to be who he really is.

Uranus in conjunction with the Moon indicates some emotional turbulence or underground shock. There's a need to become more conscious of his underlying drive (Aries) to understand his place in the world (9th House), even to espouse a new (Uranus in Aries) philosophy (9th House). The inner revolution is brought to light with the Sun. Uranus/Sun individuals assume roles and preferences that challenge prevailing assumptions. The trine from Uranus/Moon to his Sun suggests that his emotional condition is radiated (Sun) through color, self-expression, social engagement and the assuming of a large presence (Leo).

The house position of the Sun is complex. Since it is so close to, and rules, the Ascendant, it clearly is linked to it. Indeed, Warhol was a larger-than-life personality. However, his Sun is also conjoined with Mercury in the 12th House, which does make a closer trine with Uranus. This connects the Sun to the Uranus/Mercury aspect in 12th House ways. Warhol was a brilliant (Uranus/Mercury) figure who kept his personal life private (12th House). His persona was not outwardly detectable (Ascendant); rather there was a softness and removal (12th House) about him. Part of the intention of having a 12th House Leo Sun trine Uranus (in Aries, on the 9th House cusp) is to form a new relationship with Spirit—to find joy and sustenance by noticing the beauty available in life.

Uranus also makes a trine to Saturn in Sagittarius in the 5th House. Saturn has career correlates, while the 5th House is the area of artistic self-expression. The Sagittarian dimension suggests that his artistic career will be about making his point—there's a conceptual or philosophical statement that he delivers through his work. The Grand Trine formed by Saturn to his luminaries is an energetic system that dominates the chart. Warhol's life is defined by his need for personal liberation (Uranus/Moon), by assuming a countercultural presence as a personality (Uranus trine Leo Sun), and by channeling this personal energy into making bold statements through his art

(Saturn in Sagittarius in the 5th House). Uranus trine Mercury (12th House) is the unsuspecting genius that some would like to dismiss.

Gemini rules his 11th House, so Mercury (trine Uranus) is dispersed into the collective. Warhol gets people to think and talk about the meaning of things. Mercury/Uranus invites an audience (11th House) to ponder different angles and consider new implications. With his Mercury in Leo, the discussion naturally centers on art—and Leo is interested in what is welcoming and popular, thus, Pop Art. The Uranian signatures in his chart position Warhol as a progressive force within areas of public consumption (Leo). Aquarius rules his 7th House, which has much to do with his personal relationships as a gay man with anti-establishment friends and associates. Other people receive (7th House) him as somewhat bizarre, and he in turn may have some alienation (Aquarius) in his dealings with others.

Jimi Hendrix

Cultural icon of the 1960s and virtuoso guitarist, Jimi Hendrix is a Uranian figure even in a most Uranian time period! Hendrix reinvented the guitar by adding a dizzying array of effects, integrating several genres of music, and helping launch funk, heavy metal and elements of soul into the rock mainstream. He played a right-handed guitar upside-down, with his teeth, behind his back, and he took style and pyrotechnics to a new level. He was sexually provocative through his lyrics, through his lifestyle and even on stage with his guitar. He wasn't just a performer: his band was called The Jimi Hendrix *Experience.* Part Native American, he was of a mixed racial background and worked with and entertained a wide diversity of peoples. Hendrix was interested in spirituality, altered states of consciousness and other occult interests, all of which informed his career. He suddenly died at the age of 27—at the peak of his success and international acclaim.

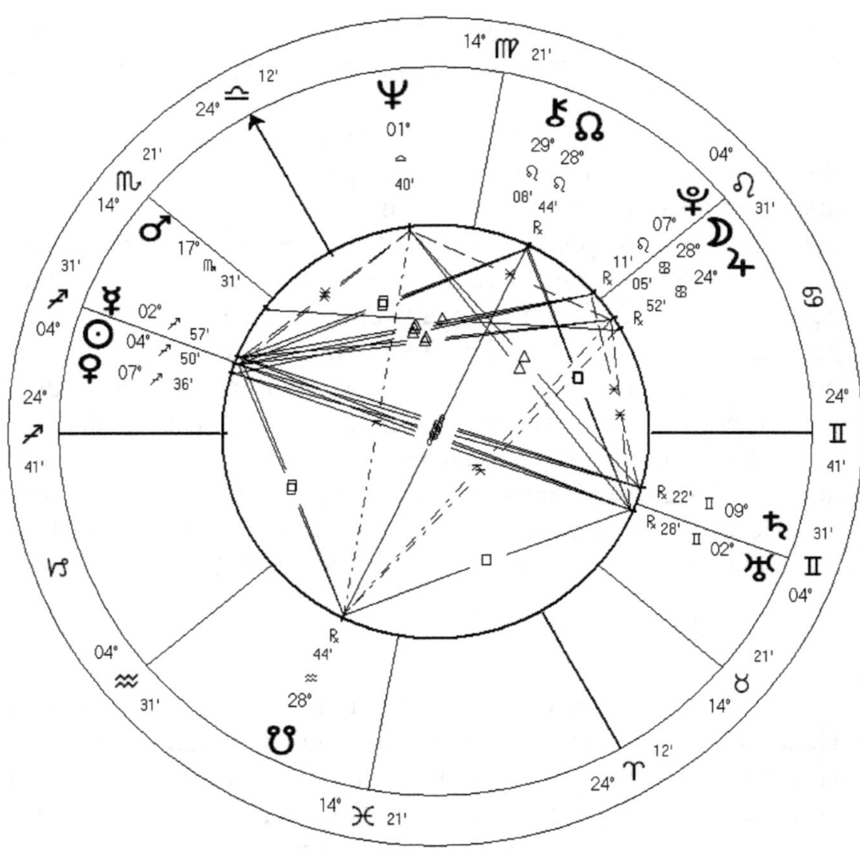

Uranian details: Hendrix has Uranus in Gemini the 5th House in conjunction with Saturn in the 6th House. Uranus is opposed Mercury/Sun/Venus in Sagittarius on the 12th House cusp. Uranus is loosely sextile his Cancer Moon and trine Neptune in Libra in the 9th House. Uranus also serves as the ruler of his 2nd House, and his Aquarius South Node is located within it. He has Mars in Scorpio in the 11th House, with Pluto, located in the 8th House in Leo, ruling his 11th House.

Uranus in Gemini in the 5th House suggests a revolutionary performer with a message and explosion of sound. The addition of Saturn in the 6th House brings method and craft to his self-expression—indeed, Hendrix was known to perfect his talent obsessively. The opposition of Uranus to his

Mercury/Sun/Venus brings this innovation to his voice, life force and art. Sagittarius in the 12th House concerns inspiration, spiritually uplifting creativity as well as experimentation and recklessness, all of which could contribute to his undoing. Hendrix is a public Uranian figure, particularly in terms of art and social relations, because his Venus rules his vocational 10th House.

His sensitive Cancer Moon has a revolutionary need deep within (it sextiles Uranus) but likely hasn't experienced realization in prior lifetimes. In fact, a South Node in Aquarius in the 2nd House shows a degree of turbulence and estrangement, a shaky sense of self (2nd House). With a Leo North Node in the 8th House, he is meant to be charismatic and make an impact on others. Uranus, squaring the Nodal Axis, is at the crossroads of this lesson. Through self-expression and risk-taking, he can fulfill the underlying need in his soul for breakthrough.

Neptune in Libra in the 9th House is trine his Uranus. This Neptune longs for spiritual peace, meaning, and social harmony, and it actively quests for answers. The connection of his performance-oriented Uranus to Neptune indicates that he can instigate these things through his talent. Uranus/Neptune transcends the way things currently are and attempts to forge and grasp a new vision—one of togetherness, consciousness and, ultimately, oneness. Hendrix shares this Uranus/Neptune trine with many other musicians and artists of his generation.

In his 11th House, Hendrix has Mars in Scorpio. Indeed, he was blatantly sexual in his performances and was not averse to joining with many others (11th House) in intimate ways. Further echoing this theme is his 8th House Pluto in showy Leo, which serves as the ruler of the 11th House. Not only was Hendrix explicit, he was involved in mixed-race connections and was antagonized by more conservative currents in society because of his relationship choices. Also, Hendrix was a vocal opponent to the Vietnam War, and to violence in general. Many have interpreted his guitar playing, especially his famed *Star-Spangled Banner* rendition, as being aggressive, and of emulating gunfire.

Hendrix agreed with the sentiment to "make love not war," and he let his music serve as a Martial force.

Toni Morrison

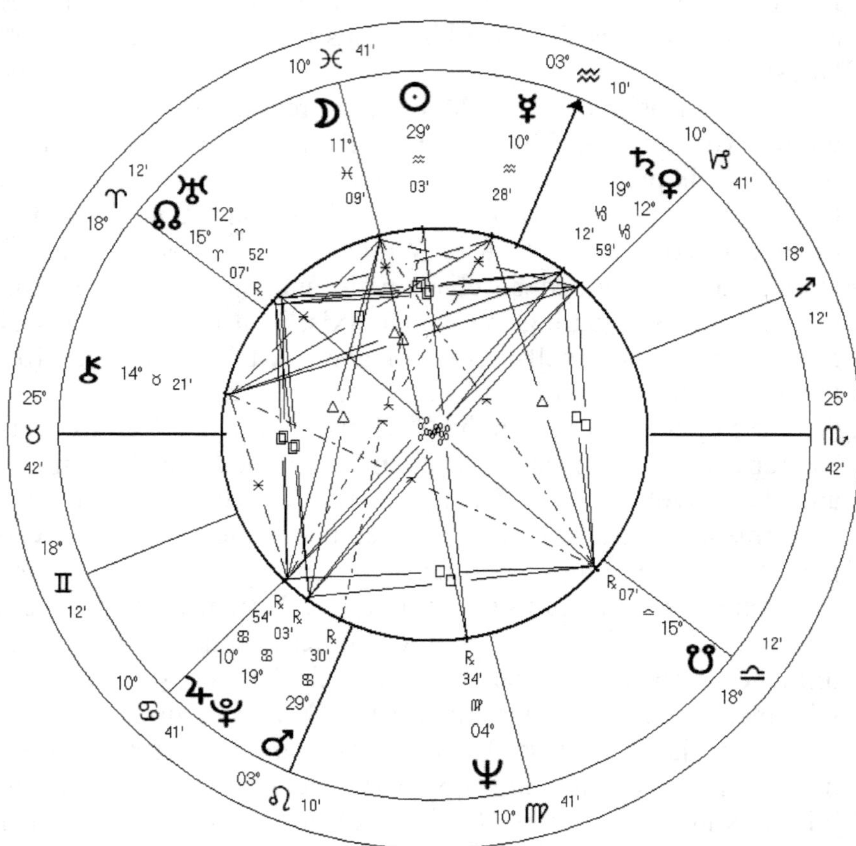

Toni Morrison is a world-renowned novelist and a winner of the Nobel Prize in Literature. A black woman born during the Depression and who came of age in the 1940s and 50s, she surmounted formidable social, racial and sexist obstacles on her way to eventual success. She became a leading figure in her field, a symbol of empowerment and inspiration to ethnic minorities and women. Morrison became a professor at Princeton University and a leading promoter of black literature. As we explore her chart and consider the worldly focus it conveys, consider her words: "I really think the range of emotions and perceptions I have had access to as a black person and as a female person are greater than those of people who are neither. . . .So it seems to me that my world did not shrink because I was a black female writer. It just got bigger."

Uranian details: Morrison has an 11th House Uranus in Aries, which rules her Midheaven, squares Jupiter/Pluto in the 3rd House, squares Venus/Saturn in the 9th House (together a T-Square), and sextiles Mercury in Aquarius in the 10th House. Uranus also forms a conjunction with an Aries North Node. (Mars, the ruler of Uranus, is in the 3rd House in Cancer.) In addition to Mercury and the MC in Aquarius, Morrison also has an Aquarian Sun. Her Moon resides in the 11th House. The ruler of the 11th House is Neptune, which is opposed the Aquarius Sun.

The 3rd House relates to writing, ideas and communication, while the 9th House involves higher education and publishing, in addition to religion and philosophy. Morrison is highly attuned to the 3-9 axis through several oppositions. Her Uranus sits in the 11th House, bringing the writing focus into areas of group and social relations, and it squares the oppositions. Saturn/Venus in Capricorn in the 9th House involves expectations to conform to traditional norms of relating. Jupiter/Pluto in Cancer in the 3rd House reveals a need to form new perspectives that stem from the heart. All of this energy is brought to the sociological realm of the 11th House. Morrison is a leader (Uranus in Aries) who challenges (square) the traditional social norms of relating (Saturn/Venus in Capricorn) to transform morally (Jupiter/Pluto) and to deepen (Cancer).

Mercury in the 10th House in Aquarius suggests a public role as a progressive writer. Not only is her Uranus the ruler of the Mercury, but it is also sextile to it. Writing is clearly the outlet for the dynamic friction of the T-Square. Furthermore, Mars is the ruler of her Uranus, and it is positioned in her 3rd House of ideas and writing. Like Mercury, Morrison's Aquarius Sun is also in the 10th House. Her life is a public symbol of change, social advancement and greater evolutionary forces.

The Pisces Moon in the 11th House suggests an underground need (Moon) to form a vision (Pisces) for greater connectedness and progress (11th House). She cares deeply about the state of the world. The ruler of the 11th House is Neptune in Virgo in the 4th House, illustrating a deep-seated need (4th House) to work diligently (Virgo) on her vision. This connects with the commanding 10th House Sun through an opposition—bringing global aspirations into sharper focus through managing her career.

David Koresh

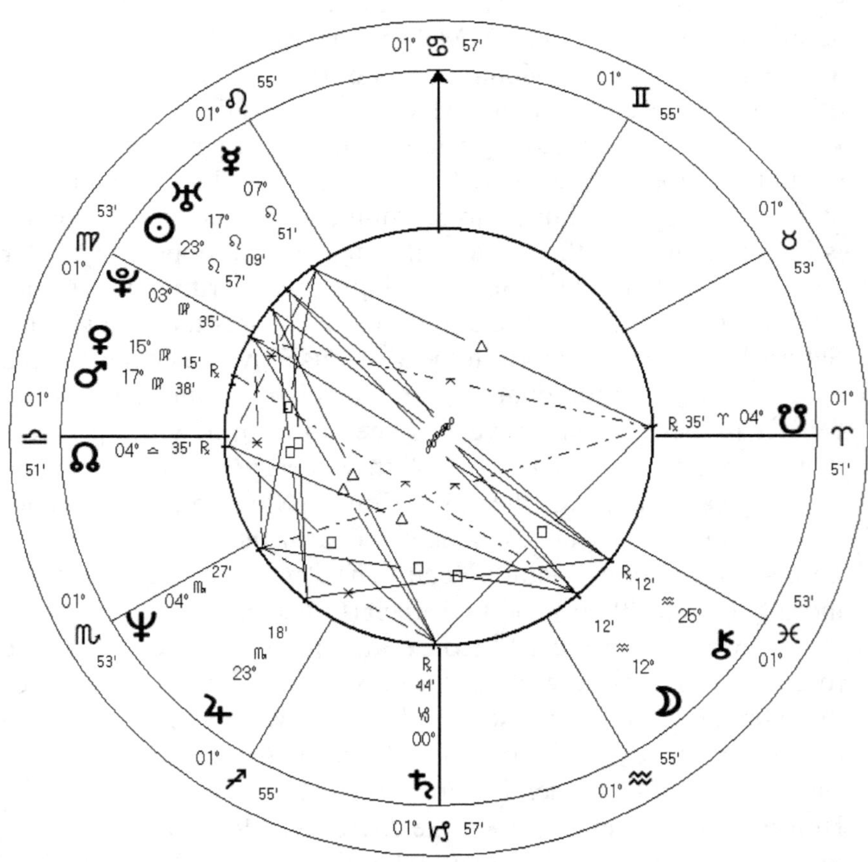

Not all individuals with a Uranian emphasis are going to be paragons of social or collective advancement. This energy is wild, unstable and often hostile to the status quo. Many renegades and rebels are wired with the Uranian need to upset the apple cart, and fanatical cult leader David Koresh is in this group. He led the controversial Branch Davidians to their fiery death after a prolonged stand-off with the U.S. government in 1993. He portrays the Uranian tendency to exist above the law, or to stubbornly challenge it, even to the point of self-destruction.

Uranian details: Koresh has a Leo Sun in conjunction with Uranus in Leo in the 11th House. His Moon is in Aquarius in the 5th House and opposes Uranus. Chiron is also in Aquarius in the 5th House. Uranus is square Jupiter in Scorpio in the 2nd House. The South Node in Aries in the 7th House squares Saturn in Capricorn near the 4th House cusp.

With the Sun and Uranus in Leo, overcompensation in the direction of narcissism is possible. The soul wants to develop and radiate its authenticity in colorful ways—the hazard is to inflate self-importance and become headstrong about it. With these two planets in the 11th House, there is a need to be visible, to form community, and to have a charismatic (Leo) role within the group. Also, the scope of the 11th House extends to the world stage, and Koresh naturally wanted to be noticed in a global sense.

His Aquarius Moon suggests the need to be rebellious. There is unfinished emotional work involving detachment, trauma or feeling different. Because the Moon is in the 5th House, he naturally expresses it. Its opposition to the 11th House Sun/Uranus sets up the dynamic of performer/audience or leader/followers. The soul intention was to develop a talent, to express warmth and to show up fully (Leo) in order to satisfy the lunar need for original (Aquarius) self-expression (5th House). His natal Chiron in Aquarius in the 5th House also suggests a soul injury in such functions.

Jupiter in Scorpio in the 2nd House squares his Sun/Uranus. His foundation (2nd House) is religious (Jupiter) passion (Scorpio). The darker potentials of Jupiter in Scorpio involve fanaticism—even leading to death (Scorpio). The intention is to embody a progressive (Uranus) philosophy (Jupiter) that touches people deeply (Scorpio) and assists them in growing. However, combined with narcissism (struggling Leo Sun), Jupiter introduces the element of grandiosity, even to the point of a messianic complex.

It is interesting to see the spiritual lessons outlined with the Nodal Axis. Koresh has the South Node in Aries in the 7th House, suggesting warlike themes (Aries) with others (7th House). Saturn in Capricorn squares the Nodes, indicating that social institutions or structures are the in the crossfire of the conflict. With a Libra North Node in the 1st House, he was here to learn how to behave in more peaceful ways.

Ellen DeGeneres

Ellen DeGeneres is a comedienne, actress, talk show host, and superstar celebrity who has hosted the Academy Awards. She is widely known for publicly embracing her homosexuality, and is one of the most famous lesbians in the world. Ellen has faced derision from conservative groups. Jerry Falwell once called her "Ellen Degenerate." Nevertheless, her star continues to rise as she brings greater tolerance of alternative lifestyles to the mainstream.

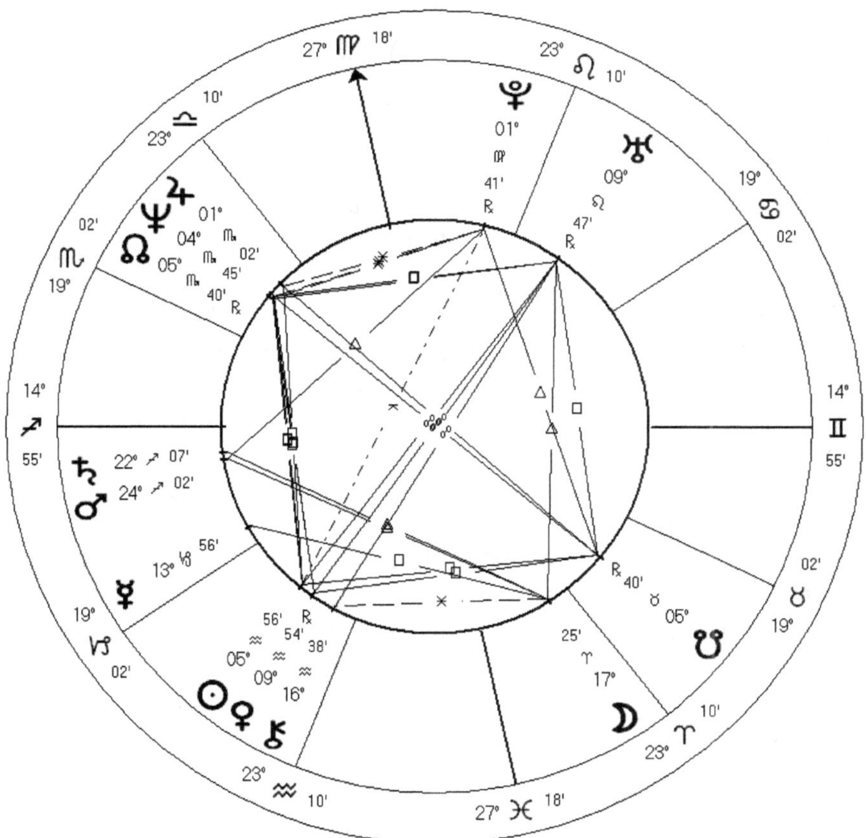

Uranian Details: Ellen has Uranus in Leo in the 8th House opposed a Sun/Venus/Chiron stellium in Aquarius in the 2nd House. Uranus is square Jupiter/Neptune/North Node in Scorpio in the 11th House. Uranus is trine the Moon in Aries in the 4th House. Uranus is the ruler of her 3rd House with Aquarius on that house cusp. Libra is on the cusp of her 11th House.

Uranus in Leo in the 8th House indicates that her individuation is accelerated by finding joy in truly being herself within the realms of intimacy and sharing. Sun/Venus/Chiron in the 2nd House in Aquarius shows that she is learning more security and confidence (2nd House) about relating (Venus) as a member of a beleaguered (Chiron) group (Aquarius). The opposition (and mutual reception between Uranus and the Sun) suggests that in order to arrive at greater self-worth (2nd House Sun) she must embody her authentic sexuality (8th House Uranus). This will stimulate healing (Chiron) and also new frontiers of socialization (Venus in Aquarius).

Venus rules the 11th House and spreads its energy into the world at large. The more confident she becomes with who she is, the greater global impact she will make. With Libra on the cusp, her progressive contribution will concern relationships. Jupiter/Neptune in Scorpio in the 11th House indicates a philosophy (Jupiter) of togetherness (Neptune) regarding underlying truths and sexuality (Scorpio). Jupiter/Neptune in aspect to the Uranus/Sun and Uranus/Venus oppositions further brings her life into public domains.

Ellen's 4th House Aries Moon is resolving some inner frustration, and has a need to be a leader. The trine to Uranus indicates that she has inner harmony regarding her alternative lifestyle—the work is to connect this successfully with the world. With Aquarius on the 3rd House cusp, her Uranus influences her language, ideas and perceptions. This is seen in her quirky and irreverent comedy. Not only does she help change people's minds about homosexuality through her voice, but she also gives the message that it's OK to be different.

When Ellen famously announced her homosexuality during an episode of her sitcom in the spring of 1997, transiting Uranus was hitting her Sun/Venus in Aquarius.

Cindy Sheehan

Cindy Sheehan is an outspoken peace activist who lost her son in the Iraq War. She has been a visible and vocal critic of the Bush Administration and has attracted both attention and scorn for her tactics. Sheehan has called Bush "the greatest terrorist in the world," and praised Hugo Chavez, the President of Venezuela, for his resistance to the United States. She tried to wear an anti-war t-shirt to the State of the Union address in 2006, which resulted in her arrest; once attempted a hunger strike; and even bought land near Bush's ranch in Crawford, Texas, to protest from. She says that she is unafraid of the consequences of her actions and continues to make headlines through her behavior.

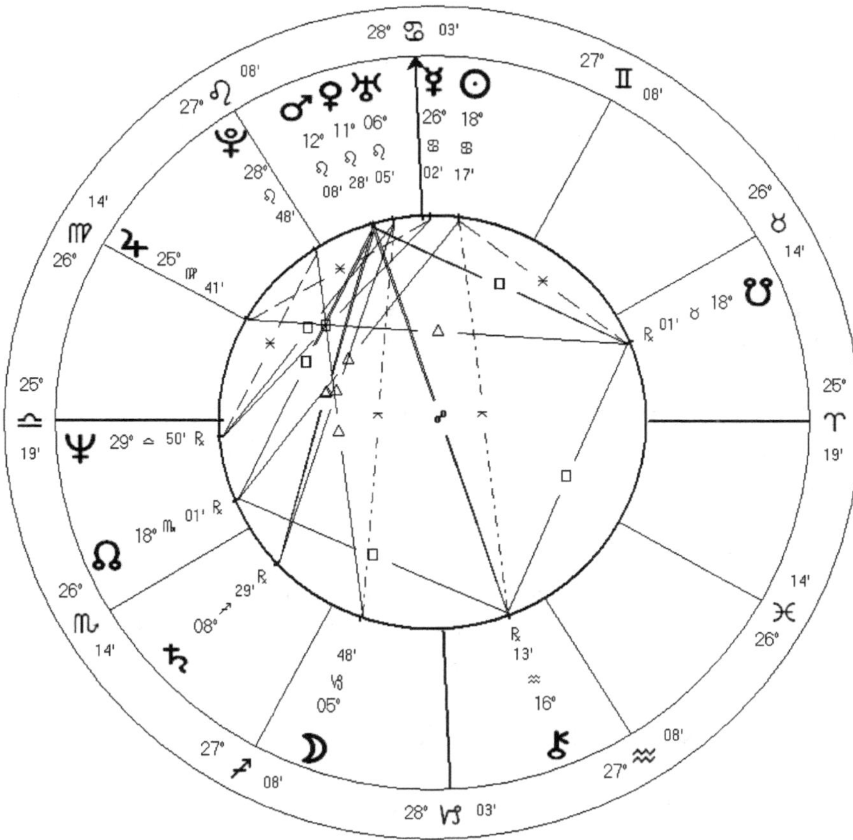

Uranian details: Sheehan has Uranus in the 10th House in conjunction with Venus and Mars as well as Mercury in the 9th House. She has Uranus square Neptune, and trine to Saturn. She has Pluto and Jupiter in the 11th House, and the Sun is the ruler of this area. Aquarius is on the 5th House cusp and Chiron in Aquarius is located in the 4th House.

Uranus in the 10th House is the most visible placement for the revolutionary planet. Sheehan embraces Uranus as a personal responsibility—to have a public role as a progressive catalyst.

Uranus in conjunction with Venus involves joining with others in causes, while the addition of Mars brings in issues of aggression, even war. Her personal individuation (Uranus) involves bringing presence and animation (Leo) while rallying people together (Venus) for action (Mars). Cancer rules her 10th House, suggesting that her maternal instincts govern her public life. The Moon is in Capricorn in the 3rd House, indicating the need for responsibility and speaking from an emotional place. Though in the 9th House, Mercury also conjoins Uranus. This is consistent with her irreverent, challenging words and insistence on truth from others.

Uranus is square Neptune in Libra, positioned on her Ascendant. She naturally behaves in accordance with a vision (Neptune) for peace and diplomacy (Libra). The connection up to Uranus in the 10th House shows sacrifice for collective reasons. She is a colorful instigator (Uranus in Leo) for greater compassion (Neptune in Libra). Saturn in Sagittarius in the 2nd House trines her Uranus. This Saturn is developing more confidence (2nd House) by adhering to a specific mission (Sagittarius). Also, Saturn/Uranus contacts tend to involve the process of challenging structures and institutions to evolve.

Pluto resides in her 11th House. This suggests a wound regarding humanitarian issues, and the potential for the greatest personal transformation to occur through making a difference on a global scale. There are intense psychological dynamics regarding her relationship with the greater world. When this aspect functions well, this makes a commanding impact on others. Jupiter in Virgo is also in the 11th House. Her mission (Jupiter) takes form in the representation of the common people (Virgo). With Leo on the cusp of the 11th House, energy is dispersed into this house by her purposeful (9th House) Sun.

With Aquarius on the 5th House cusp, her Uranus naturally informs areas of self-expression and social connecting. Interestingly, the 5th House is also the house of children. Sheehan has Chiron in Aquarius in the 4th House—and injury relating to the family system and her ability to be true to herself. This is healed by becoming more Aquarian, being rooted to her resolve and family.

Part 2 – Revolution

Part 2 comprises three chapters that address some of the social dimensions of Uranus. Reviewing some notable Uranian events illustrates how this planet enters the social dialogue as a progressive force. Then, we'll see how Uranus teams with other planets in forming cycles that challenge the collective to address evolutionary questions during specific time frames. Finally, we'll look at the upcoming astrological activity that is particularly Uranian. We are about to embark on quite a momentous period (2008-2012 and beyond) that will likely change life as we know it on this planet.

Chapter 5
Notable Uranian Events

This chapter illustrates Uranus in action through its participation in an assortment of revolutionary events. These events are split into five categories: Breakthrough Moments; Defiance and Demonstrations; The Dawn of New Eras; Shocking Occurrences; and Cultural Developments—though there is some overlap among the categories. At the beginning of each section, a particularly representative and vivid example will be discussed in detail, and the chart for the event will be displayed. Following the chart example will be other brief discussions of events in chronological order. The exact times for many of these occurrences are not known, are speculative, or in some cases, do not have a precise start time. As we'll be examining the *planetary* aspects Uranus makes (opposed to house position), exact times are unnecessary.

Breakthrough Moments

The "Discovery" of Uranus

Uranus was officially discovered on March 13, 1781, by William Herschel. However, the first recorded sighting of Uranus was by astronomer John Flamsteed (in December 1690), who erroneously catalogued it as a star. Pierre Charles Le Monnier spotted Uranus on several occasions in the 1750s and 1760s, but he also didn't realize that it was an orbiting planet in this solar system that he was watching. Herschel received credit for understanding Uranus as a planet, and, therefore, his "discovery" is relevant for the integration of it into our collective psyche.

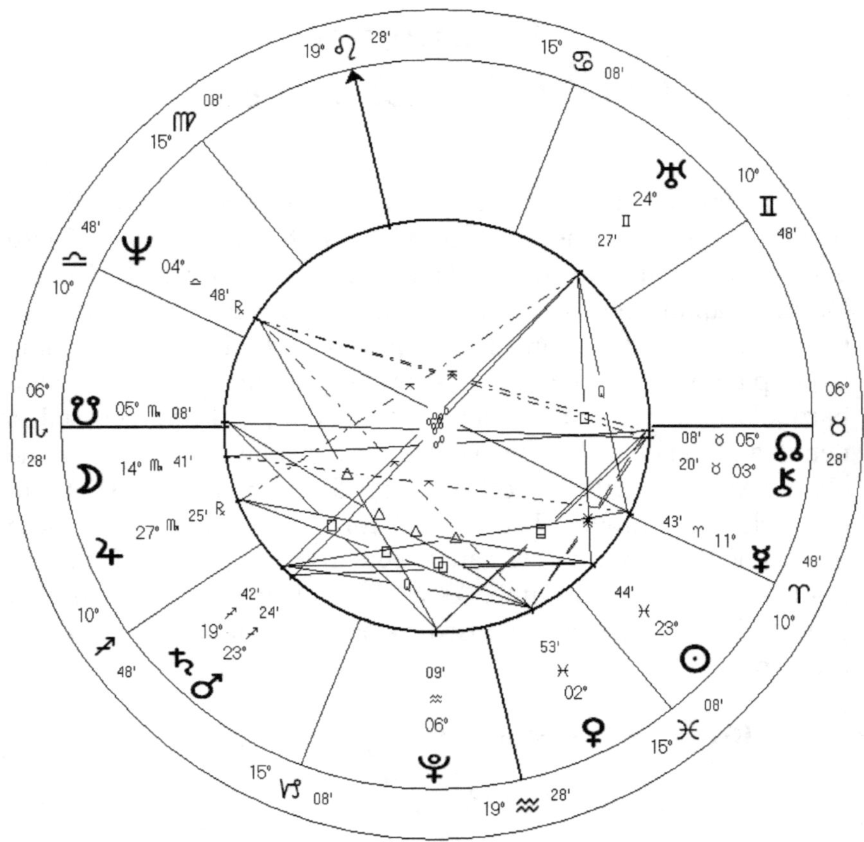

The exact time of discovery was not recorded, so the above chart is speculative. We do know that Herschel was observing the sky at night at a time when Uranus would be above. Complete darkness would have arrived around 8:30 pm, so the moment must have been after that time. The Moon rose that evening around 11:00 pm, which would have added extra illumination in the observable sky and perhaps a distraction—so the time selected for our purposes is arbitrarily 10:00 pm.

The Uranus discovery chart not only portrays the mythic tale of Uranus perfectly, but it also holds clues as to how Uranus ideally can be brought into greater manifestation and utility. As the Nodal Axis pertains to spiritual lessons, it's most appropriate to begin there. The South Node is in Scorpio on the Ascendant, in conjunction with the Moon. This speaks of familial (Moon) behavior (1st House) that's abusive, passionate and filled with hurt (Scorpio). Chiron in Taurus opposed the South Node suggests bodily (Taurus) wounding (Chiron) and the need to work diligently and in a healthy manner (6th House) to mend the pain.

Ruling the South Node is Pluto in Aquarius in the 3rd House, which is also square the Nodal axis. This Pluto is interested in reaching new paradigmatic breakthroughs, in performing the proverbial death and rebirth (Pluto) in terms of global (Aquarius) perceptions (3rd House). As the ruler of the North Node, Venus in Pisces is found in the 4th House. The Nadir and 4th House are the areas most grounded to the Earth itself. In the mythic tale, the severed genitals of Uranus are thrown into the water (4th House) and the beautiful and inspired (Pisces) Venus emerges for us to utilize on the earthly plane.

As for Uranus, it is found opposite Saturn, suggesting strongly that a major shock to the system is occurring. Saturn, in turn, is in conjunction with Mars. Saturn/Mars in Sagittarius does sound like a righteous (Sagittarius) scythe-wielding (Mars) adversary (opposed Uranus) concerned about its own security (2nd House). Uranus is in Gemini, where it is most interested in expanding thought—and in the 8th House, wanting to engage in the resolution of conflict and to awaken the mysterious or taboo. As the ruler of the 4th House, Uranus is dispersed into the area of this earthly home.

The Pisces Sun forms a T-Square with this opposition. In the 5th House, this mystically-minded energy seeks compassion and openness, and invites the broadest perspective (Pisces) to radiantly express (5th House). Because Sun-ruled Leo governs the Midheaven (10th House cusp), the best way to work with the fractious T-Square is through a public dialogue. The Pisces Sun is also trine Jupiter in Scorpio, adding the element of regenerating (Scorpio) spiritual direction (Jupiter) based upon this important work. Since this Jupiter serves as the ruler of the aggressive Saturn/Mars, it's essential for it to be fed by the more inclusive and transcendent possibilities of the Pisces Sun. Only through increasing consciousness (Pisces) can a newfound direction be found.

Neptune in Libra in the 11th House is important. This Neptune seeks broader communal togetherness, cosmic consciousness, the dissolution of boundaries, and harmony. Not only does Neptune rule the Sun (and Venus), but it also forms a Yod with Venus and the North Node, and it trines (and potentially softens) Pluto. This Neptune informs us that there is no end to the universe, no endpoint to spiritual interconnectedness. Neptune is also opposed Mercury, so connecting the personal mind (Mercury) to this lofty promise is very much the idea. (Those interested in the "minor" aspects would find it interesting that Uranus is quintile Mercury. Because both are mental planets [some call Uranus the higher octave of Mercury], the brilliant and transcendent quintile connects the personal mind with the spiritual mind.)

This chart portrays the key elements of the Uranus myth: abusive family dynamics, the wielding of weaponry and confrontation, the need for reconciliation, and the intention to appreciate and harness beauty. This chart invites the expansion of thought and new paradigms, and ultimately a more holistic and even loving worldview. Uranus in aspect to the Sun illustrates how the "new" planet is brought into awareness and presence, how it is in fact connected to the central star in this system. The T-square with Saturn/Mars shows the necessary negotiations and adjustments this landmark event entails.[4]

Other Breakthrough Moments

Abraham Lincoln's *Emancipation Proclamation* was given on September 22, 1862, which freed the slaves. Indicative of revolutionary communications, Uranus was in Gemini and trine Mercury this day. Also, Uranus was square Saturn, indicating governmental reform. Uranus was sextile Mars, suggesting newfound empowerment, and it was also square the Moon—and therefore pressing for greater emotional freedom.

Charles Lindbergh was the first to fly solo across the Atlantic Ocean in his *Spirit of St. Louis,* on May 21, 1927. Uranus in trailblazing Aries conjoined expansive Jupiter in oceanic Pisces! Furthermore, Uranus/Jupiter was sextile Sun/Mercury, which brought the adventuresome spirit to the central energy (Sun) that is teaching us (Mercury) what is possible. Uranus was also trine Saturn in Sagittarius catalyzing long-distance transportation advancements.

The United States Supreme Court ruled on May 17, 1954, that school segregation was unconstitutional, in the landmark *Brown v. Board of Education* case. Uranus in Cancer was trine a Scorpio Moon illustrating the highly emotional spirit of this event, and even the underground hostility to it. Uranus in Cancer can be a change of heart—a change in the emotional landscape we live in. Uranus was also square Neptune in Libra, a combination that presses for greater togetherness and a vision of unity. Because African-Americans have endured slavery and discrimination, it's most appropriate that the liberating quality of Uranus would be largely found within water planets and signs for this milestone event. It wasn't so much a change in mental perspectives: this breakthrough moment occurred due to shifts in what is felt inside—due to realignment with what the heart knows is right.

Wilt Chamberlain's record-breaking 100-point basketball game was on March 2 1962, and this is a sports record that is unlikely to be matched. This day found Uranus in theatrical Leo in opposition to a Jupiter/Mars conjunction in Aquarius. Jupiter amplifies athletic Mars, while Uranus takes the combination into uncharted territory. Uranus in Leo has correlates to breakthroughs in performance, while Jupiter/Mars in Aquarius takes it to distances that may never be reached again.

On June 12, 1967, the United States Supreme Court legalized interracial marriage. The Sun was in Gemini square Uranus/Pluto in Virgo. Uranus/Pluto suggests the liberation of what was once considered taboo. The Sun illuminates this territory and announces (Gemini) a change. Uranus was sextile Neptune in Scorpio, a configuration that seeks to bond intimately without restriction. The chart also features a Jupiter/Venus/Moon stellium in Leo, which correlates to increased opportunities (Jupiter) for enjoyment (Leo) in areas of love (Moon) and marriage (Venus). Four days later on June 16, 1967, was the Monterey Pop Festival. This event featured similar themes of liberation of passions and enjoyment in a more celebratory and musically expressive way.

On July 20, 1969, astronauts landed on the Moon. There was a Uranus/Jupiter/Moon conjunction, which perfectly reflects space travel (Uranus/Jupiter) to the Moon. Also, Uranus was sextile the Sun (in Moon-ruled Cancer), and sextile Mars in far-reaching Sagittarius. It would be difficult to concoct a more perfect chart for this event!

The landmark Roe v. Wade decision on January 22, 1973, legalized abortion and is seen as a climactic moment in the feminist movement. On this day, Uranus in Libra was square Jupiter in Capricorn. Uranus was stimulating advancement in areas of equality (Libra)—challenging Jupiter in conservative Capricorn to open up. The Libra/Capricorn square has much to do with laws and institutions; Uranus/Jupiter wants to make great leaps, and the square aspect provides the friction. Also note that the Sun was in Aquarius (progress) this day trine Pluto (reproductive issues) in Libra. The Moon was in Virgo, signaling feminine (Moon) health issues (Virgo).

Sally Ride took her historic flight as the first American woman to enter space on June 18, 1983, when Uranus conjoined Jupiter in Sagittarius. On this day, Uranus was also trine Venus, which is consistent with a social breakthrough. Uranus was also opposed Mercury, suggesting the scientific nature of the trip: the crew set out communication satellites and used the newly developed robot arm technology. Ride (May 26, 1951) had the Uranus/Jupiter conjunction on this day opposed her natal Sun/Mars conjunction and trine her Jupiter.

Nelson Mandela was freed from prison on February 11, 1990, after spending over 27 years behind bars. Uranus was tightly in conjunction with Mars, symbolizing a sudden breakthrough for free will. This conjunction was also a part of a larger stellium that included Neptune, Saturn, Venus, and Mercury in Capricorn, suggesting the shifting modes of governance that were taking place in Africa and around the world. Uranus was also opposed Jupiter in Cancer, another indication of busting free of restraints. The Sun conjoined the North Node in Aquarius, indicative of freedom.

Defiance and Demonstrations

The Bus stops here: Rosa stays parked

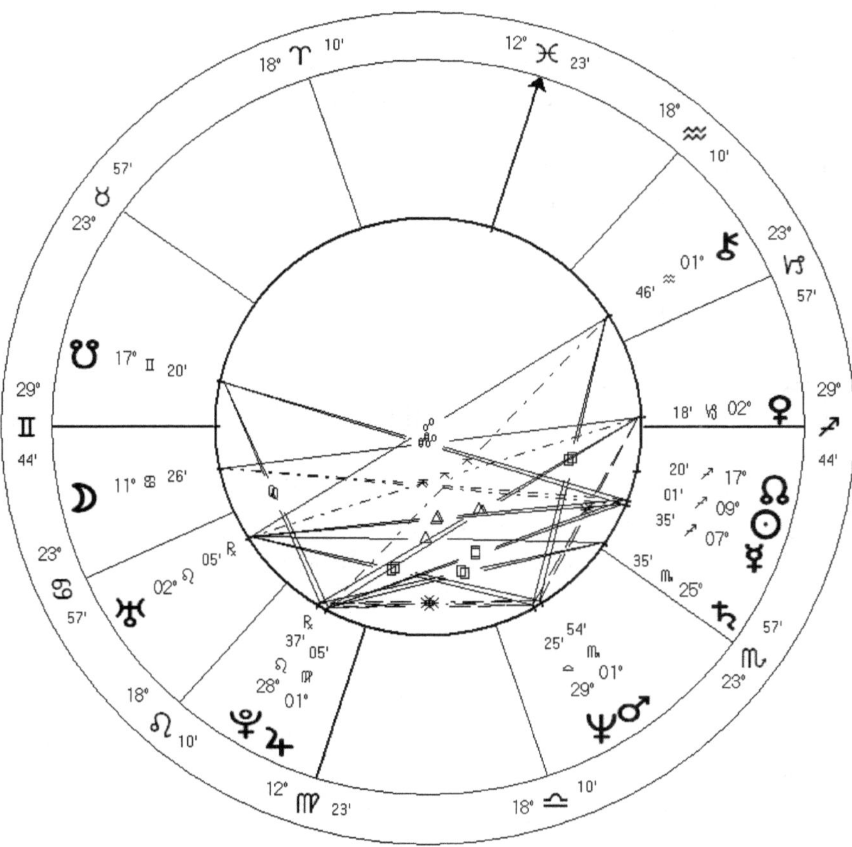

Rosa Parks refused to give up her seat for a white person on a bus in Montgomery, Alabama, on December 1, 1955. She was arrested for her actions, which garnered massive publicity. This moment is seen as the seminal event that brought momentum to the modern Civil Rights movement. The chart is cast for 6:00 p.m., the approximate time Rosa boarded the bus that December evening in Alabama.

This chart finds Uranus in the 2nd House, the area of consolidating our resources, feeling secure and confident, even feeling fortified. In Leo, Uranus is developing self-expression and visibility. This combination involves the process of displaying one's true self from a place of solidity, where one feels anchored and viable.

Uranus is trine Sun/Mercury in Sagittarius in the 6th House. Sagittarius wants to make a point and lead with moral conviction. The 6th House is a relationship house, though one that deals with unequal relations such as master/servant or mentor/apprentice. This aspect conveys making a stand, a show of strength (2nd House) connected to a purpose—asking to take a sobering look (6th House) at our assumptions and viewpoints (Sagittarius).

Saturn in Scorpio is also trine Uranus. Saturn tends to give form to whatever it touches, so the revolutionary intent is made tangible. Furthermore, Saturn in Scorpio can be rigid and controlling, even abusive—and the 6th House has been called "the house of slaves" because it deals with those in downtrodden or subservient positions. Uranus wants to obliterate this dynamic, to make Saturn progress into being mature and accountable about underlying psychological dynamics (Scorpio).

Uranus is square the conjunction of Neptune in Libra/Mars in Scorpio in the 5th House. Neptune in Libra conveys a vision of togetherness. Uranus seeks to realize this lofty intention by stimulating a breakthrough in areas of harmony. Uranus/Mars has much to do with behavioral freedom—in Scorpio, Mars is passionate and unleashed. This aspect has the spirit of unrestrained behavior, the liberation of movement based upon a broader ideal.

Uranus is also tightly quincunx Venus in Capricorn in the 7th House. Venus in Capricorn has many social norms and expectations with which it must conform. The anchored Uranus in the 2nd House connects to others (7th House) in ways that disrupt these requirements. Uranus/Venus wants a revolution in social relations, the quincunx indicating that making this adjustment is not going to be an easy task.

Other Acts of Defiance

The thwarted *Gunpowder Plot*, which attempted to blow the British Parliament to smithereens, was planned for November 5, 1605. On this day, Uranus in Taurus was in a Grand Trine with Mars in Virgo and Jupiter in Capricorn. Uranus/Mars/Jupiter correlates with political violence, while the residence in earth signs suggests that the status quo is being disrupted. Interestingly, Saturn is quite prominent in this chart—trine Pluto and square Mars, which does allude to being fortified and able to repress the violent scheme.

Nat Turner led a slave rebellion on August 21, 1831, and became a symbol of black resistance to oppression. It was a most astonishing instance of uprising in the antebellum southern United States, and it heightened the debate on slavery at this time. Turner saw an eclipse on February 12, 1831, and interpreted this as a sign to act. This chart has the eclipse in Aquarius (freedom) opposed Saturn (establishment, oppressors). The rebellion began shortly after the next solar eclipse (August 7, 1831), which occurred at 14 degrees Leo, opposed a Uranus/Jupiter (liberation) conjunction in the middle degrees of Aquarius! At the time the rebellion actually began (August 21, 1831), Uranus in Aquarius was trine Venus in Libra—consistent with the changing of social relations to achieve greater equality. Pluto in Aries was opposed Venus, a dynamic indicative of control, brutality and intense conflict. Nat Turner had Uranus trine Mars, and the first eclipse he noticed on February 12, 1831, precisely activated that natal configuration. Also note that Abraham Lincoln, who later freed the slaves, was born on February 12th, the same day Turner observed the first eclipse.

On March 12, 1930, Mahatma Gandhi began a 240-mile march in protest of the British government's rule of India. This began his campaign of non-violent protests and, eventually, the downfall of the British Empire. This day shows Uranus in Aries at the focal point of a T-Square with Saturn in Capricorn and Pluto in Cancer. The Saturn/Pluto opposition conveys oppressive governmental rule, and Uranus is applying liberating friction to this dynamic, which was largely begun by the actions of a single man (Aries). Also, Uranus was sextile traveling Jupiter on the day Gandhi began his journey.

Jesse Owens won four medals and broke three records at the Olympics on August 9, 1936, in front of Adolph Hitler, thumbing his nose at the notion of Aryan superiority. This day featured Uranus in conjunction with the Moon; square the Sun; and trine Mercury, Neptune, and the North Node. There was also a Pluto/Mars conjunction, which reflected a similar conjunction in Jesse's natal chart. Owens is a figure who may seem to defy astrological expectations because his chart is not particularly Uranian. However, his athletic contributions (Mars) do stem from psychological urgency (Pluto) and the need to right perceived wrongs in society. His victorious day had many Uranian fingerprints—particularly, breakthroughs in performance (Uranus square Leo Sun) stemming from an inner need for revolution (Uranus/Moon conjunction).

Martin Luther King delivered his "I Have a Dream" speech in front of the Lincoln Memorial at the March on Washington on August 28, 1963. About a quarter of a million people witnessed this speech that has been regarded as the most important given in the twentieth century. On this climactic day, Uranus was tightly conjoined the Sun and Venus in Virgo, with Pluto a few degrees away. Revolutionizing social relations for the disadvantaged (Virgo) is exactly what the astrology is indicating. Claiming power (Pluto) and giving illumination (Sun) to issues of race and class (Venus) is what Uranus is awakening. Saturn in Aquarius was trine Mars in Libra—providing structure (Saturn) to progressive advancement (Aquarius) through nonviolent (Mars in Libra) ways that promote equality.

The first civil rights march from Selma to Montgomery on March 7, 1965, resulted in violence and death and was later dubbed "Bloody Sunday." Here, Uranus was in conjunction with Pluto/Mars and opposed Chiron/Sun/Saturn/Venus. This shows a dramatic clashing of astrological factors pertaining to established social norms, revolutionary impulses and sudden violence. Interestingly, Uranus was also trine a Jupiter/Moon conjunction—this demonstration garnered widespread support for the movement.

The Stonewall riots on June 28, 1969, are largely considered to have launched the gay rights movement. This day featured Uranus in Libra conjoined Jupiter and Pluto in Virgo. There was an upsurge in powerful (Pluto) demonstrations (Uranus) against how people are *supposed* to live (Jupiter). This stellium promises dramatic breakthroughs regarding the oppressed (Virgo). Uranus is sextile Mars in Sagittarius, giving an energetic boost to a philosophy (Sagittarius) of sexual (Mars) freedom, as well as to unpredictable (riotous) behavior. There is a tight square between the Sun in Cancer and Chiron in Aries—illustrating vulnerability around claiming one's power. On this day, Uranus was in aspect to both of these planets (forming a T-Square), inviting or activating the uprising indicative of the Uranus/Jupiter/Pluto stellium.

Daniel Ellsberg released top-secret U.S. Defense Department documents to the *New York Times* that exposed the government's involvement in Vietnam and awakened the public to governmental deception. The *Times* began printing the "Pentagon Papers" on June 13, 1971, while Uranus in Libra was trine Mercury in Gemini, as well as trine a Moon/Mars conjunction in Aquarius. This Grand Trine does speak of the freedom (Uranus) of the press (Gemini), and of courageous action (Mars) on behalf of the public (Aquarius Moon). Ellsberg himself (born on April 7, 1931) has an Aries Sun in conjunction with Uranus at the focal point of a T-Square with Saturn in Capricorn opposed Jupiter/Pluto in Cancer. He took it upon himself to be an awakener (Sun/Uranus in Aries) that challenged the government (Sun/Uranus square Saturn in Capricorn) to liberate the underlying truth (Sun/Uranus square Jupiter/Pluto in Cancer).

Salman Rushie's *Satanic Verses* was released on September 26, 1988. Uranus was tightly in conjunction with Saturn in Sagittarius, consistent with inflaming religious institutions. Furthermore, Uranus/Saturn was also conjoined Neptune in early Capricorn, another signature of disrupting conservative religion. This stellium was square a warlike Mars in Aries, which in turn was opposed the Sun in Libra (forming a T-Square). The addition of the Sun energizes the frictional dynamic and asks if peace can be found. Uranus was sextile Mercury, most indicative of heretical communication. Uranus was also trine Venus, which goes along with the social issues triggered by a multi-national manhunt to kill an author. An Aries Moon was applying to trine Uranus throughout this day.

There were massive violent protests against the World Trade Organization on November 30, 1999, in Seattle, Washington. This day found Uranus in conjunction with Mars and Neptune in Aquarius—unruly (Uranus) violence (Mars) that couldn't be contained (Neptune). Uranus was also involved in a T-Square with Saturn in Taurus, and Mercury in Scorpio. Saturn in Taurus concerns how institutions consolidate resources/money, and this Saturn was square Uranus in Aquarius, with freedom impulses. Mercury in Scorpio can be passionate and conflict-driven in order to make its point. Also, Uranus is sextile a Pluto/Sun conjunction in Sagittarius, which conveys the fiery viewpoints and international scope of the event.

On February 15, 2003, millions around the world protested the impending U.S. invasion of Iraq. This day had the Sun conjoined Uranus in Aquarius. In addition, Mars was tightly in conjunction with Pluto—showing an awareness of the psychological dynamics of aggression, in Sagittarius, with its overseas reach and strong opinions. This day also featured Jupiter in Leo exactly opposed Neptune in Aquarius—a large-scale (Jupiter) demonstration (Leo) of worldly togetherness (Neptune in Aquarius).

Let's conclude this section where we started. *V for Vendetta*, a film that commemorates Guy Fawkes and the *Gunpowder Plot* (and brings the story to a modern context), was released on March 17, 2006. Like the original *Gunpowder* date, Uranus (in Pisces) is in major aspect to both Mars (in Gemini, square) and Jupiter (in Scorpio, trine), suggesting political violence yet again. Uranus is also in conjunction with Mercury (communications), and makes a loose stellium with the Sun. This movie is quintessentially Uranian, as the main character *V* has no human identity and speaks of himself as an idea. Also, the movie encourages the masses to band together in order to overthrow a repressive regime. This is clearly stated in the movie release chart with a Neptune/Venus conjunction in Aquarius opposed Saturn.

The Dawn of New Eras

The Bombing of Hiroshima

On August 6, 1945, the world irrevocably changed. As Hiroshima became reduced to ashes, the world saw the ominous signal of a new era, one that takes war (Mars) into technological and highly explosive (Uranus) possibilities. This chart is cast for when the first warhead was dropped from the *Enola Gay* at 8:15 a.m. over the Japanese city. The Uranus/Mars conjunction is exactly on the Midheaven, a most public message (Gemini) of chaotic and unprecedented (Uranus) weaponry (Mars). Uranus in Gemini signifies breakthroughs in intelligence, and here it's applied to force.

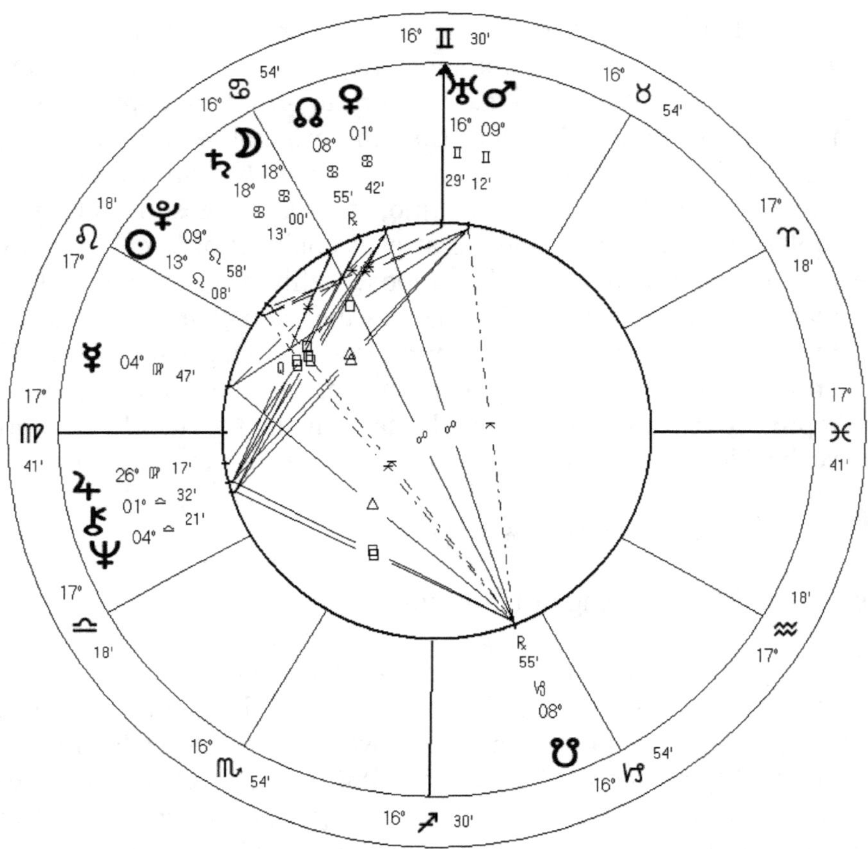

The major connection of Uranus/Mars in this chart is to the Pluto/Sun conjunction in Leo in the 11th House. As discussed previously, the addition of Pluto to this combination introduces elements of evolutionary importance, fueled by the resolution of collective disturbance—madness (or transformative healing) on a global scale. Connected to the Leo Sun, this is made dramatic and colorful, for the entire world to see (11th House). How would the royal WE (11th House), as a world family, deal with this massive new reality, the newfound evidence that we can in fact annihilate (Pluto) ourselves? Leo is supposed to be a fun, lighthearted sign, isn't it? Yes, and when the pathology that Pluto addresses connects with this playful process, we get a sobering look at what we just might obliterate—the life force itself.

The sextile between Uranus/Mars and Pluto/Sun forms a Yod that points to the South Node (Capricorn in the 4th House) in the Hiroshima chart. This South Node asks a pertinent question: how will we be responsible (Capricorn) in our stewardship of the homeland (4th House), which, in this case, is the earth itself? Are we going to restrict feeling, assert a need to icily control? Or is it possible to publicly emerge in the world (10th House North Node) through feeling (Cancer) and togetherness (Venus)? The Yod portrays the evolutionary lesson of either coming together or dramatically coming apart. Since the rulers of the Nodes (Saturn, Moon) are in conjunction, this is a lesson that couldn't be avoided at this point in history—a lesson for us all (11th House) to address.

Other examples of New Beginnings

July 4, 1776, is the original Independence Day—the day the United States officially declared autonomy from Great Britain. This day featured the South Node in Aquarius (conjoined Pluto in late Capricorn), which pertains to lessons about revolution (Aquarius) and overthrowing (Pluto) institutions (Capricorn). The Aquarius Moon portrays the emotional urgency for revolt, the need for separation from sources of sustenance (Moon). Uranus in Gemini is trine Saturn in Libra. The country was born from ideas (Gemini) of liberty and freedom (Uranus) connected to a new form of government (Saturn) based on fairness, equal opportunity and greater diplomacy (Libra).

Uranus/Mercury radio pioneer Reginald Fessenden was the first to transmit speech via radio on December 23, 1900. Uranus was tightly in conjunction with Mercury in expansive Sagittarius with Jupiter about 9 degrees later in the sign to form a stellium. This combination fits exactly with the idea of making bold leaps in communications. Also indicative of a first, Uranus was square Mars in engineering Virgo. The historical importance of the event is captured in the Uranus/Pluto opposition—Pluto being in communicative Gemini. Not far after this event, Guglielmo Marconi transmitted the first trans-Atlantic wireless signal via telegraph on December 12, 1901. Uranus was in conjunction with the Sun and Mercury in Sagittarius and was opposed Pluto in Gemini this day.

Uranus/Jupiter explorer Roald Amundsen led the first group to reach the South Pole, on December 14, 1911. Uranus in late Capricorn was sextile Jupiter in far-reaching Sagittarius, and opposed oceanic Neptune. Uranus was also trine Mars this day, which not only speaks of the event being a first, but also has much to do with the courage involved in such a freezing trek. Interestingly, Uranus was in Capricorn, a sign that has correlates to slogging through wintry or cold conditions.

On March 3, 1938, a team of explorers in Saudi Arabia discovered what would be the most lucrative supply of oil in the Middle East. The Saudi King was hoping to find water—but what they found instead would revolutionize the economy for decades. Uranus was in Taurus, the sign most related to wealth and material resources. Uranus was sextile Sun/Mercury in Pisces, a water sign. Also, Uranus was square Jupiter in Aquarius, which does correlate with exploration and with potentially fortunate discoveries.

Jackie Robinson first took the field as a Major Leaguer on April 15, 1947, breaking the color line in baseball, when Uranus was exactly square Venus. It was indeed a day of immense social change—a revolution within interpersonal relations. Uranus was also trine an Aquarius Moon, suggesting that the collective inner need for greater oneness was being awakened—along with the potential to heal prior fragmentation.

On October 4, 1957, the U.S.S.R. launched *Sputnik 1*, the first satellite put into orbit. As repeatedly seen, Uranus/Jupiter correlates with breakthroughs in air, space and travel. On this day Uranus was sextile a Jupiter/Sun/Mars stellium. Also, Uranus was trine Saturn in Sagittarius—breaking gravitational limits (Saturn) and discovering new horizons (Sagittarius). A few years later, on January 23, 1960, Jacques Piccard (who has a natal Uranus in Pisces square Mars in Sagittarius) reached the deepest point on the Earth in the Pacific Ocean, called "Challenger

Deep," at 35,838 feet below sea level. This day shows Uranus trine Jupiter in Sagittarius.

The first bungee jump occurred in Bristol, England on April 1, 1979, by the "Dangerous Sports Club." Uranus was in a Grand Trine configuration with Jupiter and Mars—precisely correlating with a revolution (Uranus) in athletic (Mars) leaps (Jupiter).

The first space shuttle flight to reach orbit occurred on April 12, 1981, when *Columbia* made its maiden voyage. Uranus was sextile Jupiter, consistent with space exploration, and trine Mercury, which correlates with technological innovation. On this day, four planets were in Aries signaling new beginnings.

A completely new era was brought in the day the Berlin Wall came down (November 9, 1989). Uranus was in conjunction with Venus, Saturn, and Neptune in Capricorn, and opposed Jupiter in Cancer. Uranus/Saturn (especially in Capricorn) correlates with the demolition of structures. Neptune adds the element of dissolving boundaries and feeling a new vision, while Venus pertains to social relations and togetherness. Jupiter seeks expansion—in Cancer, this goes along with homeland issues, and even national pride.

Shocking Occurrences

The Assassination of President Kennedy

President Kennedy was assassinated on November 22, 1963, at 12:30 p.m. in Dallas, Texas, by Lee Harvey Oswald. This event is considered one of the most shocking historical events of the last century. It was seared into the collective psyche in such a way that those alive would ask others, "Where were you when Kennedy was shot?" People reflect back on the day as the pivotal marker of the times.

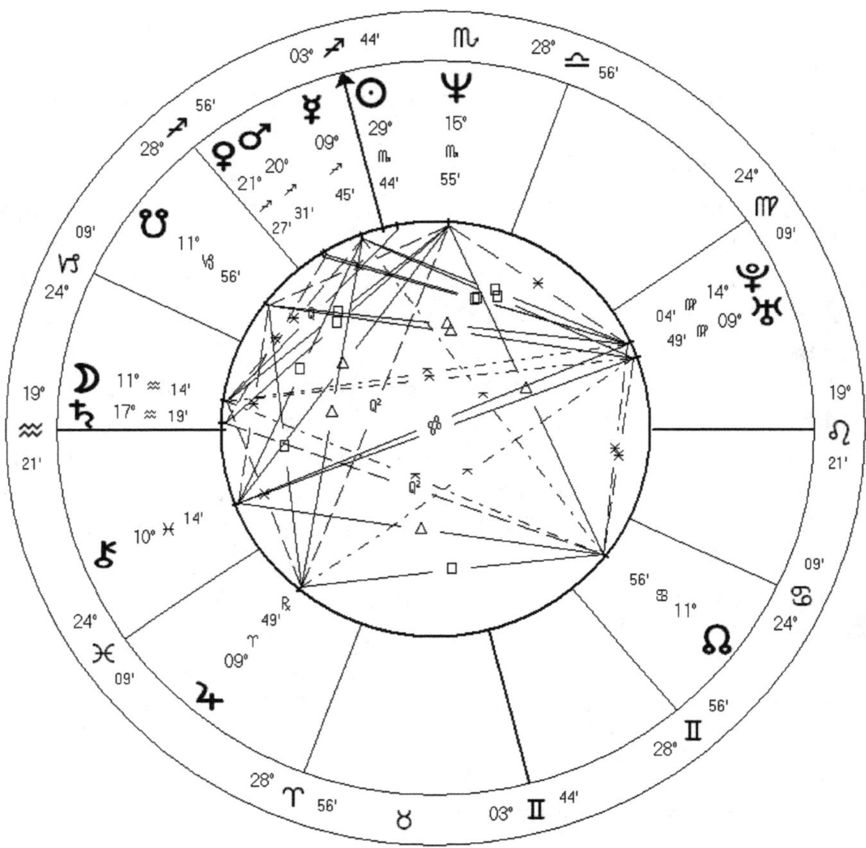

This chart shows Uranus in conjunction with Pluto in the 7th House—consistent with explosive relations. This conjunction was square a Venus/Mars conjunction in Sagittarius in the 10th House. Venus/Mars pairs violence with relating; in Sagittarius it takes on political meaning. The introduction of Uranus/Pluto adds potentially chaotic and catastrophic dimensions.

Uranus was also square Mercury in Sagittarius in the 10th House. It would be consistent that the assassination was a political message. It also goes along with the nature of shocking news of global import. There was intense media coverage, climaxing with Lee Harvey Oswald's murder by Jack Ruby, captured on live television two days later. The Kennedy assassination was a turning point in journalistic coverage of major news stories. Also, Uranus rules the Ascendant, while Mercury rules the 8th House, pairing the "chart ruler" with the house of death/transformation.

In addition to the Aquarius Ascendant, Saturn and the Moon in Aquarius were rising at the time of the shooting. This pairing illustrates the squashing (Saturn) of emotional (Moon) hope (Aquarius)—the rising of heavy feelings and uncertainty about the future, or a collective (Aquarius) emotional (Moon) burden (Saturn). Neptune (disillusionment) is square this combination.

Uranus was quincunx Jupiter in Aries in the 2nd House. Jupiter in Aries can be a philosophy of force, of taking the law into your own hands. In the 2nd House, it serves personal interest and can be inflexible. This is connected to the relational arena of the 7th House, where Uranus resides. Also note that a Scorpio Sun (death, transformation) was near the culmination point of the sky (the Midheaven) in this chart.

Kennedy had Uranus in Aquarius square Mars in Taurus, while Oswald had a 9 degree square between Uranus in Taurus and Mars in Aquarius. There were mutual conjunctions between Uranus and Mars in the charts of the two men! The composite chart of Kennedy/Oswald (not shown) has a Uranus/Mars conjunction in the 8th House (the house of death among other things). This reflects the assassination chart, which has Uranus conjoined Pluto, with the combination squaring Mars. Also, Oswald's assassin, Jack Ruby (born on March 25, 1911), has a Uranus/Mars conjunction straddling his Moon—which is prone to wild reactivity in Aquarius.

Other Shocking Occurrences

President Abraham Lincoln was assassinated on April 14, 1865. Uranus was in conjunction with Mars, opposed Jupiter, sextile the Sun, and trine Saturn. Again, we see Uranus/Mars associated with sudden violence. Uranus in Gemini opposed Jupiter in Sagittarius illustrates that a political message is tied into the violence. Saturn in Sagittarius (trine Uranus) specifically echoes this in addition to manifesting (Saturn) chaos (Uranus) in general. Uranus is sextile the Mars-ruled Sun in Aries. At the time of the shooting (moments after 9:00 p.m. in Washington D.C.), Uranus/Mars was near the 8th House cusp, with the chart featuring a Scorpio Ascendant.

The stock market suddenly crashed on October 29, 1929. Uranus in Aries was opposed financial Venus in Libra. On that fateful day, the Moon was steadily applying to also oppose Uranus, indicative of the emotional turmoil this event triggered. Uranus was also quincunx the Sun in Scorpio, the sign most involved with extremity and catastrophe. This event occurred just before the Uranus/Pluto square of the 1930s was taking hold, and can be seen as the beginning of it.

The German zeppelin called the LZ 129 Hindenburg spectacularly crashed on May 6, 1937, at 7:45 p.m. in Manchester, New Jersey. Uranus was in conjunction with the Sun, and opposed a Scorpio Ascendant. Ruling the Ascendant was Pluto in late Cancer, making a Grand Trine with Mars (Sagittarius) and Saturn (Aries) in fire signs, and also opposed aviation-minded Jupiter. In the crash chart, Uranus/Sun was not only on an angle (7th House), but together they ruled the Midheaven (Leo) and Nadir (Aquarius).

The Japanese launched a surprise attack on the United States at Pearl Harbor on December 7, 1941, beginning in the early morning. This infamous day had Uranus in conjunction with Saturn, square Venus, sextile the Moon, and trine Neptune. World War II was largely occurring during a Saturn/Uranus conjunction—a time of a "new world order." This configuration does pertain to global chaos and realignments, shifting lines in the sand. Uranus in aspect to Venus (in a global sense) has much to do with alliances, and this event did draw the United States into the War. Uranus sextile the Moon in Cancer brings disruption to the homeland, while Uranus/Neptune does correlate to existential questioning and bewilderment in light of upsetting events. Political violence can be found in the chart as well—the Sun in Sagittarius is exactly trine Mars in Aries.

The first hijacking of a plane, the *Miss Macao*, which was traveling from Macao to Hong Kong, occurred on July 16, 1948. Uranus was in conjunction with Venus and Mercury, correlating with unexpected social conditions and communications. Uranus (and the stellium) was also opposed Jupiter in travel-oriented Sagittarius and square violent Mars, forming a T-Square.

Robert F. Kennedy was assassinated on June 5, 1968, at 12:15 a.m., in Los Angeles, California. This chart displays Uranus in conjunction with both the Moon and Pluto on the 8th House cusp. Uranus is square Mars and is also the chart ruler (Aquarius rising). Uranus involved with Pluto and Mars overwhelmingly correlates with violence, while the addition of the Moon speaks to the emotional devastation this event brought.

The Pine Ridge Shootout between the American Indian Movement (AIM) and the United States government occurred on June 26, 1975. Uranus was in Libra (disruption in peace) opposed Chiron/Mars/Jupiter in Aries (war) while Saturn in Cancer (homeland) made it a T-Square. This event landed Leonard Peltier in prison for murder, where he has sat for over 30 years, despite highly questionable evidence and fairness within the legal system. Interestingly, with Mars tightly conjoined Chiron in Aries (wounding within military settings), this recalls the Wounded Knee Incident two years prior, a 71-day standoff that had begun in February of 1973, when Chiron was widely opposing Uranus. At the moment of the Pine Ridge Shootout in 1975, Chiron advanced to exactly oppose Uranus, bringing the "wounded knee" (Chiron) to its anti-establishment (Uranus) climax.

Cult leader Jim Jones initiated the mass murder/suicide known as "The Jonestown Massacre," on November 18, 1978. This day found Uranus in conjunction with the Sun and Venus in Scorpio, signifying widespread coercion and abuse of others. Religion-oriented Jupiter was squaring the stellium from charismatic Leo. This day also featured Pluto in Libra sextile Mercury/Neptune/Mars in Sagittarius, echoing themes of religious mind control.

John Hinckley attempted to assassinate President Ronald Reagan on March 30, 1981, around 2:30 p.m. in Washington D.C. Uranus was in late Scorpio sextile the Moon in early Aquarius. When Uranus rules the 7th House, it relates to interpersonal dynamics. This chart also features Sun/Venus/Mars in the 8th House. John Hinckley was trying to impress Jodie Foster, and James Brady was shot and paralyzed in the incident. Hinckley, Foster and Brady are all Uranus/Moon people who reflect the Uranus/Moon aspect in the chart. Interestingly, Uranus/Moon is about emotional instability, and Hinckley's mental illness manifested in such a way. This event did lead to awareness of and discussion about stalking and how to handle unstable people. Uranus was not in aspect to Pluto or Mars, both of which are prominent when death occurs.

A famous nuclear accident happened in Chernobyl, Ukraine on April 26, 1986 at 1:23 a.m. This chart has Uranus rising, exactly on the Ascendant, and square far-reaching Jupiter. The Sun was exactly opposed Pluto in Scorpio this day.

The Alfred P. Murrah building was bombed on April 19, 1995, in Oklahoma City, Oklahoma, at 9:02 a.m. Uranus was in Aquarius tightly square the Sun in Aries, portraying explosion and chaos with connotations of war. Uranus was exactly sextile Pluto in Sagittarius at this time, which correlates to terrorism. Venus was sextile Uranus, adding the dimension of social disruption. As for Mars, it was in fiery Leo on the 4th House cusp (homeland) trine political Jupiter in Sagittarius.

Princess Diana met a shocking death on August 31, 1997. She and her boyfriend entered the car for the fateful ride around 12:20 a.m. in Paris, France. At this time there was a T-Square with Uranus in Aquarius opposed the Moon in Leo, both squared by Mars in deadly Scorpio. Again we see Uranus/Mars equated with violence, and the Moon with the great emotional upset this event triggered. Diana herself (born July 1, 1961) had an Aquarius Moon opposed a Uranus/Mars conjunction.

Two disgruntled students attacked their school in Colorado killing 12 peers and a teacher on April 20, 1999, beginning moments after 11:00 a.m. This event is known as the

"Columbine Massacre," and it's one of the worst school shootings in U.S. history. This chart shows Uranus in Aquarius in the 8th House, consistent with random death. Uranus is trine Venus in Gemini in the 11th House, suggesting that the chaos is directed at peers (Venus) in their community (11th House). Also of note are tight oppositions between Venus and Pluto in Sagittarius, as well as Saturn in Taurus to Mars in Scorpio—both indicative of heated exchanges. (Uranus makes a loose T-Square with Saturn/Mars.) Jupiter in aggressive Aries is also sextile Uranus which shows the bravado two high school adolescents had about blowing up a school.

And now we arrive at September 11, 2001. The attacks began at 8:48 a.m. in New York City, when the first plane hit the World Trade Center. Uranus in Aquarius was opposed Venus in Leo, trine the Moon in Gemini, and quincunx the Sun in Virgo. It was also in a Grand Trine with Mercury in Libra and Saturn in Gemini. The most frictional of these aspects is the Uranus/Venus opposition, which is consistent with international alliances that are at odds with each other. Uranus/Moon goes with the emotional upset of the event, while Uranus/Sun brings the explosive nature of Uranus to animation. A 12th House Sun correlates to endings and despair. The Grand Trine in air signs goes along with the incredible media coverage. Also, Uranus trine Saturn connects Uranus to the Saturn/Pluto opposition, the dominant aspect of this chart and the most indicative of the catastrophe: the death (Pluto) of structures (Saturn) due to opposing paradigms and perceptions (Sagittarius/Gemini).

A devastating tsunami hit a large section of Southeast Asia on December 26, 2004, which submerged entire regions and killed thousands. It was a shock of epic proportions. For this cataclysmic event, Uranus in oceanic Pisces was square Mars in expansive Sagittarius—a most frictional aspect, with a broad reach in these mutable signs that dislike boundaries. The Moon was almost full for this event, and Uranus was in aspect to both luminaries, sextile the Sun and trine the Moon. The violence and tumult of Uranus square Mars was brought to the luminaries at the time the lunar cycle was nearing its climax. Also, Uranus was square Venus, which adds the element of chaos for interpersonal relations, and also the lesson of learning how to come together in a humanitarian way.

The following year brought another Uranus-in-Pisces water storm. Hurricane Katrina hit land the morning of August 29, 2005, in the Gulf Coast region of the United States. Uranus in Pisces was opposite a Virgo Sun, trine a Cancer Moon, and quincunx Saturn in Leo. The opposition from Uranus in a water sign to the Sun in an earth sign portrays the event quite literally. The levees broke in New Orleans, Louisiana, and the land in many areas of the Gulf Coast region became waterlogged. Furthermore, Virgo is the sign of the disempowered and the downtrodden. In the Deep South, many hurricane victims didn't have the means to get out of the way, or to rebuild afterwards. This event exposed and awakened (Uranus) conditions of the impoverished (Virgo). Furthermore, it occurred 42 years after Dr. Martin Luther King Jr. delivered his "I Have a Dream" speech, almost to the day. As we'll discuss in the next chapter, Uranus has an 84-year cycle, so it reaches the halfway point (opposition) at exactly 42 years. Certainly King would have agreed that the way minorities were treated in this event was more akin to a nightmare than a dream. The other aspects Uranus made echo the dominant themes of water (Uranus trine Cancer Moon) and the tension with earth (Uranus quincunx Saturn). Also, Saturn in Leo correlates with institutional arrogance (a criticism of the Bush Administration) which the hurricane (Uranus in Pisces) exposed. Uranus in aspect to a Cancer Moon goes along with homes being wrecked, and with upset over the conditions of the land itself.

On April 16, 2007, a gunman at Virginia Tech University killed 32 students and school personnel. Once again, Uranus was in aspect to Mars; here they were in conjunction. Uranus was also square Jupiter in Sagittarius—and the gunman explained his behavior as his exercising his right to correct the wrongs he perceived in society.

Cultural Developments

The Beatles appear on Ed Sullivan

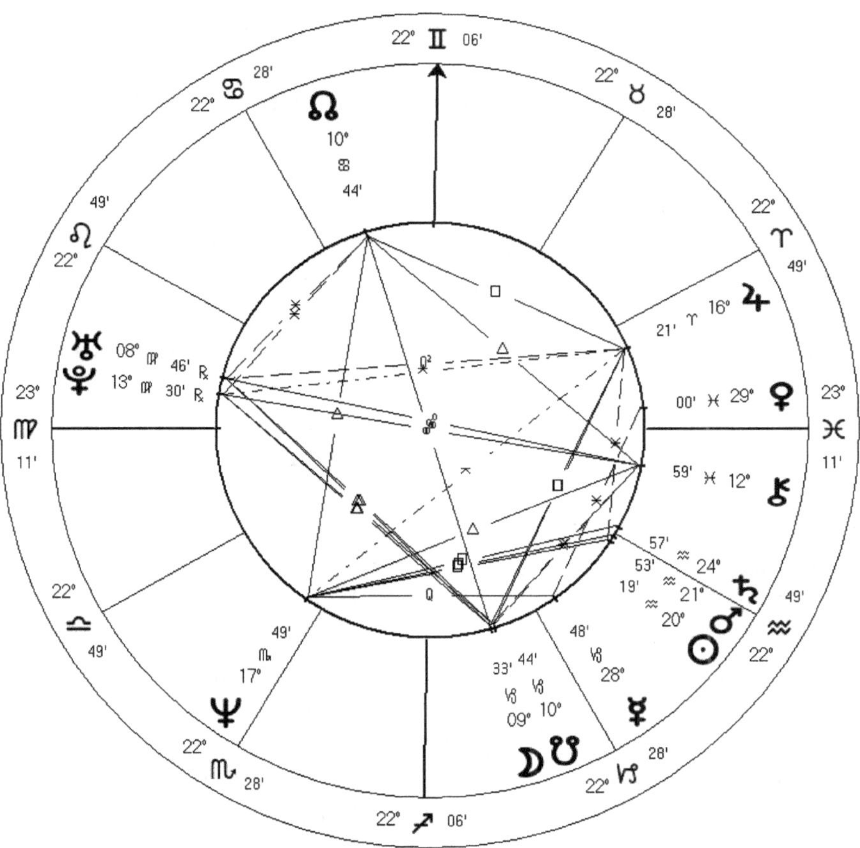

If there is one landmark moment that encapsulates the building fever of rock and roll in the 1960s, it's the Beatles' appearance on the Ed Sullivan show on February 9, 1964. Watched by an estimated 73 million people, the lovable "mop tops" were leading the British Invasion on the premier variety show of the day. It was more than just the playing of a few songs; this moment was emblematic of a new form of entertainment sweeping the globe. Though early pioneers Elvis Presley, Chuck Berry, Buddy Holly and others got the rock rolling the previous decade, there was a pervasive feeling that another wave was crashing. This was borne out with the Uranus and Pluto conjunction that was applying at the time—reaching its climax in just a few more years.

The Ed Sullivan chart is cast for 8:05 p.m. (in New York City) as the Beatles took the stage shortly after the show started. The chart features a 5th House Aquarius Sun in conjunction with Mars, and Saturn (located in the 6th House). The 5th House concerns performance, fun and self-expression, and also has a youthful, sometimes innocent feel. Aquarius situated here signifies a new type of creative force, one of potency, rawness and libido (Mars) that also is a progressive (Aquarius) institution (Saturn) in itself. Saturn's residence in the 6th House has to do with the craftsmanship required to sculpt the creativity into an art form.

The Nodal lessons portrayed speak to the emerging embrace of the rebellious cultural phenomenon of rock and roll. A Capricorn Moon in conjunction with the South Node in the 4th House has a need for family values, a conservative, nurturing dynamic that is reliable. Trine this combination is the Uranus/Pluto conjunction in the 12th House—the wild and primal energy is metaphorically banished to the closet. Nevertheless, there is a need (Moon) attached (trine) to unlocking (Uranus) this passion (Pluto), however sidelined it has been. The 10th House North Node in Cancer suggests a public demonstration of the pent-up lunar need to bust through the restrictive qualities within and, basically, to go wild. Uranus/Pluto sextile the North Node echoes this intention to go public with what had previously been hidden.

Jupiter in Aries in the 7th House squares the Nodal axis. This Jupiter seeks expansive and passionate (Aries) connections with others (7th House), the sharing of raucous (Aries) energy. This event chart speaks of the need to reclaim that prerogative, to lead with one's enthusiasm. Jupiter is also sextile the revolutionary Aquarian Sun and quincunx Pluto. The Aquarius Sun (20 degrees Aquarius) in the event chart is trine to both John

Lennon's (16 degrees Libra) and Paul McCartney's (26 degrees Gemini) Suns.

Other Cultural Developments

The Ku Klux Klan was founded on December 24, 1865. Though the hate group is not progressive, it qualifies as being Uranian because it operates outside the mainstream and is rather rebellious and unstable. Indeed, the founding chart features Uranus in Cancer—suggesting the emotionally turbulent nature of the group and its intentions to disrupt the homeland. Also, the Moon was square Uranus for most of the day. This Uranus, with its emotional instability, is directly opposed the Sun and Jupiter in controlling Capricorn. More than any other sign, Capricorn has to do with consolidating power, and tends to be conservative. Uranus opposing Sun/Jupiter suggests that this group functions as an outside force while maintaining a conservative philosophy. Furthermore, Neptune in pugnacious Aries makes the opposition a T-Square. Neptune in Aries has poor boundaries with violence, while also idealizing self-promotion. Uranus is also trine Saturn in Scorpio, which shows an agreement with parts of the status quo (Saturn) that are subversive and have hidden agendas (Scorpio).

The Statue of Liberty was dedicated on October 26, 1886, with Uranus in conjunction with Jupiter, indicative of a titanic (Jupiter) symbol (Uranus). This planetary combination precisely correlates with large overtures proclaiming freedom and reaching towards the heavens. Édouard René de Laboulaye is credited with being the intellectual creator of the piece, Frédéric Bartholdi was the principle sculptor, Richard Morris Hunt designed the pedestal, and the inscription titled *The New Colossus* was written by Emma Lazarus—all of these figures had Uranus/Jupiter! The statue was closed in 1984 to be renovated and was rededicated on July 3, 1986, with Uranus square Jupiter.

The Protocols of the Elders of Zion is an anti-Semitic manifesto that was circulated underground for years but nevertheless was highly influential. It was first published in a widely available form on August 28, 1903. Uranus was in Sagittarius, indicating an erratic philosophy not based in reality. Functioning poorly, this combination can be sanctimonious and rigid. Most suitable for a piece of propaganda, Uranus was in a remarkably tight T-Square with Pluto in communicative Gemini, and Jupiter in impressionable Pisces. Uranus/Pluto can be ruthlessly manipulative, and this pairing connects with a religious agenda (Jupiter). Mercury (writing) was in late Virgo, but close enough to make this configuration a Grand Cross. Also note that on this day, the Moon was in conjunction with Mars in Scorpio, suggesting that hidden emotional aggression was a driving force—and Moon/Mars was trine religious Jupiter.

Alcoholics Anonymous was officially instituted on June 10, 1935. This organization has been instrumental for leagues of people in breaking through to sobriety and taking control of their lives. Uranus was in Taurus on this day, signifying the need to claim composure, and to arrive at inner peace. Uranus square Venus in Leo illustrates a new type of relationship with recreation and indulgence. It also goes along with finding new friends, allies and associations. Indeed, many times when people join AA they need a new support system because the old one is filled with other substance users. Uranus sextile Mercury suggests that breakthrough occurs by speaking up, and also by learning. The North Node at this time was in sober Capricorn—signifying an intention to create good boundaries and take control of one's life. Saturn, the ruler of the North Node, is in Pisces—so the intention to reach a new level of maturation is applied to Piscean areas, which include alcohol and substance abuse.

On April 16, 1943, chemical scientist Albert Hoffman unwittingly became the first person to ingest LSD. This day featured Uranus trine Neptune, sextile Pluto, square Mars in Aquarius, and it was in a stellium with Saturn and Venus in Gemini. Uranus/Mars equates to the event being a first, while Neptune and Pluto pertain to transpersonal states of consciousness. The stellium suggests that the collective social fabric was infiltrated by a peculiar and potentially chaotic (Uranus) substance, which ended up changing not only the established order (Saturn), but culture itself (Venus). LSD brought the mind (Gemini) into new territory and instigated previously unheard of experiences. It catalyzed a dialogue about experimenting with consciousness and whether or not this should be restricted.

The birth control pill became available on May 9, 1960. Uranus was in uninhibited Leo square a pleasure-oriented Taurus Sun. This combination seeks new sensual experiences without worry—the appetite of Leo connects with the body (Taurus). Uranus was also quincunx Saturn in Capricorn, showing how this revolution (Uranus) is at odds with the conservative (Capricorn) establishment (Saturn). This chart also has Venus in Taurus exactly opposed Neptune in Scorpio—dissolving boundaries in order to be able to connect intimately.

The Woodstock Festival officially began on August 15, 1969, at 5:08 p.m. in Bethel, New York. Uranus in Libra was in the middle of a stellium with Jupiter in Libra and Pluto/Moon in Virgo, all in the 9th House. Uranus in Libra suggests advancements in togetherness, while the addition of Jupiter amplifies this to larger arenas. Moon in conjunction with Pluto has an underlying need for intense and transformative experiences, and this is brought to the more social Uranus/Jupiter in Libra. Furthermore, the 9th House correlates with travel and the proverbial quest. Making a pilgrimage to a farm in upstate New York would certainly fit. An 8th House Leo Sun square Neptune in Scorpio in the 11th illustrates recreation, sexuality, a lack of boundaries, and community.

The Rainbow Gathering is an annual countercultural festival based on community, sharing and activities that are best described as being part of the "hippie" movement. The first gathering was on July 1, 1972, when Uranus was in Libra and trine Venus/Saturn in Gemini. Uranus/Venus portrays the bohemian spirit, while the addition of Saturn goes along with the organization, social structure formed and the festival's longevity. Uranus was also square the Sun in Cancer (emotional connection, focus on tribal consciousness) at this time, bringing a sense of "free love."

The World Trade Center was officially opened on April 4, 1973. On this day, Uranus was opposed Sun/Venus and trine Saturn—a combination that does speak to an iconic and breakthrough (Uranus) artistic (Venus) structure (Saturn). Furthermore, Saturn was in Gemini suggesting duality, while Uranus in Libra opposed Venus in Aries suggests structural art that is one-of-a-kind. On the day of its demise (September 11, 2001), Saturn returned to its initial position (and was opposed Pluto in Sagittarius), while Uranus was again trine it, this time from Aquarius. Uranus/Saturn patterns formed bookends to the towers' brief existence, which was exactly one complete Saturn cycle.

On March 7, 1974, at the University of Georgia, 1549 people got together to break the record for mass streaking. For this odd nudist occasion, Uranus was in late Libra, while Venus was in early Aquarius. Not only were the planets square, they were in mutual reception. This does go along with social experimentation and unusual, norm-breaking behaviors. Uranus was also trine "anything goes" Jupiter in Aquarius, and trine organized Saturn in Gemini; the three planets form a Grand Trine. Also of note is that Mars, planet of sexual expression, was opposed Neptune, which is excellent for dissolving inhibitions. A few weeks later, on April 2, 1974, Robert Opel famously streaked at the Academy Awards. On this day, Uranus was in a Grand Trine with Venus and Mars/Saturn, and it was also sextile an entertainment-focused Leo Moon. (Natally, Opel had Uranus opposed Venus and square Mars in a T-Square. His Sun was also opposed Uranus.) On April 20, 1974, the first streaking at a major sporting event occurred at a rugby game in England. This day showed Uranus trine Saturn/Mars (correlating with organized athletics), and opposed the Sun.

The "wave" debuted at a sporting event in Oakland, California, on October 15, 1981. The wave is particularly Uranian because it requires a large group of people to act as one. This day featured Uranus square Mars (athletic) in Leo (entertainment), stimulating movement of the masses in an innovative way. Furthermore, the Moon—which is often considered in mundane charts to represent "the people"—was opposed Uranus and square Mars, forming a T-Square. This day also found the Sun conjoined both Jupiter and Pluto—a buoyant and forceful combination.

The Internet came into existence on August 6, 1991. Uranus was in conjunction with Neptune in Capricorn, giving tangible structure to our interconnectedness. Uranus was also trine Mars and Venus in Virgo. Uranus trine Mars in methodical and tech-savvy Virgo does correlate with computer innovation, while Uranus/Venus echoes the community and social outreach made possible by this invention. Saturn in Aquarius (in mutual reception with Uranus in Capricorn) also echoes the theme of providing structure for technological breakthroughs.

The O.J. Simpson verdict was announced on Oct 3, 1995. The so-called "Trial of the Century" was followed by millions and became symbolic of the state of modern race relations. Uranus in Capricorn (in conjunction with Neptune) was square Venus in Libra at this time, portraying the social turmoil, and the need to come together and heal (Neptune). Interestingly, the South Node was in Aries and ruled by Mars (conjoined Pluto) in Scorpio—a most malicious, even murderous combination. Venus in Libra was in conjunction with the North Node, indicating that moving towards a peaceful conclusion is the work, but getting there is a stretch. Squaring the Nodes was Uranus/Neptune—showing the ability to transcend differences and unite as one.

Viagra, the erectile dysfunction pill, became available on March 27, 1998. This day had Uranus conjoined Venus in Aquarius, most suitable for revolutionizing relations. The regenerative sexual potency is seen with the Aries Sun trine Pluto in Sagittarius. Uranus in Aquarius is loosely sextile both the Sun and Pluto, further connecting the scientific breakthrough in sexual prowess.

Chapter 6
Uranus Cycles

The Uranus Cycle

Uranus has an 84-year cycle, which roughly matches the human lifespan. The times that Uranus makes 4th harmonic or quadrature alignments (conjunction, square, opposition) to itself or to other planets are indicative of major life passages. At age 19-22, transiting Uranus squares an individual's natal placement. This correlates with the establishment of one's identity on one's own terms. The mid-life crisis or life review generally takes place at age 40-43; age 61-64 marks the passage into the senior years. At age 84, the time of the Uranus return, is when active engagement with the world is on the decline. One's "work" (however defined) is behind one, and a realignment with the core self can be explored. The sextiles and trines of Uranus to its natal placement are also notable times of self-alignment, though they aren't usually met with the urgency or crisis of the hard aspects.

During a typical lifespan, Uranus will transit every planet in the birthchart and travel through each of the houses. It is the only planet that will visit every area of the chart for a significant duration. Saturn will make three trips (each lasting 29.5 years) around, but the visitations to each house are relatively quick—roughly a third of the time of Uranus. Neptune and Pluto will only partially make it around the wheel. Their work is more concentrated in specific houses and planetary aspects. Since Uranus spends an average of seven years in each house and will form a conjunction with every planet for over two years (depending on orb size used), its transits are notably potent and indicative of times of accelerated growth, progress and potential breakthrough. There is hardly a time when Uranus is not doing something notable in the advancing of one's development.

Upon excitation from Uranus, a natal planet is roused to realize new qualities and ways of operating that were previously dormant or beyond one's grasp. This stimulation may manifest in a number of ways depending on the condition of the planet in question, as well as on one's natal attunement to Uranus as seen in the root message of the chart.

Since there is no endpoint to conscious evolution, every Uranus transit potentially brings newfound skills, understandings, opportunities, and life changes that position an individual closer to claiming his or her higher potential. Uranus transits frequently correlate with unexpected or "unwanted" events that recalibrate consciousness from a new vantage point. Losing a job, getting a divorce or experiencing an accident are circumstances often viewed as "difficult," but they too carry substantial evolutionary import. Through dramatic life changes, the self learns new ways of being that serve spiritual development—even when these moments are not easy for the personality.

At the completion of the Uranus transit, the lessons and experiences are a part of the individual's biography. They are brought into the person's awareness, and are no longer unfamiliar. However, if the transit is experienced chaotically and the lessons not learned, then similar lessons in different guises will be delivered until a conscious integration is achieved. When we say "here we go again," this indicates a reluctance to learn. When Uranus transits are resisted, they can be the most troubling and exasperating for the soul that is stuck.

Uranus Cycles with the Planets

The cycles of the outer planets (Jupiter through Pluto) convey collective trends, lessons, and themes—the *zeitgeist*, or spirit of the times. The passage of these planets through the signs, as well as the aspectual interactions among them, illustrates the psychological, sociological and spiritual conditions for our shared evolution. The common analogy of relating astrology to psychospiritual weather conditions is relevant here. We can extend this by construing these larger cycles as distinct seasons.

As a general rule, the faster a planet cycles through the zodiac, the less relevance it has for the collective. The inner planets move swiftly and serve as activators of larger evolutionary themes. Since these planets move so quickly, they do not have time to generate deeper levels of process. If two people walk past each other on the street, they may greet in passing, but the dialogue can't go much further. If they spend years together, the exchange has ample opportunity to incorporate many angles and previously unexplored territory. When outer planets make significant aspects to one another, they are galvanized to dialogue for extended periods, which has major impact for the host planet.

These are the durations of the outer planet cycles: Jupiter: 12 years; Saturn: 29.5 years; Uranus: 84 years; Neptune: 165 years; and Pluto: 248 years. In contrast, the Moon's cycle is one month; the Sun's one year; Mercury's and Venus' less than a year each; and Mars' roughly two years. Jupiter orbits six times more slowly than Mars—this illustrates the dramatic divide between the inner and outer planets.

Uranus holds a unique position in the outer planet pantheon. Jupiter and Saturn are faster, while Neptune and Pluto are slower. Also, Jupiter and Saturn are best thought of as "social" planets, while Neptune and Pluto are "transpersonal." The Uranus/Jupiter and Uranus/Saturn (social) cycles are much quicker than the Uranus/Neptune and Uranus/Pluto (transpersonal) cycles, and they tend to correlate with more concrete events. Jupiter and Saturn bring Uranian impulses into our familiar realms of consciousness. The Uranus/Neptune and Uranus/Pluto cycles are longer in duration and are more subtle, like background music. This music sets a particular tone, but it operates on subconscious levels. The interplay among the quicker planets catalyzes activity within the particular outer planet seasons.

Every cycle begins at the conjunction. The faster-moving planet gradually moves ahead and forms a series of aspects to the slower-moving planet. The major aspects it forms are the sextile, square, trine and opposition; then the cycle begins its waning hemicycle and forms the trine, square and sextile once again. The quadrature (90 degree) alignments tend to provide the most urgent evolutionary stimulation and, therefore, most visible effects of the planetary interchange. The sextile (60 degrees) and trine (120 degrees) do correlate with significant activity consistent with the nature of the exchange. Due to the less urgent nature of these aspects, events consistent with their flavor are often dwarfed or colored by other cycles occurring simultaneously. Here, we will focus only on the conjunction, opposition and squares, in order to witness the most vivid examples of planetary cycles.

Astrological signs are a secondary factor to note. Since planets are the actual energy, they take form in far more overt ways. For example, Uranus/Mars correlates to sudden violence (among many other things), while the signs modify and illustrate the processes and dynamics that inform the actual events. In this discussion, the focus is on the planetary exchange; signs (and houses) are considered more peripheral.[5]

Uranus/Jupiter Cycle: Boundless Exploration

This is a high-flying and rambunctious cycle that requires bold moves in order to claim its lofty promise. Since life tends to be heavy and challenging at times, this cycle inspires us to "go for it" and reach new levels of experience and breakthrough. Jupiter is interested in direction and has ample reserves of fire power to reach its destination. Uranus infuses this sense of expansion with novel, often radical ideas. Ideally, this cycle instigates exploration into the unknown. It could also result in ungrounded optimism, haywire decisions or faulty planning. Uranus/Jupiter is like an inspirational coach, but such figures come in many forms, and with a variety of agendas.

This pairing is optimally used when setting an informed agenda or developing a clear route. Those who know exactly what they want to accomplish can use this cycle like rocket fuel. One twist is that Uranus continually brings new information that awakens us to the "higher" path. What often unfolds is the incorporation of adjustments to one's direction that potentially make the endeavor even more successful. Trusting the process and seeing through adaptations bring a revolution (Uranus) in faith (Jupiter). Indeed, this pairing involves partnering with the intelligence of this universe (Uranus) to maximize one's reach (Jupiter) within our familiar world. Sometimes this pairing brings about wholesale changes in the belief system, or in the conception of the divine.

There are metaphysical/philosophical correlates to this cycle. It does register with collective breakthroughs within spheres of religion, politics and human rights. During Uranus/Jupiter times, people living in oppressive conditions may, for instance, rise and topple a tyrannical government. There could be a rallying of like-minded allies to accomplish large-scale projects, or the publishing of imaginative works that shape our collective mindset.

The Uranus/Jupiter cycle is approximately 14 years in duration. Every 3.5 years it makes a 4th harmonic, or 90 degree, aspect, (conjunction, square, opposition). Although Jupiter and Uranus are often in quadrature aspects, the most compelling interchanges occur when they are in conjunction. Though every major aspect is noteworthy, the conjunction is the only one that unifies the energies at a single point. It is a burst of new beginning, or a renewal of the cycle, and tends to correlate with clear examples. The other points of the Uranus/Jupiter cycle may become overshadowed by other cycles also occurring.

1997 Uranus/Jupiter Conjunction

This conjunction happens to coincide rather nicely with the calendar. Throughout almost the entire year, Uranus and Jupiter were within 10 degrees of separation. During Jupiter's station mid-year, it was briefly out of this range, but it returned in its retrograde motion. It then moved ahead of the 10 degree point only in the last few weeks of the year. We can safely construe 1997 as being a Uranus/Jupiter year, with the beginning few months as the highest point of the conjunction. These planets were conjoined in Aquarius, further enhancing the Uranian vibe of this year.

The year began with the inauguration of William Jefferson Clinton to his second term as President of the United States. As mentioned previously, he is a Uranus/Jupiter figure with a strong record as a progressive politician. His defeat of the conservative Robert Dole is testament to the general movement toward fresh possibilities. Clinton campaigned to "build a bridge to the twentieth century," reflecting this eye toward the future. Clinton named Madeline Albright his Secretary of State—the first woman to hold the post.

In Great Britain, the more liberal Labour Party was elected, ending Conservative rule of 18 years, and the House of Commons voted to ban handguns. Hong Kong was released from British rule, and Scotland created its own Parliament after 290 years of British rule. NATO invited the Czech Republic, Hungary and Poland to join the alliance. Tasmania became the last state in Australia to decriminalize homosexuality. Militant Serbian President Milosevic finally recognized opposition victories in the November 1996 elections. The Russian-Chechen peace treaty was signed.

In 1997, the United States economy was in wild expansion. The Clinton administration frequently touted its record of creating jobs and international economic alliances. The Dow Jones Industrial Average reached 7000 for the first time early in the year, only to eclipse 8000 a few months later. In fact, the Dow doubled its value in a period of 30 months.

The Internet became widely used this year. For the first time, many had access to endless information at their fingertips. All across the globe, people set up email accounts and familiarized themselves with the new cyber-world; the term "blog" (short for "weblog") was coined. The economic expansion entered the computer industry, and the number of new businesses created was enormous. A few years later, the "dot-com bubble" burst when many of these businesses no longer had the resources to sustain themselves. However, the general sense in 1997 was of getting aboard the growing expansion and claiming a part of the riches.

Uranus seeks interconnectedness. When combined with Jupiter, there is potential to join forces with like-minded allies. Morgan Stanley and Dean Witter merged, and WorldCom and MCI Communications teamed to become MCI WorldCom. Microsoft bought a significant portion of Apple. Boeing and McDonnell Douglass also completed their high-profile corporate merger. The Star Alliance was formed between Air Canada, Lufthansa, SAS, Thai Airways International, and United Airlines—most appropriate since Uranus/Jupiter correlates to air and space travel.

A sheep named Dolly, the first successfully cloned animal, was introduced, marking a significant scientific breakthrough. Also, IBM's *Deep Blue* defeated Garry Kasparov, the first time a computer beat a world champion in chess. NASA began repair work for the Hubble Space Telescope, and its Pathfinder landed on Mars, sending a plethora of amazing pictures that awakened many to another world. Also, scientists reported new DNA findings from a Neanderthal skeleton, which supports the "out of Africa" theory of human evolution. This "African Eve" is allegedly between 100,000 and 200,000 years old. The supersonic land speed record of 763 mph was set in the Black Rock Desert, Nevada, and the first test flight of the F/A-22 Raptor took off into the skies. The first hybrid vehicle, the Toyota Prius, made its debut in Japanese showrooms.

In other Uranus/Jupiter news, 39 people died attempting to join Haley's Comet as part of the Heaven's Gate cult suicide. A woman in Iowa successfully gave birth to septuplets. The USS Constitution sailed for the first time in 116 years. Almost a million Christian men assembled for prayer and repentance at the Promise Keepers' *Stand in the Gap* demonstration.

Many of the top films of 1997 had strong Uranus/Jupiter themes including *Contact, The Lost World: Jurassic Park, Men In Black, Tomorrow Never Dies, The Fifth Element, Amistad,* and *Austin Powers*. Production began for *Star Wars Episode 1: The Phantom Menace.*

In the world of music, Radiohead released *OK Computer*, Uranus/Jupiter figure Bob Dylan reclaimed popularity with *Time*

Out of Mind, and Phish was at the peak of its success. Both Fleetwood Mac and the Monkees reunited, and Coldplay forms. Recordable CDs are made available for the first time. Uranus/Jupiter-themed *Harry Potter* debuted, and *The Simpsons* surpassed *The Flintstones* as the longest-running animated TV show.

1983 Uranus/Jupiter Conjunction

Like the one in 1997, this conjunction was operative throughout most of the calendar year. It was beginning to form in December 1982, and was separating in December 1983. Uranus and Jupiter formed a conjunction in Sagittarius (Jupiter's home sign), emphasizing the adventuresome, political and religious. President Ronald Reagan proclaimed 1983 to be the year of the Bible.

The Uranus/Jupiter conjunction of 1983 was occurring precisely at the time of a Saturn/Pluto conjunction, which was also in effect the entire year. Saturn/Pluto is a slower cycle, and almost opposite in flavor. It concerns the consolidation of power, the psychodynamics of fear, the willingness to look unflinchingly at how systems are governed, and the manifestation of our darkest horrors. Ultimately, it promises radical shifts in structural operations, leading to greater responsibility and honesty. The early 1980s was marked by conservative (Saturn) power (Pluto), and the intensification of the Cold War illustrates one way this conjunction played out. The Uranus/Jupiter conjunction provided moments of release from the gravity of the times and helped balance fear with hope. Nevertheless, these two events inform each other, so 1983 can be seen as a study of opposites, but also a blending of planetary factors.

Many of the breakthroughs and advancements that Uranus/Jupiter typifies are within the darker terrain of Saturn/Pluto. For instance, Nazi war criminal Klaus Barbie was arrested at the beginning of the year. The United States accepted criticism for imprisoning Japanese citizens during World War II, a significant advance in the honoring of human rights

(Jupiter/Uranus), but also an acknowledgment of the abuse of governmental power (Saturn/Pluto). The movie *Gandhi* wins big at the Oscars. He is a man that liberated a country and stood for human rights (Jupiter/Uranus), and was subsequently assassinated (Saturn/Pluto). Samantha Smith, a schoolgirl from Maine, was invited to the Soviet Union to visit Secretary Uri Andropov after he read her concerns about nuclear war. Poland ended a time of martial law and granted amnesty for political prisoners. An agreement was signed withdrawing Israel from Lebanon. Pope John Paul II retracted the Catholic Church's dismissal of Galileo. In West Germany, there was a massive demonstration for nuclear disarmament.

Martin Luther King Day was established as a national holiday this year, and Ronald Reagan became the first U.S. President to address the Japanese national legislature. The Zapatista Army of National Liberation was founded in Mexico. Soviet officer Stanislav Petrov helped prevent a worldwide nuclear war by refusing to accept that the United States was attacking the Soviet Union, despite information suggesting otherwise.

Astronauts performed the first space shuttle spacewalk. Pioneer 10 was the first manmade object to leave the confines of our solar system. Sally Ride became the first American woman in space, and Dick Smith performed a circumnavigation of the Earth in a helicopter. Six men walked underwater across the Sydney Harbor in 48 hours. Richard Noble set a land speed record of 633 mph at the Black Rock Desert in Nevada. The Denver Nuggets and Detroit Pistons scored 370 points in a game, setting a record. Environmental artists Christo and Jeanne-Claude set up *Surrounded Islands*, a massive project which involves 11 islands and 6,500,000 square feet of fabric.

New inventions and technologies included the release of Lotus 1-2-3, the IBM PC XT, Microsoft Word, and Swatch timepieces. Tokyo Disneyland opened in Japan, and Barney Clark received the first artificial heart. A computer was recognized as TIME Magazine's *Man of the Year* at the close of 1982.

In popular culture, Michael Jackson's *Thriller* was released and became one of the most popular albums in history. Other record releases include the Police's *Synchronicity*, which addressed metaphysical questions; the Cocteau Twins' *Head over Heels*, which introduced "dream pop"; and Nena's cross-cultural (Jupiter/Uranus) and Cold War (Saturn/Pluto) anthem "99 Luft Balloons." Phish and the Red Hot Chili Peppers formed in 1983—both of which are noted for their lively, improvisational music and mixing of musical genres.

The Right Stuff, a movie that chronicles U.S. advancements in air and space exploration, was released. *Wargames* was another hit, capturing the spirit of technological advancement within the Cold War mentality. Adventure movies such as *Return of the Jedi*, *Superman 3* and *Octopussy* fared well at the box office. Notable books released include *Odyssey: A Daring Transatlantic Journey* by Susan Oliver, and *The Robots of Dawn* by Isaac Asimov. Popular game show *Wheel of Fortune* debuted on television.

October 1968-October 1969 Uranus/Jupiter Conjunction

This conjunction began in October 1968 and was separating a year later. It took place in the sign of Libra, which concerns peace, justice, the arts, relationships, and diplomacy. The more compelling Uranus/Pluto conjunction that typified the tumultuous decade of the 1960s was still operative, though gradually reducing in intensity. Just when Uranus and Pluto were getting some breathing room between them, Jupiter came along and formed a triple conjunction with the two. This had the effect of bridging Uranus and Pluto, thereby prolonging the primal and instinctual drive (Pluto) towards liberation and subversion (Uranus), and adding the distinctive Jupiterian flavor of optimism, bravado, expansion, and faith. The Jupiter/Uranus conjunction with Pluto is rare, and 1969 was one of the most cataclysmic years in history.

The wildness and urge for breakthrough typical of Jupiter/Uranus became exaggerated this year. There were mass demonstrations for peace, feminism, the environment, and civil and homosexual rights. The sexual revolution was in full swing, and the culture was agog with rock and roll and recreational drug use. Curiously, during this time Richard Nixon was elected and installed as President—hardly a figure representative of the times. Or was he? Nixon's paranoid and controlling style, his escalation of the war in Vietnam, and eventual criminality represents the shadow side of boundary-ignoring Uranus/Jupiter combined with secretive Pluto. In many ways Nixon was the perfect figure to rally the progressive troops to mobilize into specific causes. Despite, or because of, Nixon, 1969 was uncompromisingly cathartic.

The events of the year include major advances in air and space exploration, culminating with the Moon landing by the Apollo 11 mission. Earlier in the year, Apollo 7 and 8 were launched, with the latter giving humans the first chance to see the far side of the Moon and the Earth as a whole. Interestingly, the crew read passages from the Bible—a mix of technology (Uranus) and religion (Jupiter). Apollo 9 took flight and tested the lunar module; Apollo 10 also had a mission. The Mariner 6 Mars probe was launched. A Soviet space probe called Venera 5 landed on Venus this year, and the Soviets also launched Soyuz 5. In France, the first Concorde test flight took off. On the seas, Robin Knox-Johnston became the first to sail around the world, solo, without stopping, and Tom McClean crossed the Atlantic in a rowboat.

Some of the events that capture the freewheeling and turbulent spirit of the year include the Beatles' impromptu concert on the roof of Apple Records, which was halted by the police, Jim Morrison's public indecency incident in Miami, and the gathering of about a half a million people at the Woodstock music festival. The Stonewall riots launched the gay rights movement, and John Lennon and Yoko Ono had their "bed-in" for peace. Lennon's song "Give Peace a Chance" is emblematic of the times and a clear reference to the conjunction taking place in peaceable Libra. In April, the first anniversary of the musical *Hair* was celebrated in New York City with a free concert.

In October of 1969, hundreds of thousands joined together for the National Moratorium antiwar demonstrations throughout the United States. A student in Prague set himself on fire to protest the Soviet invasion of Czechoslovakia. The communist group "The Weathermen" seized control of the Students for Democratic Society offices at the University of Michigan. Ted Kennedy's infamous Chappaquiddick incident resulted in the death of Mary Jo Kopechne in July. Charles Manson's cult followers carried out the gruesome murder of five innocent people. People demonstrated in Chicago in connection with the trial of the "Chicago Eight."

In other events, Golda Meir was installed as Prime Minister of Israel, and Yasser Arafat assumed control of the Palestine Liberation Organization. The first temporary artificial heart was implanted; ARPANET, the predecessor to the Internet, was created, and the first automatic teller machine was introduced. Wal-Mart was incorporated and would go on to be one of the largest corporations in world history. The improbable "miracle" Mets won the World Series, which matches the feat of the New York Jets winning the Super Bowl earlier in the year—both are unexpected (Uranus) triumphs (Jupiter).

Movies released under the Uranus/Jupiter conjunction of 1969 that capture its flavor include *Easy Rider, Midnight Cowboy, Butch Cassidy and the Sundance Kid, The Wild Bunch,* and *Alice's Restaurant*—they echo the themes of individual expression, adventure, travel in search of meaning, standing up for one's ideals, and confronting or overthrowing the norms of society.

Within music, progressive rock was at its height, with such acts as Jimi Hendrix, Pink Floyd, the Grateful Dead, King Crimson, Frank Zappa, Yes, Jethro Tull, and the Moody Blues. Led Zeppelin formed and released its seminal self-titled first album, and Bob Marley emerged on the scene. The Who released *Tommy*, the first rock opera, and David Bowie put forth his "Space Oddity," which paralleled the space exploration occurring this year. The Fifth Dimension's "Age of Aquarius/Let the Sunshine In" was emblematic of the times.

Uranus/Saturn Cycle: New World Order

Saturn relates to the physical world, the prevailing organizational structure that is in place at any given time. It allows us to have a sense of continuity and solidity, to trust in the preservation of our institutions and social norms. Uranus demandingly insists that structure and organization not be calcified in ways that stifle necessary change. The Uranus/Saturn cycle concerns the dynamic confrontation between resistance and change, the catalytic boost toward reforming, and sometimes destroying, what we have come to rely on. Because Saturn is an earthy planet, the Uranus/Saturn cycle is the most observable Uranus cycle in our visible world. It parallels with striking events that leave us wondering, "what in the world is next?"

Revolutionary events tend to recalibrate consciousness in the direction of forward movement—and help us anticipate how reform is going to unfold. However, with the introduction of the "unknown," there is a sense of widespread trepidation. In contrast to Neptune, which gradually dissolves, Uranus can suddenly strike, leaving many in shock and uncertainty. These alienating jolts serve to orient the collective toward the implementation of a newfound (Uranus) plan (Saturn). The integration between these planets calls for a new world (Uranus) order (Saturn)—one that is more attuned with where we are going rather than where we have been. Uranus/Saturn events are some of the hardest to fathom—in the midst of them, many struggle to attain a sense of security.

Though Uranus/Saturn is difficult for us to manage, it is of prime evolutionary importance. The Uranus/Jupiter cycle may thrill us, but it is fleeting. The Uranus interchanges with Neptune and Pluto relate to more prolonged passages of evolution, but these operate on more subtle levels and require the social and inner planets to carry out their spirit. The Uranus/Saturn cycle is the most edgy, dramatic, confrontational, and urgent of all. There are times when a poorly constructed building needs to face the wrecking ball. After the moment of impact, we pick up the pieces and begin to rebuild. The stronger the resistance (Saturn) to the necessary demolition, the more perplexing and disturbing

(Uranus) the change becomes. Breaking new ground can fill us with optimism and possibilities if we cooperate.

The duration of the Uranus/Saturn cycle is 45 to 46 years. Approximately every 11 to 12 years these planets form a 4th harmonic aspect, which tends to be the most compelling example of this interchange. This cycle guards against complacency. Almost every decade will have some sort of confrontation between the current state of the world, and what the world ideally could be. The Uranus/Saturn cycle continually moves forward, instigating this evaluation, but other cycles are mitigating factors as to how this is played out.

As seen in the mythic tale in which Saturn castrates Uranus, this dynamic is highly antagonistic. The opposition aspect in particular carries the spirit of enmity and possible resolution, and therefore illustrates the interplay of these planets graphically. The conjunction forces a fusion of these energies, which are otherwise hostile to one another. Like two fighting fish forced to share the same aquarium, when mixed together, Uranus and Saturn produce a burst of events that are similarly spectacular. Here, we will examine the Uranus/Saturn conjunction of 1987-1989, the opposition of 1964-1967, and the conjunction of 1941-1943. Later on, the opposition spanning late 2007-2011 will be addressed as part of upcoming Uranian activity.

1987-1989 Uranus/Saturn Conjunction

This conjunction actually began during the last couple of weeks of 1986, but it gained momentum at the onset of 1987. It released precisely at the end of 1989. This event occurred in late Sagittarius, then moved forward to early Capricorn. We would expect to see increased activity within realms of political movements, the structure of governments, religious institutions, and ideology. During much of this time, Saturn was also in conjunction with Neptune, which was then positioned a bit farther ahead in Capricorn. Again, we have a triple conjunction in effect, with Saturn playing the role of bridger of the other two planets. This adds the Neptunian influence of dissolution, grief and letting go, while conceiving of a new vision. It potentially increases the theme of alienation or despair, while also delivering a sense of hope for those who are lost. Saturn's bridging of Uranus and Neptune also grounds the beginning of the Uranus/Neptune conjunction, which was just forming.

The final three years of the 1980s were marked by worldwide political turmoil and restructuring, economic turbulence, social unrest, dramatic breakthroughs, shocking revelations, and an improbable series of accidents, explosions and catastrophes. The interchange between Uranus and Saturn was unmistakable in this relatively brief time frame that catalyzed an entirely new world order.

The political events are most striking. The Soviet Union held its first free elections, which went against the Communist Party. The Soviet Union fractured and soon would split into separate countries. The Berlin Wall was torn down, and Germany was beginning its reunification. Apartheid ended in South Africa. The Intifada began in the Middle East, and an independent State of Palestine was proclaimed by the Palestinian National Council. Lebanon and Syria become embroiled in conflict. The Soviets withdrew from Afghanistan, and the European Union passed the Single European Act. Portugal and China agree to return Macau to China. The Constitution of the Philippines went into effect. Hungary opened its borders to western Europe. Solidarity is victorious in the first free elections in Poland. The Velvet Revolution in Czechoslovakia successfully ended Communist rule in that country, and Bulgaria and Romania followed suit. Mongolia, the second oldest Communist country, peacefully transitioned to a democracy. In China, students demonstrated fo democracy in Tiananmen Square. Brazil held its first fre Presidential election since 1960. Korean President Chun Do Hwan admitted to corruption and went into exile. T Netherlands restructured its political parties.

In the United States, the Reagan Administration rocked by the Iran-Contra scandal. The Tower Commis reprimanded Reagan for the mismanagement of his nati security staff. John Poindexter and Oliver North were indicted on charges of conspiracy. Conservative Supreme Court nominee Robert Bork was defeated. In late 1987, Reagan and Gorbachev signed the Intermediate-Range Nuclear Forces Treaty. Two years later, President George H.W. Bush and Gorbachev announced that the Cold War between the superpowers was coming to an end. On October 19, 1987, termed "Black Monday," stock market levels plummeted, causing instability for the global markets.

Part of the scope of Uranian energy is rallying the collective toward progress and breakthrough. When paired with Saturn, the result is overthrowing worn-out structures and political regimes. Throughout Europe and Asia there were demonstrations, riots and protests—most notable are the tank-defying heroics in China and the East German protests for political reform.

Other revolutionary events include mass protests against the governments in both Algeria and Burma, which resulted in 'housands of deaths. The Soviet Red Army massacred Georgian emonstrators who were non-violently protesting. In the Baltics, people of Estonia, Latvia and Lithuania formed an unbroken 'n spanning 600 kilometers, roughly two million people, in a of independence from the Soviet Union. In a far different f demonstration, the Harmonic Convergence was observed the globe—the spirit of which was to enter a new age. police arrested 250 citizens for observing the Summer t Stonehenge.

other facet of this interchange is the cementation breakthrough (Uranus). Indeed, many "firsts" are this time. Aretha Franklin became the first woman d into the Rock and Roll Hall of Fame. In Great he Order of the Garter and Magdalene College ors to women. Benazir Bhutto became the first nister of Pakistan, as well as the first woman to ent of an Islamic state. Barbara Clementine first female bishop in the Episcopal Church. ibution of RU-486, the "abortion pill," and ights resumed after the Challenger disaster.

Gaby Kennard became the first Australian woman to fly non-stop around the world.

Ron Brown was installed as chairman of the Democratic National Committee, the first African-American to lead a major American political party. Virginia elected Douglas Wilder as governor, the first African-American to run a state. David Dinkins was elected the first African-American mayor of New York City. Jesse Jackson almost became the nominee for the Democrat Party in the 1988 Presidential race. Surprisingly, Sonny Bono was elected mayor of Palm Springs, California.

Other notable breakthrough events include the discovery of a 4400-year-old mummy in the Great Pyramid of Giza. An official new agency in the Soviet Union reported that a UFO had landed in Voronezh, and scientists at the University of Utah achieved cold fusion. Europe announced intentions to ban all chlorofluorocarbons by the end of the twentieth century. Voyager II reached Neptune and its moon Triton.

The explosive quality of Uranus takes on literal meanings when paired with Saturn. During this transit, there were unprecedented numbers of transportation accidents, catastrophes at factories and other startling events that made graphic news headlines. Some of the most notable are the Exxon Valdez oil spill, which dumped 11 million gallons of oil into Prince William Sound. A United Airlines airplane's door opened during flight, resulting in the ejection of nine passengers and crew members from the plane. The Hillsborough disaster, a massive European football tragedy, occurred. The United States military detonated an atomic bomb in Nevada, which paralleled the rampage of the Unabomber, Ted Kaczynski, who was very active during this time with his anti-establishment (Uranus/Saturn) bombings.

One would expect many shocking revelations when Uranus is paired with Saturn. The religious structure in particular faced many scandals: Jim Bakker was defrocked by the Assemblies of God, Jimmy Swaggart confessed his sins and left the pulpit, and televangelist John Nunes was found guilty of embezzling $158 million dollars. In politics, Gary Hart left the 1988 Presidential race amid allegations of an extramarital affair.

In Israel, Mordechai Vanunu is sentenced to 18 years in prison for leaking Israel's nuclear program. President George H.W. Bush unexpectedly held up a bag of cocaine, purchased across the street from the White House, in a televised speech to the nation.

The United States Supreme Court decides to protect free speech in *Hustler Magazine v. Falwell.* Robert Tappan Morris was indicted for releasing a computer virus, the first person to be prosecuted under the Computer Fraud and Abuse Act. The "Police Riots" occur in New York City's Tompkins Square Park. Australia's domestic airline pilots resigned over a dispute. Iranian leaders encouraged Muslims to kill Salman Rushdie, heretical author of *The Satanic Verses.*

Uranus/Saturn Opposition 1964-1968

Using a 10 degree orb, this event would have begun in March 1964 and separated in February of 1968. Saturn's comparatively wide swings of retrograde and direct movement position these planets as further than 10 degrees apart at some points during this four-year time frame. Saturn was in Pisces for most of this time, then ingressed into Aries for the later stages; Uranus was in Virgo for its entirety. The Virgo/Pisces axis deals with issues of health care, spiritual or transcendent experiences, working toward some ideal, populism, technological vision, and rallying the downtrodden to overcome restrictions in finding liberation.

The political climate during this opposition was one of unrest, leading to war, political realignment and struggles for freedom. At the beginning of this event, the United States pledged to offer South Vietnam economic and military aid, only to become embroiled in a nightmarish quagmire in years to follow. Military coups occurred in Brazil, the Dominican Republic, Syria, Ghana, Nigeria, and Sierra Leone. A rebel army in Congo took 1000 western hostages. India and Pakistan resumed fighting. Martial law was declared in Rhodesia. Freedom Fights in Cuba began, leading to a massive tide of immigration to the United States. Castro announced martial law in Cuba. The Irish Republican Army's terrorist campaign was active in Dublin. France decided to leave NATO. The Soviet Union requested that Chinese students leave the country, then sent troops to the Chinese border a few months later. The Six-Day War occurred in the Middle East. Greece was taken over by a military dictatorship. Revolutionary Che Guevara was captured in Bolivia and subsequently executed. Botswana became an independent state. South Yemen, Malawi, Malta, and the Gambia declared independence from Great Britain. Israel and Jordan experienced border clashes.

Uranus/Saturn, particularly in opposition, correlates with collective demonstrations for change against what is perceived as oppressive leadership. The protests and demands made for greater freedom during the middle years of the 1960s are legendary. Martin Luther King Jr. was most active during these years in leading the modern Civil Rights movement in the United States. There were marches, sit-ins, demonstrations, and protests of many kinds. Malcolm X led a more radical form of black empowerment that is sympathetic to violence. The Watts Riots occurred in Los Angeles, California; the Hough Riots broke out in Cleveland, Ohio, and riots occurred elsewhere including Lansing, Michigan; Tampa, Florida; and Buffalo, New York—all in response to racial oppression. In Detroit, Michigan, 43 people died in the 12th Street Riot—hundreds were injured, and over a thousand buildings were burned. A protest at a white-only bowling alley in Orangeburg, South Carolina, led to the deaths of three college students. Three civil rights workers were murdered in Mississippi by segregationist officials. In South Africa, Nelson Mandela delivered his "I Am Prepared to Die" speech as part of the anti-apartheid movement.

Other notable demonstrations include the railroad strikes against the Illinois Central Railroad, and a strike of public transportation workers in New York City. Thousands marched against the Vietnam War in San Francisco, Washington, D.C., and other cities. Allen Ginsberg and Benjamin Spock were two noted celebrities arrested for protesting the war. China began its

Cultural Revolution. In separate events, football fans in Peru and Turkey rioted, injuring and killing hundreds. Anti-Communist demonstrations took place in Indonesia. Protesters marched in Algiers in support of their deposed President. Martial law was declared in South Korea after thousands of student demonstrators overpowered law enforcement. Hundreds of student demonstrators took hold of an administration building at Cheyney State College.

Anti-establishment and rule-breaking activity took on many forms. Jimmy Hoffa was convicted of tampering with a Federal jury. The Black Panther Party was founded. The Church of Satan was formed in San Francisco, and experimental LSD "Acid Tests" began. Pirate radio was started off the coast of England, which led to an official government ban. Muhammad Ali refused military service, and John Lennon elicited controversy and protests by suggesting of the Beatles that, "We're more popular than Jesus now." Bob Dylan played an electric guitar and alienated a large segment of his audience. The New York Times rattled the government by reporting that the Army was covertly conducting germ warfare experiments.

The theme of freedom versus oppression becomes emphasized during Saturn/Uranus times. The U.S. Supreme Court upheld the First Amendment by protecting critical speech toward political figures. The Civil Rights Act of 1964 and Voting Rights Act of 1965 were signed into law. President Lyndon Johnson pledged to create "The Great Society," which promised equality for all. The Social Security Act of 1965 became law and established Medicare and Medicaid. The Freedom of Information Act was enacted. The famous *Miranda v. Arizona* case was decided by the Supreme Court in favor of informing suspects of their rights. *Loving v. Virginia* declared any law that prohibits interracial marriage to be unconstitutional. In another case, the Supreme Court decided that businesses providing accommodations cannot discriminate on racial terms. In Great Britain, the Parliament decriminalized homosexuality and passed an abortion bill. The Vatican addressed contraception and decided to condemn (Saturn) the birth control pill (Uranus).

Athletic recruiting became desegregated at the collegiate level. Other evidence of racial integration includes some important firsts for African-Americans. Robert Weaver became the first African-American Cabinet member; Edward Brooke, the first Senator since the Reconstruction; Carl B. Stokes, the first mayor of a major U.S. city; and Thurgood Marshall, the first Supreme Court Justice. Dr. Zakir Hussain became the first Muslim to preside over India.

Some notable technological breakthroughs include the completion of the Gateway Arch in St. Louis, Missouri. IBM debuted its System/360 computer. The first color television broadcasts were made and Public Broadcasting began. The first artificial heart was installed. The first person was cryonically preserved in hopes of future revival. The first Kwanzaa was celebrated. China announced a hydrogen bomb test and also detonated an atomic bomb in Sinkiang.

The number and severity of accidents, disasters and explosions rival that of the Uranus/Saturn conjunction of the late 1980s. Among the most notable is the Good Friday Earthquake in Alaska that registered a 9.2 on the Richter scale. Two massive earthquakes hit Turkey, destroying whole cities and killing thousands. Mining accidents in India and Bosnia-Herzegovina killed hundreds. There was a deadly fire at an oil refinery in France, and a department store in Belgium burned down, killing over 300 people. A B-52 bomber collided with a jet tanker over Spain, dropping hydrogen bombs. Three Apollo astronauts were killed by an explosion during a test. A Delta rocket ignited at Cape Canaveral, which also took three lives. A suicidal passenger shot the pilots of a Pacific Air Lines flight and subsequently killed all aboard. A Swiss turboprop crashed in Cyprus, killing 126 people.

Uranus/Saturn Conjunction 1941-1943

This conjunction was operative between April 1941 and June 1943 in the later degrees of Taurus and the early degrees of Gemini. The shorter duration, compared to the opposition detailed earlier, is attributed to retrograde motion. When planets travel together, they station direct or retrograde around the same time. With the quicker orbit, Saturn gradually moves away from its conjunction to Uranus. When opposed, planets station at different times, therefore producing a see-saw effect that prolongs the event. In the applying time frame, Saturn moves forward as Uranus retrogrades, bringing the planets together. During the separating time frame, Saturn retrogrades back as Uranus moves forward, prolonging the opposition.

As an earth sign, Taurus deals with issues of land, resources, money, security, and the status quo. Gemini, an air sign, involves communications, ideas, perceptions, information, and change. The disruptive reverberations of this pairing did shake up the fixity (Taurus) of the world order, then catalyzed a new way of thinking (Gemini) about it. The procession from Taurus to Gemini is akin to emerging into greater possibilities and complexity, to dialoguing and learning how to create workable (Saturn) progress (Uranus).

The dominant event of this time was World War II, arguably the greatest example of armed conflict and international restructuring in world history. This was the first modern civilian war, and it influenced the trends of world events in its aftermath. The war is noted for its intense and widespread chaos and human suffering, propaganda and indoctrination, as well as its use of new technologies and weapons, which amplified the destruction. If we extend the modest 10 degree orb a bit further out, the Saturn/Uranus conjunction would have been in effect for almost the entire war. Saturn and Uranus are not usually associated with the levels of atrocity and depravity witnessed in the Holocaust and related events, which have more of a Plutonian dimension. However, right at the onset of the war, transiting Pluto entered Leo and became more overt and expressive in the sign of the Lion. Pluto formed a sextile to the Uranus/Saturn conjunction from 1941 to 1943. Though classically thought of as "supportive" in a benign sort of way, the sextile doesn't alter the fact that it is Pluto, the so-called "Lord of the Underworld," that is supporting the worldwide chaos and ultimate reorganization.

From 1941 to 1943 the news was completely dominated by the war. Countries were collaborating and strategizing, leaders were changing, and political and geographical lines were being crossed. Assassinations and surprise attacks, including Pearl Harbor, were taking place. It seemed that one country declared war on another nearly every week. Massive military campaigns were waged across the globe, with countless fatalities.

Uranus/Saturn initiates a new structural beginning. In the early 1940s, The Great Depression ended. Efforts toward the war created millions of jobs, and a renewed economic optimism took hold. Instead of wallowing in despair, people joined together for a common purpose. Unlike other wars, the Allies saw a clear-cut enemy and threat to global security. The name "United Nations" debuted for the Allied pact, and the institution bearing the same name was formed after the war concluded. The war paved the way for India and Australia to achieve their independence, as well as for the nation of Israel to form. A civil disobedience movement spread across India, resulting in Gandhi, a revolutionary Uranian figure, being arrested by the British government (Saturn). Consistent with the Uranus/Saturn conjunction occurring in Gemini, Anne Frank famously captured the essence of the times in her diary. The Warsaw Ghetto uprising is one event that illustrates the dramatic tension between freedom (Uranus) and control (Saturn) that was so widespread during this time.

Indicative of Uranus, nuclear weaponry entered the picture. The Manhattan Project, led by Enrico Fermi, took place in secrecy. Fermi sent to President Roosevelt the following message: "The Italian navigator has landed in the new world." Bombs used in Hiroshima and Nagasaki devastated Japan, and the war ended shortly after. In November 1942, the Soviets launched *Operation Uranus* counterattacks in Stalingrad, which secured them a military advantage in the region. In the United States, The Women's Auxiliary Army Corps was established, and the first African-Americans joined the U.S. Navy.

Some technological and mathematical breakthroughs during this time include the construction of the first electronic and computer, and the development of quantum electrodynamics, cybernetics, game theory, and cryptology. The first report detailing the properties of LSD was written. Also indicative of Uranus/Saturn, the first emergency ejection from an aircraft occurred. Roosevelt became the first President to travel by airplane. Innovative and seminal movies *Citizen Kane* (1941) and *Casablanca* (1942) were released, and the landmark *Oklahoma!* opened on Broadway. *The Voice of America* began broadcasting. In other communications news, the Office of War Information began censoring movies. Daylight savings time in the United States is instituted.

Uranian accidents and infrastructure disasters also occurred. Some of the more noteworthy are a coal dust explosion in China that killed 1549, hurricanes and flooding in Bombay, India, that killed 40,000, and a fire in a Boston nightclub that killed nearly 500.

Uranus/Neptune Cycle: Collective Interconnectedness

The Uranus cycles with Neptune and Pluto vary significantly from the Uranus cycles with the social planets Saturn and Jupiter. Orbiting outside the confines of Saturn, the transpersonal planets (Uranus, Neptune and Pluto) do not manifest *tangibly* in the world. They are suggestive of broader themes that we must strive to understand and implement. The interactions the transpersonal planets have with the social and personal planets bring them down into the familiar dimensions of our earthbound reality. For instance, at some point during a major Uranus/Neptune interaction, Saturn or Jupiter will make major aspects to the combination. This is when we will see the Uranus/Neptune spirit on the social level. The faster-moving inner planets will continually move in and out of aspect to the outer planet combination, creating many moments when the theme is personally felt.

Examining the cycles of the outer planet cycles reveals meta-evolutionary periods that last several years. It is imprudent to discuss any specific event(s) as being indicative of the planetary combination, the way we did earlier. Rather, we will use a more removed lens to understand the larger picture. We will see that certain phases of human history are marked by global advancement consistent with these collective cycles.

The Uranus/Neptune Conjunction of the 1990s

For this discussion, we will focus on the conjunction between these planets that began to apply in the late 1980s and separated in 1999, touching the signs of Capricorn and Aquarius. The Uranus/Saturn conjunction reviewed earlier overlaps with the start of this seminal event. In fact, Uranus/Saturn/Neptune formed a triple conjunction at the conclusion of the 1980s—and with Saturn involved, events manifested graphically and heralded a new world order. The dissolution of the Soviet Union, the fall of the Berlin Wall and the end of the Cold War are notable events of this time.

At the start of 1990, Saturn moved out of range of Uranus, while the Uranus/Neptune conjunction was tightening. The 1990s is noted as a time of dissolving boundaries, greater world connectivity and the proliferation of new mediums that make possible a sense of widespread and instantaneous unity. Comparatively peaceful and occasionally sublime, this decade opened a new era in realizing our *shared* Earthbound experience. In the 1990s, the world we trek upon seemed to get smaller.

Personal computers became popular, and for many, necessary. Prices decreased, accessibility increased, and a wave of "plugging in" swept the globe. Millions began to log on to the Internet and correspond via email. Internet business (E-commerce) quickly created the .com boom. The world was finally at our fingertips. This instant proliferation of information seduced many into a new cyber world. Addictions (Neptune) of all stripes flowed through computer screens (Uranus). And through computers, members of the interconnected world family could engage with each other.

Along with this new medium arrived greater optimism and hope. After communism began to recede, a new beginning emerged. There was greater economic development around the world, as well as higher standards of living and increased trade among nations. GATT and NAFTA were instrumental in expanding trade. Oil prices were low, and it appeared that resources were in abundance. Politically, the 1990s was an era of increased democracy. Former countries of the Warsaw Pact moved from totalitarian regimes to democratically-elected governments. The same happened in other non-communist countries, such as Taiwan, Chile, South Africa, and Indonesia. The improvement in relations between the countries of NATO and the former members of the Warsaw Pact ended the Cold War, both in Europe and in other parts of the world. The Oslo Accords resulted in an agreement by Israel to allow Palestinian self-government.

Apartheid ended, and Nelson Mandela assumed power in South Africa. The European Union was declared in 1992, followed by Clinton's bringing Rabin and Arafat together for historic gains in Middle East peace. Israel and Jordan also reached a new peace agreement. Talks for a peaceful resolution in Northern Ireland commenced. Demonstrations for Tibetan liberation from China occurred on a global scale. "Civil Unions" for gay couples were legalized in several European countries. Visibility and acceptance of alternative lifestyles entered the mass media. Multi-cultural awareness spread, and a blending of lifestyles emerged. Multi-racial figures like Tiger Woods, Derek Jeter and Mariah Carey were popular. Environmentalism flourished: biodegradable products proliferated, substitutions for ozone-depleting Styrofoam were instituted and recycling became practiced by many.

Technology exploded. Cell and video phones, digital cameras, DVDs, and a plethora of Internet-oriented inventions all contributed to a consciousness plugged into another realm. "Infotainment" is perhaps the best description. Those things touched by Neptune tend to have an allure, a force that sucks our focus away. The 1990s was a time when many became distracted by fancy gizmos, to the exclusion of paying attention to the immediate environment.

In science, “string theory” in physics challenged us to imagine a bizarre energetic field of life, black holes were confirmed, and dozens of planets orbiting other stars were discovered. The Hubble Space Telescope revolutionized astronomy, while the Mars Pathfinder thrilled us with new images. The Global Positioning System became operational and allowed us to navigate by signals from above. Cloning became a reality, and the Human Genome Project took off.

In entertainment, reality television burst on the scene—another illustration that the membrane that separates personal lives is thinning. Popular music became socially active and political again. Furthermore, music was easily downloaded for instant access and sharing. 3-D graphics advanced the sophistication of video. Drug use increased in the 1990s, along with a fascination for new designer drugs such as Ecstasy, GHB and methamphetamine. Sexual curiosity moved away from the primal intensity indicative of the 1960s to the ethereal, glorified and fantastic mood of the times. Internet dating, romances, images and personas craft a world where it’s all right, often encouraged, to be anonymous.

Uranus/Neptune calls us to become more aware of our interconnectedness, to feel a humanitarian impulse and realize community. It diminishes the importance of the personal self while inviting us to transcend any boundaries or limitations that have been created among us. The feeling that we are all plugged into something (nature, Spirit, cosmos) that contains us all can be exhilarating at times, but also confusing. The lesson of this time frame was to develop the consciousness to feel truly uplifted and a part of the global community.

Uranus/Pluto Cycle: Progressive Evolution

Uranus/Pluto is the outer planet combination most involved with catalyzing radical or intense collective growth. When these slow-moving and uncompromising planets interact, their urgency is palpable with the broadest of reach. Integrating reform (Uranus) with survival (Pluto) results in dramatic advances, but also the exposing of unconscious and subversive forces that limit progress.

Uranus and Pluto last formed a conjunction in the 1960s and will be detailed below. The waning square occurred in the 1930s, another notably extreme decade that included the New Deal and the Great Depression. The next square will be active from 2008 to 2019 and will be discussed later.

The Uranus/Pluto Conjunction of the 1960s

Using a 10 degree orb, the conjunction would have begun applying in 1962 and was separating in late 1969. Throughout much of this time, Uranus was also opposed Saturn, boosting the significance and bringing many concrete examples. The conjunction occurred in Virgo; Uranus entered Libra as it was nearing completion. In almost every conceivable way, modern life changed drastically. Comparing life before and after the conjunction is a graphic illustration of the power of this collective event. This era was noted for its urgent (Pluto) change (Uranus), beginning with the Cuban Missile Crisis, Bay of Pigs situation, tragic death of Marilyn Monroe, build-up of involvement in Vietnam, and assassination of President Kennedy. Before leaving office in 1961, President Eisenhower warned of a potential "military industrial complex" if military power were to combine with corporate gain in irresponsible ways. The decade ended with the inauguration of President Nixon, the Stonewall rebellion, the Moon landing, Woodstock, and the tragedy at Altamont. In between these events were massive strife, reform and the surfacing of everything previously submerged.

The 1950s is noted for conservatism. The traditional family was the norm, people generally went to church on Sunday, and men and women respectively wore only short or only long hair. There was politeness and decorum, and the taboo was not discussed. Culture was tame and reflected the inoffensive virtues of the day. The hip moving of Elvis Presley was controversial! There was a general social agreement to almost pretend that homosexuality, sexual abuse, masturbation, mental illness, and other "deviations" didn't exist. In fact, the rise of McCarthyism was largely an attempt to ensure that the public might maintain homogeneity—and adhere to the white, patriarchal, capitalistic version of the "American Dream." If you worked hard and played by the rules, you would be just fine. In short, life was sanitized.

Uranus/Pluto is the liberation of the primal and taboo, the psychological and the sexual—the urge to insane-itize! In the 1960s, a revolution of the social norms unfolded: alternative lifestyles flourished, and civil rights, feminism, and religious diversity were demanded. Pluto's intensity and urgency was seen in culture, epitomized by the electrification (Uranus) of music. The volume of life was turned up, insisting that conservatism loosen its hold.

The modern Civil Rights movement began to gather momentum in the 1950s at the Jupiter/Uranus conjunction of 1954. This coincided with the *Brown v. Board of Education* ruling about school integration. However, it wasn't until the early 1960s that the movement became impassioned and forceful, with mass demonstrations, marches and protests—often with the hostility, and in some cases brutality, suggestive of Uranus/Pluto. Deep within the psyche is an innate understanding that all members of the species are united. It is a truth at the most primal level (Pluto), which was awakened (Uranus).

Technological advances (Uranus) in areas of reproductive health (Pluto) led to the proliferation of the birth control pill and other contraceptive measures, abortion, instructional sex books, videos, and a massive surge of pornography. The taboos mentioned above came out of the closet and were confronted as parts of the human experience. Instead of as just a method of reproduction, sexuality was beginning to be understood for its connections to individuality and higher growth (Uranus). The feminist movement not only empowered female sexuality, but it also challenged the traditional gender designations. The "glass ceiling" was recognized, and thousands of women began cracking it with stiletto heels.

Uranus/Pluto involves the individuation into our raw, primordial and ancestral identity. The rise of the "Hippie" subculture can be seen as an attempt to get back to our authentic roots and live off of the land. Indeed, the parallels between the Hippies and Native American culture and life are substantial. Both emphasize ritual, music and dance, adornments, long hair, less emphasis on sanitization in favor of living "naturally," mind-altering substances, distrusting those in power, and spirituality based on our interconnectedness with nature. In addition to the Hippies, the emergence of a greater diversity of peoples, the fascination with foreign and esoteric interests, and the propagation of alternative lifestyle choices brought the flavor of Uranus/Pluto to culture and society. Whatever was unorthodox and thought to be authentic was championed.

This era is noted for being overtly psychological. Therapy attained greater acceptance—many began to explore their psychic wounding (Pluto) as a way to find the "higher self" (Uranus). The idea of catharsis, the release of intense emotion, was evident on a broad scale. Primal screaming, sexual healing, extreme states of consciousness attained through substances, or even the exploration of the darker potentials of humankind stimulated a connection to these psychic areas that were no longer off-limits.

The assassinations of public figures (John and Robert Kennedy, Martin Luther King Jr.) the Vietnam War, riots, clashes, acts of cruelty or abuse, and infamous crimes such as the Manson Family murders invited the public to probe the most destructive (Pluto) potentials of the human character. Some were simply overwhelmed, and others extended significant energy toward repressing any darkness within. However managed, it was a time that people awoke (Uranus) to human extremes (Pluto), and many became motivated to heal (Pluto) by discovering unconditioned truths (Uranus). This combination may be best described as explosive—which can take the form of destruction or of ecstasy, depending on how it's utilized. Uranus/Pluto is a massive, collective call to wake up and take responsibility for making changes, or else face the unappetizing truths (and often consequences) of staying in a regressed or unconscious state.

Chapter 7
What's Ahead for Uranus?

At the time of this writing (2007-08), we are on the verge of several important events for Uranus. In late 2007, Saturn entered Virgo, and it will make its way toward opposing Uranus in Pisces. This opposition will be exact on Election Day in 2008, quite appropriate for the tension between overturning and maintaining the status quo. Around this time, Uranus will also begin its long square to Pluto, which will last for many years. In 2010 Uranus, Saturn and Pluto will be in a T-Square configuration, while Jupiter will move into a conjunction with Uranus—quite an extraordinary year! In 2010 and 2011 Uranus will enter Aries and begin a new tour through the 12 signs of the zodiac.

Uranus/Saturn Opposition 2007-2011

Using a 10 degree orb, this event would begin in November 2007 and release in September 2011. The times that the opposition reaches exactitude are November 2008, February 2009, September 2009, April 2010, and July 2010. Saturn will be in Virgo at the start of this opposition before moving to Libra at the conclusion. Uranus will reside in Pisces at the start and will enter Aries at the end.

Even without the Uranus/Pluto square that is starting to form at this time, the opposition of Uranus and Saturn is of the highest import. The addition of Pluto to the mix only intensifies this clashing and reflects the conditions of the mid 1960s, when these three planets were in challenging aspect to one another. This section will focus on the interchange of Uranus/Saturn, with occasional reference to Pluto.

As illustrated previously, this pairing is the most visible of any Uranus combinations with the social and outer planets. The late 1980s, mid 1960s and early 1940s are three examples of times of tumultuous change. What is to come shouldn't be any different from these times; in fact, it may be more extreme (given the other planetary activity occurring). There is no way to precisely predict what will unfold since events are shaped by a multitude of factors and play out according to the conditions of the day. However, we can survey the dominant sociological themes or currents leading up to the opposition and make some educated assumptions.

The polarization between rich and poor, religious and secular, conservative and progressive, Republican and Democrat, and their respective "red" and "blue" states has widened significantly in recent years. With the opposition, divides tend to become more extreme, bringing evolutionary urgency. The question is posed: "are we going to come together or come apart?" This Uranus/Saturn opposition begins to apply right around the campaigning for the early primaries and is exact on Election Day, making for an unusually divisive, heated campaign season with the highest of stakes. In the 2000 election, many believed there were few differences between the parties or candidates—the monikers "Bore" and "Gush" were bandied about. In 2008, there will be no mistaking vast differences between the candidates, and voters will decide on markedly different visions of our future.

Uranus/Saturn suggests that the ways we are running things need to change in order to ensure that we continue to move forward in harmony with nature. The issue of global warming is gaining traction. The practice of building gas-guzzling automobiles that harm the environment, fueled by the dwindling resource of oil located in a hotbed of political strife, is likely to be reformed. Uranus/Saturn suggests the implementation of alternative technologies, forcing the auto and oil industries to adapt to a new reality. This is likely to take many years to unfold, but this opposition heralds the beginning of the process. Our collective survival (Pluto) depends on the Earth, and the prolonged Uranus/Pluto square in effect for over a decade will likely see this change through.

Another area ripe for reform is healthcare. Instead of maximizing care and promoting optimal health, profits seem to be the driving force. Institutions that want to consolidate power and resist change are particularly Saturnian. The introduction of Uranian stimulation demolishes "business as usual" in order to open to wider inclusiveness. Universal healthcare fits this event quite literally, considering the polarity of signs involved are Virgo (health) and Pisces (universality). Furthermore, Pluto's entrance into Capricorn deals with changing corporate power structures.

Uranus/Saturn suggests shifts in demographics. In the present day, conservatives (Saturn) are holding fast to a traditional model of who should attain and secure power—mainly, those who are wealthy, white, heterosexual, and Christian. Similar to the 1960s, the Uranus/Saturn opposition suggests a modification in the direction of greater inclusiveness. Middle- or lower-class citizens, non-whites, or those with alternative lifestyles or differing religious views may insist on greater acknowledgment and integration into spheres of influence.

The next wave of societal tolerance of differences (and the inevitable backlash) will enter the collective psyche. Whereas the last Uranus/Saturn opposition (in the mid 1960s) addressed issues of equality for African-Americans and women, the current opposition involves other groups, including Hispanics, homosexuals and Muslims. Hispanics in the United States are growing rapidly into a sizable group. A more progressive immigration policy is certain to face vitriolic opposition from conservative factions. Racial and economic issues, undertones of discrimination and closed-mindedness are likely to be exposed. How much does the U.S. welcome "your tired, your poor, the huddled masses yearning to breathe free?"

In many ways, homosexuals have made great strides toward being accepted into society. Still, there is much discrimination, judgment and fear. Note the homophobia surrounding the Larry Craig (2007) and Ted Haggard (2006) stories, or even the use of gay-bashing to secure votes in the 2004 election. The strange situation of conservatives advocating family values while wanting to forbid homosexuals to have stable, monogamous and loving families could reach the next level of resolution. Marriage or Civil Unions are emblematic ways to address this issue but greater tolerance across the board is ready to be addressed.

Religious diversity is a major issue that is not talked about nearly enough. When issues of salvation or damnation are at play, people get very passionate. As a result, there is an in-group mentality with religion that many consider to be more important than race, gender, class, or ethnicity. In the United States, a sizable percentage of citizens sees the country as a "Christian Nation." This creates a hierarchy in which Christianity is at the top and other religions, based on fewer numbers, often feel marginalized or oppressed. The hubbub over "Merry Christmas" versus the more inclusive "Happy Holidays" is one example of this friction. Uranus/Saturn tends to expose the issue of dominance or control (Saturn) versus greater community and oneness (Uranus). We can expect voices on both sides of this divide to become louder and more insistent, thereby leading to greater reconciliation, polarization, or a mix of both.

Religious issues form the crux of another global issue: international terrorism. Christianity and Islam are not particularly comfortable with one another, and religious terrorism is one manifestation of this clashing. Many Muslims feel bullied by Christian political and economic dominance. A violent response by the more militant factions of Islam exposes the general enmity that many in the religion share. An "us versus them" mentality is the opposition at its most literal. If steps are not taken to come together, things could come apart. The course we have been on is likely to face radical change or possibly a climactic conclusion. This has Plutonian dimensions, which we'll now address in detail.

Uranus/Pluto Square 2008-2019

Orientation

Due to Pluto's irregular elliptical orbit, it speeds up and slows down at various points in its cycle. Its passage through Libra, Scorpio and Sagittarius is *relatively* quick, while in Aries, Taurus and Gemini it slows dramatically. At the time of this writing (Pluto transiting late Sagittarius), Pluto is moving quickly, thereby catching up a bit to Uranus and extending the period of time during which they are in aspect. The Uranus/Pluto conjunction of the 1960s was active during a shorter time frame (about eight years) because Uranus was moving quicker relative to Pluto. Now that Pluto has sped up some, the square will be in effect for about 11 years.

In 2008, Uranus and Pluto will slowly begin to form a square while Uranus is opposite Saturn. These three planets will make a T-Square between 2009 and 2011. The Uranus/Pluto square will reach exactitude, in Aries and Capricorn, respectively in June 2012 at 8 degrees, September 2012 at 7 degrees, May 2013 at 11 degrees, November 2013 at 9 degrees, April 2014 at 13 degrees, December 2014 at 12 degrees, and March 2015 at 15 degrees, for 7 exact squares! Uranus and Pluto will be within an 8 degree orb up until 2019. There are three segments to this event: four years applying, three years of exact squares, and four years of separation. There is more planetary activity during the first segment (2008-2011) making for a most colorful entry to the climactic moments of the event (2012-2015).

Meaning

The manifestation of an astrology event is contingent upon the conditions and contexts of how evolution is unfolding. We can understand the thematic meaning but not the precise ways in which it will play out. At a thematic or archetypal level, Uranus/Pluto has to do with unlocking secrets, liberating what has been pushed into the unconscious, rebelling collectively, using technology and other advances to promote survival, awakening to the human condition and our place in the cosmos, dealing with issues of physical, economic, social, and political destruction or realignment, and perhaps even shifting the ways we organize and construe this existence. As witnessed during the conjunction of the 1960s, all of these issues were pertinent in some way. The square will pick up on these themes and bring them to the next level.

The waxing square is a time of confrontation and hard work, facing crisis, and finding necessary solutions in order to move forward. Pluto suggests the death of stagnant modes of operating, while Uranus points to the development of new ways of being. The square has the flavor of urgency—our lives may depend upon it. Astrologically, the pieces are in place for a most dramatic time period with the largest stakes. We are dealing with two heavy hitters and a gritty, in-your-face aspect.

The signs involved (Aries, Capricorn) provide an exclamation point! Cardinal in nature, the square between the 1st and 10th signs is immediate and restless, full of competition and power issues. Pluto in Capricorn is working on evolving corporate structures, changing any and all institutions whose power is damaging progress. Also, traditional paradigms (Capricorn) that suffocate expansion are scheduled to face Plutonian transformation. Capricorn is interested in solidification, preservation and the centralization of power. While Pluto transits this sign, it will expose detrimental excesses of this nature in order to catalyze reform, if not a complete overhaul of business operations. Uranus points to technological advances, communal thinking and the empowering of the masses instead of plutocratic control from a wealthy few. Furthermore, Uranus in Aries suggests the implementation of anything new, an upsurge of excitement for revolution.

The great triumph of capitalism also has shown a dark side, mainly corporate greed, the exploitation of people and resources, a deleterious impact on the environment, and the polarization of rich and poor. It is difficult to construe the collective as a human family, or as a community when power is so concentrated in the current state. The Uranus/Pluto square promises to expose the divisions that keep us apart, even in volatile ways if necessary. Resisting a greater sense of world unity will only make this time more painful and explosive. Considering that cherished businesses, legacies, paradigms, and familiar social organization are at stake, there is bound to be marked resistance to reform from those in power.

Uranus will be transiting Aries: the sign of war, conflict, empowerment, and the individual. If there is any astrological combination that is representative of masses of people demonstrating with pitchforks fueled by anger, this is it. "We're not going to take it anymore!" or "Power to the people!" can be rallying cries, which pick up where the 1960s left off. In short, Uranus/Pluto transiting Aries/Capricorn suggests culture war—a battle between the "haves" and the "have nots." Pluto in Capricorn can ruthlessly concentrate power, while Uranus in Aries takes up arms for change. It is appropriate to see conservative versus progressive here, but it's far broader than that. We are entering a time when "past" is clashing with "future" in a more general sense.

One of the most obvious areas where we see the beginnings of this clashing is the climate crisis of global warming. All the Uranus/Pluto signatures are clear: survival of the planet, the need to change our ways, and the implementation of a collective effort. The Aries/Capricorn square places the impetus on business and industry (Capricorn) to reform, but also on the individual (Aries) to carry out changes in everyday living. The depletion of oil as a resource brings the urgency indicative of the square. Blindly continuing as we have only furthers a ruinous path of costly energy, environmental degradation and war—until the eventual depletion of oil. Failure to plan for oil depletion would be a worldwide disaster on economic, social and political levels. The Uranus/Pluto square is the time to avoid this calamity and live in greater harmony with each other while taking care of the environment.

Uranus/Pluto precisely correlates to using alternative fuels and technologies for collective survival. Solar, wind-based, geothermal, vegetable-based, and hydrogen-based bio-fuels are becoming increasingly more developed and ready for widespread implementation. The Uranus/Pluto square promises such innovation, though Big Business is likely to resist the process, kicking and screaming. The political system has become increasingly corporate and privatized—favoring the mighty dollar instead of what could be most collectively advantageous to all. This dynamic will be further exposed, potentially leading to breakdown or revolution of the political system. The emergence of a viable third party is absolutely within the realm of possibility. Demonstrations, protests and other social movements are quite likely to occur. Decentralization of power is the theme.

At the Uranus/Pluto conjunction, Jim Morrison asked, "What have they done to the Earth? What have they done to our fair sister? Ravaged and plundered and ripped her and bit her / Stuck her with knives in the side of the dawn / And tied her with fences / And dragged her down." Now at the first quarter Uranus/Pluto square, time has arrived for us to answer this question.

Economic Unrest

The last Uranus/Pluto square (1928-1937) correlated with the stock market crash and the Great Depression. We cannot assuredly predict a similar downfall because the conditions are completely different today. However, we still might expect economic instability. The economy is affected in times of political and social unrest. If Big Business is to be reformed in favor of decentralization and communal economic empowerment, the economy must go through a period of adaptation. The break-up of powerful monopolies or oligarchies is sure to create a ripple effect throughout the United States and the world.

Social Reorganization

The Uranus/Pluto conjunction of the 1960s saw the climax of the Civil Rights movement and the rise of Feminism.

Since then, African-Americans and women have bolstered their standing in society. We can expect these groups to further enhance their standing at this next critical point of the Uranus/Pluto cycle. Indeed, at the time of this writing, the two leading Democrats running for President—Barack Obama and Hillary Clinton—are members of these groups. We can reasonably expect more inclusion and leadership within the ranks of government, entertainment, academia, media, and other institutions.

There are still some marginalized groups, most notably Hispanics, immigrants, homosexuals, Muslims, and the elderly. As the numbers of these groups continue to grow the social fabric must adjust. As discussed with Uranus/Saturn, some of the more conservative currents seem intent on propagating a white, Christian, heterosexual vision of the United States. During the Uranus/Pluto square, we can expect the friction between the conservative vision and the realities of modern life to reach a boiling point—especially so when Saturn makes the configuration a T-Square.

The aging of the population will continue to present challenges. The increase in the average lifespan, as a result of medical advancements, has ballooned both the numbers of seniors in need of care and those who deserve to receive government benefits. To state the conundrum bluntly: Who is going to take care of these people, and who will be paying for it? Elder care is simply not a preferred occupation for many. The longer people live, the greater their chances of developing debilitating physical and mental conditions that require round-the-clock care. There is also the issue of resources. The dwindling treasury sets up nothing less than age warfare. Politicians are reluctant to raise taxes or cut benefits for key constituencies—and sooner or later, something has to break. Continuing to borrow from other countries is not a long-term viable strategy. This puts the bill on future generations, which only increases the likelihood of a very real crisis between members of different age groups.

Uranus/Pluto does correlate with new attitudes about death and dying—including the liberation (Uranus) through death (Pluto). It is quite possible that a movement towards euthanasia will gather momentum, especially if there is a shift in understanding around reincarnation and the afterlife. The Plutonian reality is that some people will need to die in order for the rest of us to thrive. During this square, there may be an unspoken, underground war between different age groups, with money, healthcare and other resources at stake. The "losers" will literally die off. Those in less favorable positions, such as the poor, weak or disadvantaged, may face ruthless realities.

The markings of what some would call a "culture war" are there. As discussed with Uranus/Saturn, this time frame deals with the realities brought by shifting demographics and attitudes. The addition of Pluto adds a psychological element—how we wound or dishonor each other. Will the fear of Muslims, immigrants or homosexuals trigger overt waves of discrimination and brutality? What are the global implications of xenophobia and intolerance? The prospects for a culture war are matched by the prospects of World War.

The Unthinkable

The Uranus/Pluto conjunction of the 1960s occurred during the Vietnam War. The Uranus/Pluto square of the 1930s saw the rise of Nazism and Fascism in Europe. However, the Uranus/Pluto opposition at the beginning of the twentieth century (1898-1905) was not marked by conflict. One could argue that it set the conditions for World War I, just like the 1930s set the stage for World War II. It appears that Saturn is necessary to concretize conflict: World War I had a Saturn/Pluto conjunction, while World War II had a Saturn/Uranus conjunction. Also note that Saturn was opposed Uranus/Pluto for the most dramatic moments of the 1960s, including the escalation of, and opposition to, the Vietnam conflict. During the upcoming Uranus/Pluto square, Saturn is involved (in a T-Square) for about a three-year-period. We must address the possibility of global conflict.

Already-existing hostility in the Middle East is exacerbated by American presence in Iraq. There is hostility between the United States and Iran and ongoing American distrust of North Korea. Pakistan is a politically unstable nuclear state. The reputation of the United States has been compromised; its alliances have weakened, and so has its military might. Also, the strain on America's pocketbook would make financing another conflict difficult.

Terrorism is another pertinent issue. At this point, United States foreign policy has been militaristic in pursuit of "smoking out" terrorism and "fighting the enemy over there." A continuation of this course during the Uranus/Pluto square would bring this dynamic to increasing levels of crisis. The religious overtones are impossible to ignore—this conflict is largely Christian versus Muslim. Some sort of Holy War is a possibility, which would satisfy the fanatical cravings of Fundamentalist factions on both sides. The specter of nuclear catastrophe unfortunately fits Uranus (technological) and Pluto (destruction). The weapons held by governing nations are at least protected. Nuclear warheads on the black market are unregulated and horrific to fathom. Furthermore, Uranus is entering Aries, the sign of war. It would be difficult to maintain optimism in light of previous Uranus/Pluto cycles and our current global situation.

Other Dark Possibilities

With infinite possibilities for manifestation, we can never know what this titanic event will trigger. Our only clue is the thematic meanings of the planets. We apply this meaning to current events and see what emerges. Issues of survival, destruction and rebirth, and opening to a new world are evident. In addition to war, famine and disease are possible.

The evolutionary purpose of famine and disease is hard to swallow. The collective is interested in maintaining evolutionary momentum. That said, the herd must be thinned at times so the greater whole can prosper. Pluto deals with shared resources.

Sometimes the survival components of food, water and even land are brought to crisis and emergency.

Overpopulation breeds imbalance. Of course it is sex, a most Plutonian subject, that propagates the species. The other favorite Plutonian subject is death, and these two are intimately related. Sex leads to birth, which leads to death—the eternal cycle of life. When reproduction (birth) is unbalanced, then the correcting mechanism is death. On a very primal and unconscious level, the species will see to its own preservation. Allowing a disease to wipe out scores of people paradoxically promotes survival.

Harmony with nature is an ideal. Crowding the planet and sapping its resources throws nature out of balance, with great consequence. Outer planet energies are not immediate or personal; there is no empathy. Uranus is particularly unsentimental. However, noticing large-scale tragedy stirs us to behave differently because it personally touches us. We are encased in human sentiment—and only by being moved through the atrocities of war, the outbreak of pandemic disease, or the gradual loss of people through starvation are we motivated to change the collective course. The Uranus/Pluto square may awaken us to how we need to be better caretakers of nature.

A Bit Brighter and More Cosmic

On a brighter note, let's review some of the more fascinating possibilities of a Uranus/Pluto square. I must state upfront that I'm not particularly engaged with the hoopla surrounding the purported end of the Mayan calendar on December 21, 2012. I'm sure this will increasingly receive more attention as the date nears. What I do notice is that this date is right smack in the middle of the Uranus/Pluto square. So let's consider some of the phenomenal speculations (and some that have independently crossed my mind) in light of this historic planetary clashing.

There is much chatter about our relationship to time changing in some way. Time is a dimension. Changes in consciousness result in changes in the perception of the passing of time. We notice this in dreams or meditation, with drug use, or during any other alteration of consciousness. With a collective change in consciousness, we certainly would have a different relationship with time. I would argue that we are always changing our relationship with time. We notice this as we age: when we are young, time passes slowly, and as we age, it tends to be perceived as moving more quickly. With so much Uranus activity in the upcoming years, we will likely feel that evolution is accelerating and that time, therefore, is changing.

The calendar is how we organize the passage of time. We measure time by the Earth's rotation (day), the Moon's orbit around the Earth (month), and the Earth's orbit around the Sun (year). If there were to be an actual change in the calendar, there would need to be a change in the celestial conditions that inform the calendar. And here's where we swallow the blue pill and enter the rabbit hole.

Imagine one of these scenarios: The relative position of the Earth to the Sun changes when the Earth orbits either further away or closer. The orbital position of the Moon relative to the Earth is altered. Also consider if the tilt of the Earth's axis were to change, which would change our spatial relationship to nature, rather than our temporal relationship. It's difficult to fathom what would cause something like this, perhaps the result of some celestial body or event interfering with the system. The ramifications of any of these possibilities would be enormous.

First and foremost, we would conceive of and implement a new system to organize our relationship to nature, time and space. It would launch a new epic. People would think in terms of "before" and "after" this historic turning point. Astrologers would certainly claim that the event ushered in the Aquarian Age. Other New Age thinkers would (rightfully) tout a shift in consciousness. More religious types would see it in Biblical proportions. A wave of hysteria and excitement would sweep the globe.

An event of this magnitude would awaken (Uranus) our fundamental connection to the rhythms of life (Pluto). We would remember that we're on a little pebble hurtling through space, relative to other planets, stars and galaxies. Many would fathom the meaning of our unique position in the grander expanse. Interest in the metaphysical or cosmic, to anything that helps people make sense of life, would be ramped up. What might unfold would be a renaissance period for astrology and other pursuits. During the conjunction of Uranus/Pluto in the 1960s, interest in these matters accelerated and proliferated. With or without some form of calendar-changing cosmic event, the Uranus/Pluto square promises a new wave of metaphysical interest and experimentation with the extraordinary. These transpersonal planets are simply going to help us get out of ourselves and into something bigger.

Let's consider a potential shift of the Earth's polar axis. Apparently, the astronomical conditions on or near December 21, 2012, may trigger a different tilt—some have speculated that the Earth could even flip on its axis. As far-fetched as this may sound, there is agreement among astronomers that the polar axis of Uranus went through some sort of change since it now *rolls* instead of spins. If the Earth changes its tilt, it would be "pointing" at a different astrological constellation. Now, we are gradually entering the Aquarian Age as we move away from the Piscean Age. We may end up pointing somewhere else, thereby beginning a new era. This would be consistent with the end of one calendar and the start of a new one. The terrestrial, environmental, climatic, social, economic and political shifts that would accompany some kind of new celestial orientation are impossible to predict or even imagine, but they would be enormous. It would fit the essence of Uranus/Pluto.

Another possibility to consider is making contact with other life forms in the universe. This would potentially unleash a variety of Uranus/Pluto emotions, such as hysteria, euphoria, fear, a deeply felt connection with the universe, or wide-eyed intrigue. It would instantly engage a shift in consciousness about the composition of the universe and our place in it, and potentially begin a new epoch of collaborative outreach with other life forms.

It is fun to speculate on these possibilities, and there are many more to enthrall us. The point is that our fundamental connection to the cosmos itself will be reevaluated during this time period. Whether or not this manifests in actual astronomical terms, or through making contact with other life, we cannot predict. However, we can be sure that a resurgence of interest in metaphysical matters is a thematically sound assumption.

Culture Shock

Many are nostalgic for the flowering of culture that occurred during the 1960s, and decry a current culture than is often perceived as synthetic, insipid, or overly profit-driven. Instead of artistic purity and inventiveness, many see a popularity contest. Uranus/Pluto does foretell a deep engagement with unexplored regions of the psyche, and the discovery of new material to share. Collectively, we will be ready for new forms of expression, innovative collaborations and a blending of styles. Most central is the idea of getting back to what really moves us. Art, music, theater, and other avenues of culture will be more gripping and unforgettable—displaying necessary truths and inviting us into deeper contemplation. Classic works and artistic contributions are likely to emerge.

In reflecting on what Uranus/Pluto feels like, this image comes to my mind: A soldier carrying an injured battalion-mate from the jungle, feeling the dying man's heart beating as he sees a helicopter in the distance, wondering if he'll make it in time. Anything that's "edge of the seat" theater qualifies as Uranus/Pluto. The psychic volume of life is just going to get turned up.

The Uranus/Saturn/Pluto T-Square

This event is roughly in effect from 2009-2011 with varying degrees of exactitude. As mentioned previously, the Uranus/Pluto square is applying then, with its precise squares between 2012 and 2015. So the rising energy of Uranus/Pluto is concretized into form by Saturn in this highly dramatic three-year period. Saturn is not set to form a 4th harmonic aspect with the Uranus/Pluto square again until its closing moments in 2019, when Saturn will be approaching a conjunction with Pluto in Capricorn. At this time, Uranus will be quickly separating, so it would be more appropriate to view 2019-2020 as a Saturn/Pluto period without a significant Uranus contribution.

From 2009 to 2011, the interchange among Uranus, Saturn and Pluto will be pronounced, echoing the middle years of the 1960s, which featured a Uranus/Pluto conjunction opposite Saturn. The difference between the upcoming T-Square and the opposition of the 1960s is even greater friction! This is true because Uranus and Pluto more or less joined together in confronting Saturn. There was massive conflict between emerging progressiveness and the traditional/conservative sentiments that typified the previous decade.

For the upcoming T-Square, there is no "teaming up"; rather a multi-directional conflict will be operational. Uranus opposite Saturn, Uranus square Pluto, and Saturn square Pluto will all be occurring simultaneously. Since the sum is always greater than the individual parts, we can expect this time frame to be quite extreme.

In approaching the discussion of what could unfold, it's important to remember that the most dominant configuration sets the backdrop. The Uranus/Pluto square features the two most outer planets, and therefore, the deepest evolutionary growth. Saturn, being a quicker planet and social in scope rather than transpersonal, grounds the energy of the broader event into manifestation. We will experience a tangible account of Uranus/Pluto through social, political, economic, and environmental revolutions, adaptations, and crises.

The spirit or question posed by this three-way exchange is figuring out how our institutions can adapt to the shifting tectonic plates of the collective psyche. The tipping point, when a critical mass of people understand how and why things are no longer working, will trigger large-scale revolt or reformation. There is likely to be a deep-rooted insistence on change, a willingness to destroy if need be. Some possibilities to look for include the uncovering of major governmental abuses of power. For example, the discovery that the Bush Administration was somehow complicit in September 11th tragedy would qualify, as would information that the government had been involved in the assassination of John F. Kennedy.

Another possibility is the formation of a new political or social movement that forcefully challenges the reigning systems. There might be shifting demographics, increased grass-roots organization available through the Internet, and a widespread mistrust or suspicion of government operations. The emergence of a viable new movement is quite possible. As discussed above, the encroachment of corporate rulership into public domains is one likely area that will be challenged. The decentralization of power is certainly a major possibility.

If the "climate crisis" of global warming continues to build momentum, there will be needed global changes in infrastructure and business operations (Saturn) in order to survive (Pluto) and progress (Uranus). The inclusion of Saturn suggests that the rhythm of everyday living will be disrupted (Uranus) as we collectively feel our connection to the need to further our species (Pluto). Saturn suggests a period of responsibility, of taking a sober account that we could be in an irreversible dilemma. Those who resist this reality (Saturn) are simply going to be overmatched by sweeping tides of urgency. If we should keep heads buried in the sand and attempt to cling to the established order (Saturn), nature itself (Uranus/Pluto) will deliver its message in ways that cannot be ignored.

Uranus enters Aries (conjunction with Jupiter) 2010-2011

Uranus enters Aries on May 27, 2010, only to retrograde back into Pisces on August 14, 2010. It settles into Aries for good on March 11, 2011. The ingress from Pisces to Aries renews the planetary relationship with the zodiac. A new 84-year Uranus cycle through the signs is about to be born—the spiral has circled back. At this level of evolution, we address personal concerns.

Uranus in Aries manifests behaviorally. Are we living our truth? How brave are we willing to be? What can we do to take an active, hands-on role in changing our lives and, therefore, changing the world? The intention of this transit is to reinvigorate our assertive function so that we sculpt reality in ways that reflect the visionary processes of the Pisces period.

The movement is from the impersonal, transcendent, dreamy, and passive Pisces to the driven, passionate, leap-before-looking, and fiery bravado of Aries. Pisces is prone to deception, a collective suspension of critical thinking, and blind trust of authority. Like the tsunamis and hurricanes that are prevalent while Uranus is in Pisces, many may feel impotent, surrendering to forces that appear too great to surmount. A collective malaise or alienation occurs when breakthrough (Uranus) is out to sea (Pisces). Since few are skilled at contemplative or mystical practices, accessing the promise of Uranus is difficult in the sign of the fishes.

Uranus entering Aries is like returning from the recesses of consciousness, sitting on a Harley and ready to rumble. The purpose is self-empowerment after the dystopia that many may have been experiencing. The reclamation of autonomy, with a renewed sense of personal entitlement, is the idea. The primal, red-meat flavor of rugged individuation lurks just out of grasp (Uranus), coaxing us to grow towards its instinctual urgency. It is as if a faint smell of blood will be detected, and like sharks, we ready ourselves to satisfy previously dormant appetites. There is a return to being blunt and unapologetically direct. Free will is championed, though the hazards are plenty.

Overcompensation results in unchecked, competitive, impulsive, if not aggressive, behaviors. Fueled by the desire to assert itself, Aries can pick fights or unnecessarily ruffle feathers. It is important during this transit to courageously right what has been wronged, but choosing the proper battles is essential. There may be uprisings, erratic displays of rebellion, experimental sexuality, and eruptions of violence. Many times explosions can and should be avoided. Uranus has an affinity for explosions, so this time period does promise a certain degree of recklessness, if not outright mayhem. The prospect of conflict and war is chilling to consider. Through this, we may learn more judicious uses of Aries functions.

The last time Uranus entered Aries was 1927-1928 and it similarly was in conjunction with Jupiter (as it will in 2010-2011). This correlated with the "Roaring 20s," or Jazz Age. There were magnificent advances in science, including the discovery of penicillin. The quantum revolution peaked this year, with significant advances put forth by Heisenberg and Bohr that were captured in the Copenhagen interpretation. Charles Lindberg made his historic Transatlantic flight; the first motion picture with sound—*The Jazz Singer*—debuted; and Ford Motors unveiled its Model A. The 1927 Yankees, known as Murderer's Row and widely regarded as the most offensively potent lineup ever assembled, swept the World Series. The spirit of this time was living large, advancing confidently and not looking back. However, this conjunction is short-lived and quickly gave way to the applying Uranus/Pluto square that was about to form. Nevertheless, Uranus entering Aries in the late 1920s did correlate with a time of seizing new opportunities, taking bold leaps and feeling enthused by possibilities.

The upcoming Uranus/Saturn/Pluto T-Square is heavy stuff—necessary, but not a walk in the park. The addition of Jupiter to the mix allows us to feel like progress is actually being made! We will see expansion, the opening of doors and successful innovations. The Jupiter flavor of optimism and hope, the "can do" mentality, will balance the edginess and conflict of the other planetary clashing. The best comparison is 1969, when Jupiter joined the separating Uranus/Pluto conjunction. As reviewed earlier, this year brought the Moon Landing and Woodstock among other BIG events. In 2010 and 2011, though, the inclusion of Saturn to the T-Square configuration suggests that governmental, institutional or other structural reforms will take similar dramatic big steps.

The Next Boss

How this upcoming time frame plays out will be influenced by those in power, particularly the Administration installed in January 2009 that will govern for four years. At this moment of writing, the election is completely up for grabs. We can look at the Inauguration chart for the next Administration and see what the astrology is illustrating. Whoever gets elected will have his or her hands full—as they say, "be careful what you wish for!" Presidents governing in other Uranus/Pluto times (Teddy Roosevelt during the opposition, Franklin Roosevelt during the square, Kennedy and Johnson during the conjunction) are remembered for significantly shaping world events, for better or for worse. Whoever is elected is likely to reach a similar level of magnitude.

The next occupant of the Oval Office will be presiding during this remarkable time of change. As discussed, the years leading up to the exact hits of the Uranus/Pluto square are potentially more revolutionary than the years when the aspect perfects. This is due in large part to the grounding that Saturn introduces. Looking at the condition of the chart, and Uranus (plus Aquarius and the 11th House) in particular, gives many clues to what we might expect during this potentially historic time.

U.S. Presidential Inauguration Chart: January 20, 2009, 12:00 p.m., Washington, D.C.

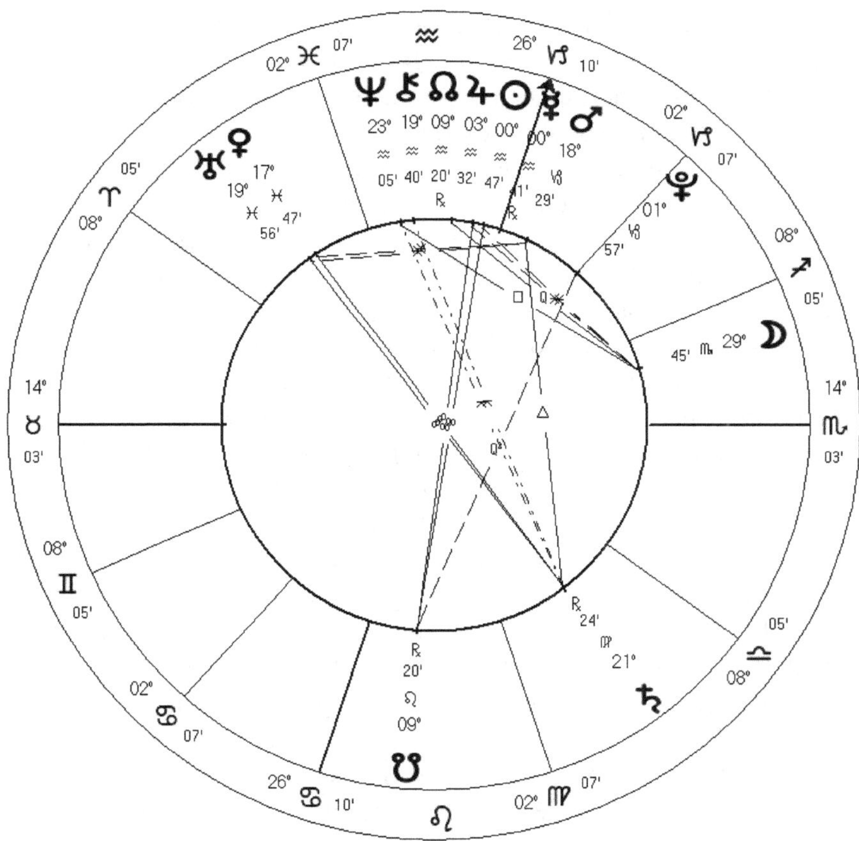

This chart features four planets (Mercury, Sun, Jupiter and Neptune), the North Node and Chiron in Aquarius in the 10th House—suggesting fresh ideas and progressive management. Jupiter and Mercury in Aquarius conjoined so prominently with the solar life force of the administration strongly indicates a philosophical/intellectual attunement with governing that has an eye toward the future. This 10th House is radical, though the inclusion of Chiron and the North Node indicates that reaching the promise of lofty intentions will be an uphill climb.

As the ruler of all of these Aquarian signatures, Uranus sits in the 11th House conjoined Venus in Pisces, the ruler of the Taurus Ascendant. Through this connection to Venus, Uranus is brought directly into behavioral manifestation as it naturally directs its energy into the 1st House. Venus ruling the Taurus Ascendant modifies this in a practical and resourceful direction, but the Uranian impetus remains as a central part of the mix. In its home domicile of the 11th, Uranus joins with Venus to produce highly spirited networking, humanitarian and inclusive energy that promises new international relations based on a broader spiritual vision (Pisces). This administration will likely seek to make reparations around the globe.

Uranus is opposed Saturn in Virgo in the 5th House. Marked by a Uranus/Saturn opposition, this administration will be a departure from business as usual, changing the structure of Presidential operations as it has previously been defined. This aspect speaks of historical importance, for good or ill, depending on the governing and the dictates of the day. The polarization between reform (Uranus) and conservatism (Saturn) is sure to be an issue. This opposition does portend major tug-of-wars in regard to implementing an agenda. Since Uranus is attempting to modernize a Saturn in Virgo, issues of healthcare, the poor and other downtrodden groups are salient. Uranus in Pisces wants to dissolve barriers among us, and this is specifically applied to helping those in subservient (Virgo) positions.

The tight sextile between Uranus and Mars in Capricorn in the 9th House speaks of a new type of leader, but also one who is steadfast, tough and politically driven—able to follow the structures that are in place. Uranus/Mars can be ruthless—however, this is tempered by the prominent Venus in Pisces attached to this aspect. Nevertheless, this sextile is most formidable, a joining of the two planets most interested in sticking to their guns. The administration is likely to have a clear agenda and make no bones about implementing it.

The progressive spirit of this chart favors a Democrat for President. If a Republican should be elected instead, the spirit of the Uranus/Saturn opposition would make governing a conservative agenda fraught with conflict. The force of antagonism to such governance would be similar to the widespread discord Richard Nixon faced early in his first term. The Uranus/Saturn opposition would take on the quality of demonstrating against conservatism (Saturn) by the masses (Uranus). If a Democrat assumes power, he or she would likely institute a progressive agenda consistent with the spirit of this time. The opposition would then play out in the form of resistance to and confrontation from conservative factions in the government and media. Current policies of the Bush Administration regarding stem cell research, the environment, immigration, the Iraq War, and national security are likely to be reversed or altered, and the polarization between the parties will only widen.

Part 3 – The Intelligence of Nature

In this section we'll address the transpersonal facets of Uranus, the characteristics that transcend personal relevance or social domains. Along with the archetype of Aquarius, and the 11th House, Uranus describes the overarching intelligence of nature. As science informs us, we are enveloped in an interconnected energetic web or matrix. Uranus pertains to the intellectual properties of this matrix, specifically how nature itself continually *knows* how to evolve. This is a humbling discussion to attempt because we are dealing with nothing less than God's mind! We can never fully reach omniscience; nevertheless, the course of evolution insists that we try to align with this macro-intelligence so we can chart the most informed course. It is with this sense of humility and perspective that we leave the self behind and try to see things from a loftier view.

Chapter 8
The Spiritual Mind

The Matrix

Uranus correlates with the metaphysical container that envelops us, a vast matrix of interconnected energy. A useful analogy for this matrix is the Internet, which everything and everyone is plugged in to. A popular movie series called *The Matrix* depicts life inside an energetic web. Also note that this idea is not science fiction or something Hollywood conjured up—the interconnectedness of all energy is a scientific fact.

Another way to comprehend this matrix is to think of it as the cosmic mind. Every individual thing then would be akin to nerve endings that connect to the oneness of this mind. The activity within the mind is *metaphysical*, just like our thoughts. Therefore, grasping the energetic linkages among the various parts is elusive. Within this vast, crackling, unified network, we generally perceive the *illusion* of separateness. This is because the energetic linkages that connect everything together are metaphysical.

The matrix holds endless ideas and possibilities circulating within its neural framework. None of it is subject to verification or feasibility in concrete reality. All potentials are evident, and anything is possible! All of creation begins with the spark of ideas. The idea of monkeys playing trombones standing on the U.S. Capitol wearing space suits is ridiculous and has no relevance in reality as we know it. This idea (and all others) is one of the endless creative possibilities. We notice with the monkey example that Uranian ideas are often wild or erratic—this is because all rules can be broken when you transcend the limitations of space and time. As we'll review later, the matrix does interface with the physical world. For now, we'll address the intellectual rather than the structural components since the integration with Saturn is needed for the latter.

The Uranian matrix is the overarching intelligence of nature on a scale that is overwhelming to everyday cognition. Every branch of science and mathematics, from the realm of astronomy to the intricacies of the quantum world, are part of its reach. Many are not accustomed to thinking of nature as "intelligent," but once we approach the world as meaningful instead of random, it becomes dizzying in its creative brilliance.

At the micro-level, quantum physics reveals a world that boggles our everyday notions of space and time. Time has been found to be neither linear nor unidirectional, space is curved, and all measurements of space and time are relative. In Uranian fashion, nature at this level is full of paradoxes. Subatomic phenomena can appear as either particles or waves. There are no definite places or times for matter to exist. Instead, there are only "tendencies" to exist, or to occur. Even more puzzling (and Uranian) is that everything is connected non-locally—meaning that there are imperceptible connections among *everything*, through all space and time. Simply stated, quantum physics reveals a unified and all-pervasive energetic web. At this level, there is no separateness.

The scientific law of the conservation of energy affirms that energy can never be created or destroyed, but only transformed. Though the totality of energy stays the same at the transpersonal level, activity within the matrix is continually in flux. We have the constant (energy) of change (in motion). This metaphysical structural stability is indicative of Aquarius (Uranus-ruled), being a fixed sign. Also, since nothing is ever destroyed, this colossal energetic container is quite the recycler. The birth or death of anything and everything is just another change.

At the chemical level, the intelligence of nature is unmistakable—though one must approach the subject matter with the mindset of perceiving this intelligence to see it. Glancing at the Periodic Table, we see that all of nature's elements are impeccably categorized. Each has a unique quality and role as one of the "building blocks" that enable life to exist and flourish. There are intricate rules for joining the elements together to build other compounds. For instance, sodium combines with chlorine to make salt. Atoms join into molecules and the building blocks create the material of the physical world. Most of us don't bother studying chemistry all that much because, frankly, it's hard. Nature is one smart cookie, and you have to be the same in order to open the cookie jar.

Our awareness is primarily attuned to the biological level of life, to the familiar world around us. Everything is part of the great web of life, the interconnectedness of nature at the biological level—the ecosystem. Sun and rain nurture life, seeds sprout from fertile soil, bees pollinate flowers, vegetation feeds animals, and trees provide shelter. It's a marvelous, sustaining system in which everything is necessary and serves a function. Humans tune in with the natural flow of the seasons in order to maximize the yield of the harvest. Here we also notice recycling. Life emerges from the earth, lives to fullness, dies, and returns. Seasons go round and endlessly repeat. Life reproduces itself, never really giving birth to anything "new" but continuing a process that's been in motion indefinitely. As evolution marches on, there is an obvious advancement. This is made possible only because of our innate interconnectedness. We evolve *together*—there are no Cro-Magnon men anymore. Underlying the biological level is our DNA, the genetic code—another example of a vast intelligence of breathtaking proportions.

Consciousness itself is interconnected. The next level of the matrix is psychological. The terms *noosphere* or *collective unconscious* have been applied to this notion of psychic interconnectedness. Whereas traditional psychology sees consciousness as only personal, transpersonal psychology addresses the collective dimensions of consciousness. Here, universal archetypes are shared by all sentient beings. A collective understanding of consciousness allows us to feel connected to all of humanity, not only around the globe, but also throughout history and into the future. This sense of collectivity encourages us to steward the Earth for each other and for our children. Resistance to or denial of this idea leads to the championing of the individual over nature—which, of course, has led to imbalances in many ways.

This idea of a collective consciousness is still incredibly controversial, even threatening, to mainstream academia, science, most mainstream religions, and our governing policy-makers. It opens the door to the theoretical possibility of all types of parapsychological or extrasensory phenomena. It leads to a greater organizing system within nature that both includes and transcends individual cognition and consciousness. It becomes our responsibility to think and act collectively, and to dissolve whatever barriers keep us apart. Since the matrix is bigger and more sophisticated than we are, it points directly to spiritual questions that cannot be grasped rationally. This is where the individual finds his limitation. He must either disavow that there could be more transcendent levels that envelop him, or he must choose to proceed further into Uranian territory and realize he is no longer master of his domain—another organizing system is.

Spiritual Lessons in the Matrix

So, before entering this discussion it's important to reflect on this awesome intelligence of nature. At the quantum level, there is confirmation of interconnectedness—one massive, unified energetic field. At the chemical level, we find an intricate system of elements that "miraculously" combine to form the substances of life. At the biological level, there's an ecosystem or web of life.

Every level is intelligently organized far beyond what any human can fathom; that's why most can't see it, or doubt it altogether. Nature "knows" how to heal broken bones, hearts involuntary pump blood that nourish the system, and male and female body parts fit together to reproduce life. Penguins in Antarctica know just how far to march inland to survive the winter, chameleons change color in order to survive, and skunks have the ability to spray their foes—and on and on it goes. Nothing eludes nature's intelligent grasp; everything is in its rhythm. As Leonardo da Vinci noted about nature, "in her inventions, nothing is lacking and nothing is superfluous."

This same vast intelligence functions at the soul or spiritual level, just as it does at the physical, chemical, and biological. The difference is that the transpersonal dimension is now engaged. The matrix serves as a behind-the-scenes coordinator of our growth. Everything is "plugged-in" to the matrix. Everything. It cannot be transcended or escaped as it's God's mind, and we're akin to nerve endings within it. We are in relationship with this intelligence that organizes life in necessary ways to maximize growth. An individual contributes to collective evolution by participating with this giant mind. From this view, there are no accidents, only synchronicities. Everything has some kind of purpose and potentially catalyzes greater integration—whatever is occurring in our lives is exactly what we need.

Isn't it uncanny how we seem to connect with the right people and find ourselves in the right situations to catalyze our growth? "Right" doesn't mean easy; in fact, the lessons may be unpleasant and difficult. Though the personality may resist, the matrix connects us to those things that will further awaken us. This viewpoint sees the universe as doing things for us, not to us. If we can trust and align with this intelligence, we understand that life will never present more than we can handle. In fact, the events that seem the most trying are the most needed and the most filled with opportunity.

The matrix is a colossal mirror for the self because it reflects back exactly who we are. We are continuously "meeting self" as we approach life. The matrix is a *neutral* energetic web. When we experience some form of a "charge" (something that gets our attention, triggers a response) about *anything*, we are confronting the part of the self that is seeking greater integration. It's as if Spirit is continually saying, "Hey, take a look at this, and find yourself in it."

If we are unresolved about an issue, we will meet it in the world in some way. There is a wide range of responses we might make. Fear and avoidance will only make an issue larger, potentially overwhelm us and probably make it worse. An attitude of curiosity, courage and a willingness to stretch oneself from the comfort zone allows one to befriend the issue, own it, and utilize the power within it. Gifts are presented in the most unlikely packages and disguises. When we believe that the world out there is separate from the self, there is no way to recognize how entangled we are with nature. There is confusion, and a tendency to feel alienated and disconnected, to see the world as devoid of meaning.

At the soul level, nothing is "negative"—everything serves the purposes of awakening, liberation and soul alignment. Uranus obliterates the dualistic concepts of "bad" and "good." Everything is pro-growth—no matter how difficult, perplexing and camouflaged it may appear. Saturn creates divisions and polarities; Uranus holds everything in equal value as part of the One. There is no comparing of anything. When we see something in negative terms, we are just not understanding or perceiving its purpose. From the Uranian view, reality is always beneficial—our interpretations of reality are what tend to cause us so much stress and suffering.

An individual is always the center of growth-promoting processes. Therefore, even in a dispute with another, personal growth has to do with how an individual manages it. From this view, experiences never really have to do with another's perceived role, as they are part of us! The division of self/other is just another separation into a polarity. We can only truly meet another when we go beyond the personal self and recognize Spirit in each other. When the entire world is seen as the individual, then everything is "my body" or "my mind." We may potentially *become* or join with the oneness.

Projection is a common term used in psychology to describe how an individual sees himself in others and in the universe. As with many psychological concepts, this discounts the transpersonal dimension—mainly that consciousness exists apart or away from the individual. From the Uranian view, we are in a *relationship* with nature. We are playing our hand (individual), as is Spirit (collective), in a mutually beneficial connection. The universe continually reveals itself to the individual—inviting greater wisdom and understanding, and a variety of experiences, all in the name of developing consciousness. This positions the individual to be an agent for evolution. The individual recognizes the self as part of the One. Everything is the self—and paradoxically, nothing is *really* ours. From this view, it's not so much that the individual projects into the world; it is more of a two-way exchange. The individual dynamically meets the self rather than simply projecting onto an indifferent or meaningless world.

The relationship between the personal and the collective is seen in the astrology system in the polarity of Aquarius/11th House and Leo/5th House, and in their ruling planets Uranus and the Sun, respectively. As is the case with all oppositions, each side contains a piece of the other. (This is similar to the yin/yang symbol.) The personal and the collective mirror each other—the commonality is that both Uranus and the Sun concern awakening, the development of awareness. When we increase personal awareness (Sun), we meet the self throughout the collective. When we are able to align with the collective intelligence (Uranus), the personal life force is seen to be a useful vehicle in helping to further collective evolution. (Notice that the word Sun is at the end of Uranus.) The 11th House concerns the collective, but it's situated on the eastern (left) side of the chart, which concerns personal matters. This can lead to confusion if one doesn't see this symbiotic relationship between the self and the collective. What we meet in the world (11th House) is the self!

Furthermore, Neptune/Pisces/12th House come directly after Uranus/Aquarius/11th House. The Uranian matrix (Aquarius) is a container like an aquarium that houses fish (Pisces). When we elevate consciousness toward the transpersonal (Uranus), we can learn to swim in the flow of life (Neptune, Pisces). When we resist the conditions of the container, we have an increasingly hard time trying to exist within it—we are much like fish out of water.

Non-attachment

Living in a non-attached way means that we believe that whatever life brings us is perfect and necessary, and opens the self into continual breakthrough. The self does not impose an agenda onto this transpersonal intelligence that envelops us—rather, there is trust in and surrender to the conditions of the present moment. When we resist reality, we inadvertently take on the role of God. "No God, life should be *this* way!"

The Moon is the astrological indicator of attachment, and it serves the essential function of seeing to our survival. "Once bitten, twice shy"—we learn from our experiences and rightfully develop protective emotions that enable us to navigate through life. The Moon suggests how one's experiences and entire spiritual history have been absorbed and consolidated. The purpose of the Moon is to ensure that our most basic and fundamental needs are met. When they're not met, the unconscious retains a memory, and this is quite useful. The struggle of the Moon is in clutching to these memories, which prevents embracing the present moment.

In order to arrive at non-attachment, the Moon must be acknowledged, felt and brought to the present. This means embracing whatever feelings are part of the soul's history, rather than keeping them unconscious. This produces an integrated rather than fragmented psyche. A protective strategy might be to not feel anger, sadness, hurt or fear. Many desperately want to maintain composure or follow through with a task. They want to avoid the perceived unpleasantness of these states, rather than seeing any value of their acknowledgement. However, the soul has still absorbed the experiences that led to these feeling states, whether they're acknowledged or not. Since they're part of the system anyway, being conscious and honoring them releases the protective strategies designed for survival.

What's done is done—it's no longer threatening anymore unless we stay preoccupied with it by trying to avoid it. Through avoidance, the individual stays haunted by whatever trying events are in his or her past, and approaches the present in survival mode. The Moon's initial purpose of alerting us to what is potentially threatening is never turned off. Simply being with the impact that life has delivered allows emotions to lose their urgency—kind of like releasing the pause button. Emotion is energy in motion—the consolidated emotional energy *moves through us* when we bring presence and awareness to it. What usually occurs is some form of catharsis. Universally, people claim to feel "better" or "lighter" after a release. They are no longer attached to their past because it's been processed. Ideally, there is an honoring of experience when we let go—the wisdom and lessons that life delivered are understood, and this allows us to grow. Refusing to be integrated with one's absorbed experiences restricts growth, and non-attachment becomes impossible.

When we are still unfinished with past events, we are in thrall to Saturn. Reality is resisted, and the soul is desperately trying to find outcomes that it believes would be more satisfactory than what are actually occurring. Subsequently, we are unable to break through to Uranian territory. Saturn is the gatekeeper that forbids entrance to Uranus, but it's also the *gateway*. When we have the attitude that "There is no place in the world I'd rather be," then the world opens up to us. Once reality is completely welcomed, we are able to perceive and experience the intelligence of the present moment. The soul transcends egoic needs in order for soul development to proceed. Spiritual growth is not concerned with life being "easy" or "hard," and it has no use for other dualistic terms, such as "bad" or "good," that label experience. If the past is reconciled and successful closure is achieved, there would be no emotional preferences to have life unfold in a particular way. Every experience is approached and received as being beneficial. What we defend against or fear shows us where we are stuck in our suffering.

Freedom (Uranus) arrives when we give up the idea that we are in charge of our lives. When we become aware that we are unfinished students, we welcome the teacher in all of its many forms, including, and especially, the difficult ones. There is awareness that whatever challenging events happened in the past were spiritually necessary. We change our perceptions and interpretations about these past events, with the realization that what happened may not have been what it appeared to be at the time. It was actually purposeful and designed to trigger awakening and growth. This is the spirit of Uranus. When we integrate this, we then become excited about life, even about the "worst" that could possibly happen! Being "spiritual," then, means accepting all of life, even when events do not unfold to our liking.

So, freedom (Uranus) is the release of the personal. We identify as being part of Nature, which just exists. Whether it's hot or cold, dry or windy, the grass and trees don't seem to mind. If nuclear bombs fell from the sky, how does the sand in the desert *react*? It just goes along. And we can go along, too, no matter what should unfold. In a benevolent world, it's all good. There is less and less need for rules or for the imposing of an order. Problems are for the Saturnian world. When we transcend this, nothing is really a problem because everything is welcome.

This is a challenging concept for more many to agree with. One might wonder, "What if a chainsaw was shredding your arm? Would you just be *curious* about the bits of flesh and bone splattering? Would you really welcome that?" The problem with this question is that a chainsaw isn't shredding anybody's arm. Non-attachment has to do with accepting *reality,* not hypotheticals. If this unlikely event were to happen, there would be some definite reasons why—particularly; the relationship of the wielder of the chainsaw with the victim would be relevant. This is not included in the hypothetical question.

What about death? Annihilation is the ultimate threat to the ego and most people continually strategize to avoid it. This is more imprisonment from Saturn, known as the Reaper himself. Uranus informs us about the recycling of energy. It happens at every other level, and it must occur here. Since energy can never be created or destroyed, it must be transformed in some way. This begins a discussion of the idea of reincarnation, which most people have strong opinions about. It boils down to one question: in light of this mind-boggling benevolent intelligence, should death be feared as the final blow of a harsh existence, or should death be viewed as liberation, as a chance for further growth? Which makes more sense? My view is that until we see death as the tremendous gift or opportunity it is, we will be imprisoned, with Saturn as the jailor.

Non-attachment is the understanding that ultimately nothing belongs to us. Everything is "borrowed" from Spirit, and all is bound to return. When we hold on to what wasn't ours in the first place, there can only be pain. Eventually we'll have to give it back, so why not free the self *now* through non-attachment? Our essential nature is infinite and free, though temporarily confined within the Saturnian world through incarnation. Bringing the transpersonal (Uranus and out) into the personal (Saturn and in) is how we give the gift of life back to Spirit. By being agents for conscious spiritual evolution, we become part of the solution on this planet, not the problem. This has nothing to do with religion (Jupiter) and everything to do with the development of consciousness (which often leads to a trans-denominational approach). Along with the other transpersonal planets, Uranus is universal.

Non-attachment is vastly different from detachment. With non-attachment, there is no apathy or impotence—instead, the self is allowed to come home. Then, engagement with life becomes *even more* vivid, invested, animated, and meaningful. The egoic self can be used skillfully—it can be a trickster (Uranus), a vehicle for change. Furthermore, Neptune is the planet that comes after Uranus. Neptune involves compassion and a love for nature and humanity; it is an emotionalizing energy that is impersonal yet beautiful. Allowing this love to flow through the self brings an even deeper engagement with life. Pluto then brings a greater urgency, a spiritual responsibility to assume power and help shape the collective destiny. Those who approach the outer planet energies from the ego are prone to being erratic (Uranus), delusional (Neptune), or controlling (Pluto), among many other hazards. Through non-attachment, these energies are honored and used intentionally.

Integration with the Physical World

Albert Einstein's famous equation $E=mc^2$ is helpful in understanding the interface between the matrix (Uranus) and our everyday reality (Saturn). Essentially, Einstein suggested that matter (m [Saturn]) is a crystallization of energy (E [Uranus]). The universal intelligence is concretized though Saturn and renders it temporary in the familiar dimensions. Anything material (m) is impermanent (E), meaning that it will eventually return to being energy without tangibility. One example of this is the simple degradation of a fallen leaf, or the decomposition of a corpse. Over time, everything will perish and leave no trace of its existence.

The other part of Einstein's equation is c^2, the speed of light squared. My astrological interpretation is that c^2 equates to the Sun, the source of light and heat in this system. In a more universal sense, the Sun is indicative of the presence and awareness of Spirit. So *E* (Energy, Uranus) = *m* (Saturn, reality) c^2 (illuminated in the present). The planetary correlations of Sun to c^2, Uranus to *E,* and Saturn to *m* are specific to the energetic operations in this solar system, whereas these planetary principles are a microcosm of universal processes that transcend and include this one little system.

The Sun, represented by c^2 in this equation, correlates to the present moment, to how spiritual awareness is being organized (m [Saturn]) in the now. Without the vital present, there can be no transactions between energetic potential (Uranus) and material reality (Saturn). The speed of light (c^2) is the constant in this equation. Indeed, the speed of light remains uniform (approximately 186,000 miles per second), which is analogous to how Spirit is the universal constant of this existence. The Sun is the agent of awareness (light) and vitality/presence (heat) that radiates this life essence of Spirit into our solar system.

So Uranus is dependent on Saturn to have relevance in the familiar world. The great split (castration in the mythic tale) is mended through cooperation with reality. As discussed before, most people resist reality and thereby don't have access to the growth and awakening available in any given moment. Saturn is often feared and given the title of being the "lord of karma," and thought of as "the keeper of the Akashic records." However, Uranus is more of the universal mind in a metaphysical sense, while Saturn is the deliverer of our karma into the manifest world.

Karma is an exotic word that is used in a variety of ways. Science teaches us about cause and effect—every force is met with an equal force. We see this with the famous example of billiard balls. When one billiard ball strikes another, the second ball's directed movement is contingent upon the stimulation of the first ball. This is cause and effect in the Saturnian world, where the laws of classical physics have relevance. Karma is a metaphysical principle, more relevant to the complexity and multi-dimensionality of the quantum world.

In a metaphysical sense, what we put out comes back to us. Due to the fact that the matrix is multidimensional, it's not as orderly as billiard balls. How we impact the world returns to us in mysterious and perplexing ways that transcend time, space and the immediate reality—perhaps even the present lifetime. Through transits, progressions and other techniques, we can see what themes and lessons are relevant within the sphere of incarnation (Saturn) as we go through life.

Some don't believe that we can actively "create reality" in such a vast and complex universe. Certainly, what we put out will return in some form, but this does not mean we are sitting ducks just waiting for our comeuppance. Since it is a relationship *between* the individual and collective, between the self and nature, we are empowered to take an active role in designing how life unfolds. We reap and sow in an endless exchange. When we learn and integrate lessons, we're empowered to assertively impact our lot in life through informed behavior. When we personally evolve, we then teach what we have learned. This is how we can "clear" the karma accrued in states of less soul wisdom.

The matrix is available for us to use skillfully when we put out clear intentions. These intentions *cause* some form of *effect*. This is often called the "law of attraction" and was featured in the movie *The Secret*. The universe meets us where we are at, so be careful what you wish for—or be conscious what you wish for because the universe is even in harmony, mostly so, with what's unconscious.

Planets and the Matrix

I'm not a scientist, and most likely, you're not one either. The good news is that we don't need to be in order to grasp the essential point of this section—that the planets play a central role in the matrix. In a book about Uranus, one should "expect the unexpected." Here comes some unexpected and Uranian information that will, I hope, make sense and provide another piece of the proverbial puzzle.

In perhaps the greatest synchronicity in my entire life, I came into contact with a remarkable scientist—a very Uranian physicist from Ukraine whose innovative, and largely unknown, work has major implications for not only science, but also astrology. Dr. Volodomyr Krasnoholovets' research has led to a new understanding of the gravitational field, one that is far more comprehensive, and that is consistent with our changing understanding of nature.

We are so accustomed to merely living within the Earth's gravitational field that we hardly ever consider that it connects us to the other planets. All celestial objects are pulling on each other. The greater its mass, the more pull an object has on others. This is why the planets orbit the Sun—it's simply bigger than they are. You can't see, hear, taste, smell, or touch gravity. It's a force that can't be screened—we just see the effect of it, such as an apple falling from a tree. Consider the *obvious* situation that we have on this planet, one that few ever stop to think about. The Earth is in the middle of the vast gravitational pull of everything in the solar system. All planets and asteroids, comets, and other heavenly objects are connected through gravity and together compose a system. Another step back reveals that the Sun is also connected to the other stars in the same way, but our focus is to remain in this particular solar system.

I like the analogy of seeing this particular system like a cell in a body. The Sun is at the center of this cell, like a nucleus, with the planets orbiting about—everything interconnected through gravity. So, the energy of Jupiter, Mercury and the rest join together to form an invisible field that is within everything including you and me—that's the irrefutable situation to begin with. This alone should give any open-minded person pause to begin considering astrology and our connection to the planets. Skeptics cry out that this is no big deal—that the gravity between two people is far stronger than an individual's connection to Pluto. Skeptics wonder why an obstetrician isn't included on the natal astrology chart if a gravitational connection is relevant.

Enter Dr. Krasnoholovets, who discovered a field contained *within* the gravitational pull that he terms "the inerton field." The inerton field is not only composed of all the planets' gravity (as well as the other objects in the solar system—which for our purposes play a secondary role and will be excluded from this discussion) meshed together, but it also responds to consciousness! The inerton field is a vast connective network. The inert energy that forms this invisible field responds to the impulses that stimulate it. Thoughts and feelings, the contents held in consciousness, enter the inerton field and form connections. When the inerton field is activated, "inertons" carry the stimulation through the field. We are enveloped and intimately engaged with the energy of the planets, and we use them to form connections. (The gravitational connection between baby and obstetrician is irrelevant as both are enveloped within the larger field. Like two minnows in the Pacific Ocean, what happens between them will have a negligible impact on the tides.)

Dr. Krasnoholovets states that inertons have been "unambiguously" confirmed by his research. (In fact, he has helped develop inerton measuring devices.) He conceives of the inerton field as a series of "clouds" around subatomic particles—

this is why it has been elusive and difficult to find. Also, he believes that most scientists don't question the theoretical foundation of their research. By and large, the concept of aether (dynamic rather than empty space) is dismissed by scientists—space is considered to be vacant rather than full of Spirit. Most scientists do not operate from a mindset that includes shared consciousness, and therefore they wouldn't set out to affirm the aether hypothesis. Perhaps we weren't ready to have this information until now—just like Uranus was always orbiting in space but wasn't discovered until the collective was ready to find it.

There are many definitions to aether, sometimes spelled ether. The way in which it's used here is different from the "luminiferous aether," which is a disproved scientific theory about the propagation of light. Our usage concerns an omni-pervasive connective field—a neutral organizing container. Instead of seeing space as vacant or lifeless, the presence of the aether suggests that the realm of space is another dimension of Spirit. Coincidentally, Aether is the mythological God of space or the "upper sky." He is one of the "Protogenoi," the primary beings of existence that form the fabric of the universe. In fact, many mythological interpretations posit that Aether is the father of Ouranos. The synchronicity of bringing back this "debunked" idea of aether is seen in the wireless Ethernet, which connects computers to local area networks, similar to cell phones. We are freeing ourselves from dependency on cables to tap the connective fabric of space itself.

The inerton field is analogous to the matrix or the concept of the aether. It's a neutral, connective web that pervades this solar system because it's embedded within the gravitational interplay of our familiar planets. Of course, this particular system is part of a larger one; our world is a world within worlds. Transpersonal in scope and occupying space, the inerton field correlates well with the air sign Aquarius and Uranus, which, of course, resides in our solar system. The ways in which we move within this field are completely optional because we participate in a *relationship* to it. Consciousness enters the field, and inertons carry thoughts and emotions through it. Everything enters mysterious pathways that reside within a matrix of planetary energy. One implication to this finding is the idea that the collective unconscious is all around, not just in our heads. This connects well with the idea of the noosphere, the realm of mind that connects to the biosphere, the realm of life.

Dr. Krasnoholovets points out that the discovery of the electromagnetic field in the nineteenth century radically changed life on this planet. Since then, the technological explosion has been unprecedented, positioning us as powerful collaborators with nature. Here at the beginning of the twenty-first century, a new field has been discovered that could do the same for our spiritual growth. The fabric of this unending universe is woven together, activated by consciousness. We are full participants and co-creators with the universe—all we have to do is accept the responsibility of our roles. The matrix is the container (Aquarius) while we are the mystics (Pisces) swimming in an ocean—intimately in touch with the energies of the universe. We can develop this sense of touch: to connect the world back together, to strengthen our relationship with Spirit, and to fulfill our evolutionary purpose in this universe (for more information about Dr. Krasnoholovets and the inerton field visit www.inerton.kiev.ua).

Astrology and the Matrix

This section will speculate on the relationship between astrology and the matrix. How does this inerton field composed of planetary energy interact with consciousness? How do the shifting arrangements of the planets pertain to our relationship with the matrix? This leads to a broader discussion about the scope of astrology and how it works.

At one level, the spatial relationships of the planets conceivably change the composition of the matrix by setting up energetic channels. Consider the situation in which two planets are in opposition. Here, the Earth is directly in the middle of the gravitational pull between them. Bring in the Moon. We know its influence on the tides is contingent upon its spatial relationship to the Earth. In more subtle ways, the Earth also has a gravitational relationship with the other planets. The shifting arrangements of the planets change our relationship with the matrix from our position on Earth.

When planets are in opposition, or any other aspect, energetic channels based on geometric delineations become relevant. Presumably, spatial relations that form precise and perfect designs (conjunctions, oppositions, squares, trines) are more relevant than non-geometrically precise patterns. Straight lines, square, and triangles, for instance, are fundamental in mathematics, and are used extensively in architecture and engineering, among other fields. When aspects become perfect, they replicate an aesthetic found in nature that also has usefulness in forming connections.

We can speculate that the energetic channels created by such patterns activate the energy that is consistent with the *type* of aspect. For instance, a conjunction is the fusion of two energies at a single *point*. An opposition creates a polarization between two planets and resembles a *straight line*. The planets involved can either come apart or come together; a tug-of-war or a joining. The trine shows the harmony found in the *equilateral triangle*—all three sides are balanced and support each other. A square sets up a pattern of *perpendicular lines* similar to an intersection. There need to be traffic lights (rules for handling potential conflict), or the energies at cross purposes are bound to clash. The sextile is found in the *hexagon* or honeycomb, which is used advantageously by bees. Minor aspects would also have relevance, such as the quintile, which shows the precision of a 5-pointed *star*.

Points, lines, triangles, squares, hexagons, and stars all have particular energetic qualities. When these patterns are formed between and among the planets in relation to our position on Earth, the resulting energetic qualities found in nature become activated. In these angular relations, planets are connected in an immediate way that they are not when the planets are not in aspect. The immediacy of the planetary relationship creates an energetic dialogue in both social and personal ways. Through the medium of the inerton field, we are full participants in this dialogue.

Planetary cycles are most relevant at the social level. As explained in Part 2, Uranus has a unique cycle in relation with each of the planets. Indeed, all of the planets have cycles with each of the others. The essential point to remember is that the spatial relations of these cycles, which move from conjunction to opposition back to conjunction, is from our vantage point on Earth. The energetic channels formed are relevant to us all, the collective, as a macro-being. Together we address the dynamics and lessons pertinent to the planetary dialogues.

In addition to the social or collective reference point, there is also a personal reference point—the natal birth chart. Each of us embodies our energetic relationship to the universe. The shifting dance of the planets impacts individual attunement. A person may, for example, have Venus at 20 degrees Aquarius. When a planet makes an aspect to this degree, the person will experience a transit. For instance, Neptune was recently at 20 degrees of Aquarius. During this time, a direct energetic connection between Neptune and a part of this person's essential energy (Venus) became active. This person attracted energetic currents to fulfill the evolutionary purpose of the event. If this is a person who tends to lose herself in relationships, for instance, lessons of that nature might have appeared on physical, emotional, intellectual, and/or spiritual levels in a synchronistic fashion.

Since there is a dialogue between the individual and the universe mediated by the neutral inerton field, there is no predicting how the transit will unfold. There is a wide range of possibilities in direct proportion to a person's awareness and willingness to grow. Certainly knowledge of one's energetic relationship to the universe and of what transits will be arriving can ready a person to address the lessons to be presented. There is free will in our approach or response to transits, but these transits are guaranteed to occur as long as the planets follow their orbits.

Energetic channels are activated by the precise geometrical patterns created by the planets in our solar system. The matrix itself is in a continual state of flux. As conscious beings, we are full participants in this cosmic carnival through our energetic relationship to the inerton field that is embedded in the gravitational interplay of the planets. The individual relates to this field in highly personal ways, while the collective addresses evolutionary themes in a more general way. Group or social consciousness has a tone, psychic dynamics, and its own course of evolution, just like the individual does.

The Scope of Astrology

The energetic view of planetary influences presented here is direct, observational and rational. It goes along with the idea of astrology being rooted in science, which is not accepted by the scientist, the skeptic or the vast majority of astrologers either. Many skeptics joke that the planets "beam down" some sort of influence, or that we are like "puppets on strings." Since this sounds preposterous, astrology has not, for the most part, protested and has gone in another direction. Most contemporary astrologers see the system in symbolic terms. They see metaphor, poetry and archetypes that are not bound to scientific analyses. This protects the astrologer from the criticism of the scientist or the skeptic, and it also severs our direct connection to nature.

We cannot look at astrology only in a rational, scientific or linear way. Whatever relevance astrology has to science is likely to be a small part of a much larger and multi-leveled understanding. Just as there are two hemispheres to the brain, so do the poetic, artistic, symbolic, and irrational inform astrology as much as anything quantifiable, rational and literal. Would it make more sense for astrology to function strictly in either rational or irrational ways, or for both of these qualities to be relevant to the field, just as they are relevant to and inherent in nature?

Taking sides creates polarization and antagonism, and this is exactly what has happened with science and astrology. As discussed earlier, separations are only relevant in the Saturnian world; Uranus holds the oneness of nature. To arrive there, we must seek ways to integrate. So, the Uranian view would suggest that astrology isn't "puppets-on-strings," and that it's not purely symbolic either. In fact, it may be far more complicated than any simplistic paradigm.

Consistent with Uranus and the idea of an overarching intelligence of nature, astrology would function at many levels and, conceivably, many dimensions. Our connection to the planets through gravity is but one small part of it—and it does fall more on the left-brain or observational side. Other parts of nature are also relevant, such as our direct relationship with solar energy, the Sun. Daytime *feels* different from night—there is a subjective connection with solar energy that causes humans to be diurnal beings. With the supposition that astrology is broad in its function and etiology, *all forces of nature would be part of its scope*.

There is no question that much of astrology has nothing to do with the physicality of the planets. However, in a unified world, astronomy integrates with astrology; how could it not? The fracture between science and astrology is bound to mend—I think the discovery of the inerton field is a major step in this direction. Science informs us about the structure of nature, while we get to participate in it.

I do think that over time, astrology and science will become more integrated and will move toward realizing the oneness of nature. Science would need to accept that it is just one facet of nature, not its entirety. Astrology would have to find ways to integrate directly with science and nature. Of course, astrology is relevant in non-scientific ways. As is commonly stated, astrology can be thought of as a symbolic system. It reaches into archetypal realms and construes planetary energies as mythological gods and goddesses. The signs of the zodiac point to universal processes that form the storyline of evolution.

There are many examples of how astrology functions seemingly apart from the physical world. As examples, many astrological techniques do not use any physical connections to the actual planets seen in the sky. Mundane astrology may be used to cast charts for understanding the thematic structure of the beginning of an event. Mundane charts are initially cast as a direct representation of observable phenomena. The resonance continues through the collective consciousness after the astronomical conditions are no longer present. For example, the United States has a birth chart. The planets are no longer near the positions that they occupied in 1776, but the chart maintains relevance in the collective consciousness of the people of the United States.

A composite chart results from the combining of two other charts by using the midpoints between each of the respective planets and house cusps of the two separate charts. It is possible to have a composite chart that defies the laws of physical nature. For instance, the Sun can be in opposition to Mercury; in nature, of course, these two planets are never more than one zodiac sign away from each other, from our perspective.

Astrological progressions have no physical correlations to what is actually occurring energetically in the external world. For an individual, secondary progressions, as seen in the actual sky, physically occurred during the first few weeks of life. Miraculously they have relevance 20 or even 80 years later. Progressions work so well because the cyclical rhythm of the planets becomes encoded in human psyches and is best understood at the symbolic level. Techniques that function independently of the physical world are mental manipulations of the energetic realities, just like mathematics uses imaginary numbers and other phenomena that lack a correlation to anything "real."

All these non-physical astrological processes, however, in no way prove that astrology lacks a physical connection. They merely show that some phenomena are applicable to certain levels. Although distinct, all astrological layers simply must be connected due to the fundamental interconnectedness of nature. We cannot reduce astrology to only linear, rational, three-dimensional viewpoints—though these, too, are a part of it.

If astrology is this broad, no one individual could ever fully say how it works. Each of us approaches it from a unique reference point, with various personal skills and interests. No one can have the breadth and depth of knowledge of every field and discipline. Astrology is so all-encompassing that we must share, must forge a collective endeavor that integrates astronomy, physics, psychology, cosmology, poetry, ecology, biology, mythology, religion, and everything else. Since we are at the infant stages of really understanding all of these fields, how can we possibly understand how they all might unify? We'll be working it out for centuries to come, and perhaps this is what we've been doing all along. Wouldn't it be something if, unbeknown to almost everyone involved, the collective evolutionary project has revealed, and will continue to reveal, the facets of nature in every conceivable way within this meta-organizing system of astrology? If astrology is the meta-functioning of nature, then all of us (scientist, psychologist, artist, poet, and shaman) illustrate how it works—the key is to find the points of integration. All of us are microcosms that connect to the One in all that we do—all of us revealing the magnificent scope and intelligence of nature.

From this view, astrology is everywhere. The signs of the zodiac have the broadest reach since they are constellations of stars in the sky. Through rulership, the planets connect the signs to the cell of this solar system, while the houses compose our immediate environment. People, too, embody different archetypes. We notice the warrior or the healer—every field is aligned with the various themes, from athletics to science to business. We have a synastry linkage with every person we come into contact with. There's also a composite chart between any two people, including those who are deceased, or those who have never met. Once we broaden our conception of astrology, we find that nothing exists apart from it.

Losing Your Mind

Some might say that you've lost your mind if you study astrology. Well, that's precisely the point. How wonderful to get out from under the limitations of the human intellect! From the viewpoint of the ego, "losing your mind" is a pejorative term; from the view of the soul, it's quite the compliment. We need to transcend the personal to have a God's-eye view on things. The Uranian perspective allows us to see that there is much more to grasp when we free ourselves. For those oriented only within the familiar personal and social realms, transpersonal territory is unknown and, therefore, perceived as mythical or even scary.

It actually is both. Astrology is one way to study the intelligence of nature. Like all things Uranian, astrology is dangerous. If a skeptic begins to study astrology in depth and opens to it, he will lose his mind. The rational, scientific mind (Mercury) will be brought to the edge. Crossing the edge is scary; it's a remarkable moment of releasing control and accepting that there's a larger mind enveloping the individual. Refusing to cross this edge forces the person in defending the intelligence of the individual mind in relation to the macro-intelligence, and good luck!

One example of how this may play out can be seen through the following metaphor. Imagine walking on a beach on a deserted island and finding an intricate sand painting similar to one that monks sometimes painstakingly create. The actual sand on the beach is precisely ordered in such a way that an image is unmistakable. Is there a deliberate design, or was it created by chance? A skeptic may say that since there aren't any people on the island, the logical conclusion must be that the wind blew the sand—a one in a million chance, but statistically guaranteed to happen sooner or later. Maybe one time you could see something that ornate and sophisticated and brush it off as "one of those things." But what if you repeatedly ran into similar paintings on every deserted island? Perhaps at the bottom of one sand painting you even saw the message, "Yeah you, pay attention. This isn't accidental!!" Could you still dismiss this? Sooner or later you will lose your mind in a proactive or regressive way.

The proactive way allows one to surrender the intellect and grasp a larger order, to connect with the intelligence of nature. The regressive way involves losing the mind to existential confusion, unresolvable cognitive dissonance or maybe even psychosis. If there is no framework to contain the larger order, then the mind is at risk for pathology. Studying astrology is like running into sand paintings on deserted islands and learning that the islands really weren't deserted after all. This is analogous to thinking that there isn't any God or Spirit (or whatever name you use for the intelligence of nature) and being forced to see the opposite. There reaches a point where the view of meaningless coincidences becomes untenable.

The other assumption from the skeptic is that the transpersonal is mythical, just like Santa Claus. "Mythical" can be defined as "fictitious," or as "existing within myth." And here the skeptic is correct—myth is very much a part of astrology, and of the nature of life it reveals. Not only is the individual living the mythology of his or her soul growth, but collectively we are also joined through these energies or forces that all have mythological dimensions. Let's remember that Jupiter is the mythological god Zeus, Venus is Aphrodite. The system is given storyline and animation through these characters that do have deep archetypal resonance to all of life.

If an individual is able to see that there is good reason to be scared (but proceeds anyway), and that there are dimensions of life that are indeed mythical, then she can feel very good about losing her mind. Integrating the personal mind with the transpersonal attunes the individual to the organization that is naturally there, rather than imposing the personal mindset and assumptions on nature. This liberates the individual and allows her to see that everything is purposeful—there are no accidents, just synchronicities. Astrology provides an impeccable framework to understand life. I like to think of it as Spirit's way of giving us a backstage pass, a behind-the-scenes view of how things are organized. As in the sand painting example, astrology will shatter the ego, but it does provide the overarching metaphysical organization necessary to avoid any negative impact. In fact, the pleasure and fascination it bestows are as infinite as the system is deep.

When the individual loses his mind, he sees that he's in the middle of both worlds that get bigger and worlds that get smaller. Time marches forward in lockstep precision, but there are also dimensions of timelessness. There are dimensions that are dense and simple, as well as dimensions that are more complex than we can ever imagine. Once the ego lets go of making things rational, there is no endpoint to contemplate or experience. It's an endless universe with potentially parallel realities—worlds in our dreams, and worlds in who knows what other systems, other galaxies, or the billions of stars that are out there! It's so colossal, but we are stuck approaching it from the limitations of a certain vantage point. Indeed, some may criticize Part 3 of this book, the transpersonal chapters, as irresponsibly stretching astrology. My view is that my account of the breadth of astrology is so embarrassingly limited that to say it "scratches the surface" would be generous. We are simply involved in the most paradoxical, wonderful, endless mystery ever.

The Continual Lightning Storm

The concept of synchronicity is no longer fringe. In addition to being a staple within spiritually progressive circles, it can be heard in mainstream conversations, and even in popular culture. It was the title of the best-selling *Police* album in 1983. The term is generally credited to Jung, though he doesn't claim to be the first to notice the phenomenon. There are references to it in older texts and within the esoteric branches of some religions and spiritual systems. We have seen the idea of synchronicity register in the collective *zeitgeist* most profoundly in the last few decades. This is, well synchronicitous, with the collective awakening to the transpersonal currently happening.

The basic idea of synchronicity is that the interconnectedness of nature can be noticed in an assortment of ways—a message printed on the side of a truck, a song that gets your attention, or the symbolism of an animal sighting (or about a trillion other things). Synchronicities are a bridge between our familiar experience and the numinous—a multi-leveled connecting principle among the various parts of existence. Sometimes synchronicities are subtle, while other times they are unmistakable. Oftentimes they are humorous. Since they can take any form, nothing is off-limits. You can even experience synchronicities around scatology! Anything. This form of connecting with Spirit is a far different communication from the humble,—on-your-knees, hands-clasped, eyes-closed prayer. Synchronicities suggest that we are always in connection with Spirit—even while sitting in a dirty public bathroom reading graffiti that gets our attention. Anywhere. Synchronicities challenge us to either deny their existence—to essentially see the universe as random—or to accept their reality and see a larger order.

Most do shrug off coincidences as meaningless and never give them a second thought, as if to say, "We shouldn't go around pretending that every little accident has some huge purpose!" Well, yes, not all synchronicities are equal—there're various levels or dimensions to the phenomenon. Some do notice synchronicities but take a conservative approach. They're "one of those things" that happen infrequently and perhaps stimulate awakenings around major life changes. Certainly synchronicities can be detected during transitional times only, but in a psychically interconnected universe, synchronicities are continually operable. Similar to how the nervous system in the mind and body is connected throughout the system and never turns off, so too is this larger mind always turned on. However, one's individual, subjective orientation to the wider matrix determines the quality of the synchronistic experience. There is no way to objectively measure them. Depending on the inner psychic state of the individual, some synchronicities register more deeply than others. Some may be trivial, some may be urgent—in either case, the universe is merely echoing back the personal psyche.

Synchronicities connect us to the larger matrix. Since the matrix is a mirror for the individual, we are really venturing into our own psyches, and synchronicities are the signposts along the way. Within this larger mind, synchronicities are **not** infrequent—in fact, they're like a continual lightning storm. Like storm chasers running down tornadoes, we can assertively follow them. When we are able to watch the synchronistic wheels go round, we are led into the self. However, like storm chasers, we face certain risks. Synchronicities can be "cool" and exciting and produce many "a ha" moments. However, they nonetheless mirror the inner self in whatever state it's in. Synchronicities may invite thrilling expansion, or may welcome you into the repressed urges, the buried pain, the memories you wish you had never gathered. Unconscious material is hidden for a reason! Synchronicities are about awakening to it all.

Like storm hunters, we even have a map to assist us in chasing down synchronicities—the natal astrology chart. You can look at transits to see what the psychic weather is like, and then go where the activity is. The chart is like a compass, with north, south, east, and west arranging the houses. Instead of pointing out literal spatial directions, the houses show the arenas of life in which there is spiritual work to address. Go to these places, and you'll find synchronistic occurrences to help guide your way. By integrating the lessons that synchronicities convey, we reach greater oneness within ourselves. By so doing, we assist the collective convergence toward unity, which is the point of this evolutionary project. Synchronicities are how the spiritual mind communicates—in a fantastic, endless, metaphysical lightning storm.

Regarding Intelligent Design

Much of the discussion in this section of the book has to do with a conception of an intelligently organized universe. To recall what da Vinci said about nature: "in her inventions, nothing is lacking and nothing is superfluous." How do we conceive of the inventor? There are obvious religious overtones to address. The intention here is to locate belief systems in the astrological system, to help distinguish paradigms (Jupiter) from the overarching intelligence of nature (Uranus) we've been exploring.

The idea of Intelligent Design (ID) has entered our national dialogue. In particular, those who posit Creationism see this concept as a tenet that confirms their beliefs. If the fundamental structure of the universe seems to convey the designs of a divine maker, shouldn't we teach this? Why would science object? Science is supposed to be in pursuit of the truth, whatever that should turn out to be. This is a most contentious discussion, and astrology has something to add.

Astrology does point towards some sort of supreme intelligence, but astrology in itself is non-denominational. Those who are advocating ID are mixing a particular religious agenda with a far more universal concept. The intelligence of the universe does not automatically validate any belief systems or religions. Religious or philosophical beliefs are associated with the planet Jupiter and the sign of Sagittarius; how we make sense of the world and arrive at a clear life direction is part of this theme.

Jupiter orbits within the parameters of the Saturnian status quo and has a social rather than a transpersonal scope. It allows us to expand into and speculate about frontiers of the unknown, but Jupiter operates within the jurisdiction of our familiar dimensions. Jupiter reminds us that discovery can be endless, and it stimulates our urge to break through limitations. Saturn is the container of our mundane world and pulls the spirited arrows that Sagittarius launches back down to earth. This allows us to work tangibly with our intentions, but it also keeps spiritual seekers from operating outside the parameters of their everyday world. They may fall short of venturing into the heightened states of consciousness and universal themes suggested by the outer planets.

Busting through Saturnian boundaries leads to the multi-dimensional or transpersonal territory of Uranus. Whereas Jupiter informs us that the world is far vaster than what we may immediately perceive, Uranus completely shatters ego concerns so that we might arrive at a state of spiritual liberation. Jupiter, for all its wondrous speculations and intentions, is still rooted to developing a personal and/or social mission.

But the intelligence of nature transcends personal and social concerns. Intelligent Design should not be thought of as a belief system or a life path (Jupiter)—it is instead the overarching metaphysical structure that envelops us (Uranus). There is a categorical error in ID because it strips down a universal concept and squeezes it into the confines of a particular religious view. Nature's intelligence has no ideological agenda whatsoever.

Uranus is often baffling, shocking, or, at minimum, surprising. If we could humanize the energy, I bet it would find great humor and delight in the fact that the very people who condemn astrology (many conservative religious followers, for instance) are advocating a concept that is quite aligned with it. If people who latch onto the idea of ID *seriously* study its implications, they are likely to see order and meaning within the workings of nature. They may become open to systems, such as astrology, that elucidate a transpersonal intelligence. Ultimately, the adoption of ID by organized religious groups would eventually lead to a reevaluation, dilution, or rejection of the very religions that support it. Religion (Jupiter) would be seen as operating within the broader container of astrology (Uranus)—and how that might play out would be interesting to see unfold, to say the least.

Chapter 9
Uranus & Astrology

The previous chapter discussed the spiritual mind, the unending metaphysical container that holds all of life. This concept was linked to Uranus/Aquarius, and some commentary on the scope of astrology was offered. In this chapter, the connection between Uranus and astrology is discussed in more practical, rather than theoretical or conceptual, terms. When we focus on the nuts and bolts of the astrological system, how might we construe this theme of Uranus, Aquarius and the 11th House? As mentioned earlier, the system is cyclical—each theme builds upon the preceding one. Much of this chapter addresses the relationship between the Uranus theme and that of Saturn, Capricorn, and the 10th House.

So, the natural question is: should we designate Uranus as the principle within the system of astrology that directly pertains to that system? Or, to use common astrological jargon, does Uranus *rule* astrology? The answer to this question depends on how broad a definition of astrology we use. The most common definition currently used would answer with a definitive yes. Astrology is seen as a transcendent meta-organizing system that we understand through the intellect. This is impersonal and airy, so astrology, in this definition, fits with Uranus/Aquarius.

If our scope of astrology is broader, then we must take another look at this Uranus/astrology pairing. If astrology has expressions at other levels and/or dimensions (as suggested in the last chapter), every facet within the system then would have relevance. Saturn is how astrology descends from the heights of the transpersonal to permeate our familiar reality. Jupiter shows how astrology can inform a life path, or can yield philosophical insights. Mercury shows how the individual can understand astrology in the first place. I think that it's wise to extend the scope of astrology, but also to give astrology a home base in Uranus and Aquarius. This is no different, after all, from seeing that a planet has meaning in every sign, but is also most directly associated with one or more of those signs. As we'll explore, there are many reasons to associate Uranus with astrology.

Back to the Past and Future

Prior to the discovery of Uranus, the seven classical planets joined to form a neat system that lasted for hundreds of years. The Sun and Moon rule Leo and Cancer, respectively, and the other five planets assume rulership over two signs. For instance, Saturn is the traditional ruler of Aquarius, in addition to Capricorn.

In the eighteenth century Uranus was discovered, and this discovery introduced quite the quandary. In its activity in transits and in natal charts, Uranus appeared to have many of the same qualities previously ascribed to Aquarius. Both are mental, innovative, and unconventional, with a collective or global focus and a regard for freedom and liberation. Modern astrologers felt quite comfortable assigning rulership of Aquarius to Uranus. More traditional astrologers resist this designation and the split between older and newer forms of astrology took form.

Traditional systems consider Saturn to rule Aquarius and as being pertinent to astrology too. Saturn's organizational structure and delivery of consequence does fit with a more deterministic or literal view of astrology. With a mindset that aims to play by the rules and maximize individual power, Saturn is the overseer that grants success or delivers lessons like a whip to the side in order to toughen the one who needs the lesson. A Saturnian view of astrology is consistent with this more cause-and-effect approach to the system.

This traditional perspective naturally pervades ancient astrological systems simply because they are a product of their times. Since Uranus had yet to be discovered, of course it wasn't included. Similarly, Uranian advances, such as quantum physics or multi-dimensional perspectives, were yet to come. Social revolutions were scarce, or more readily contained, and amazing technological advances were unheard of. Individuation was not prized; rather, conformity ensured prosperity and viability.

People didn't realize that meaningful coincidences could be the delightful magician of synchronicity, and the concept that Spirit permeates all of life was far less widespread than that of a transcendent God we could never fully behold.

Life was simply less Uranian before the discovery of the planet, and astrological systems likewise had a bias toward rigidity, rules and, in some cases, even fate. The quintessential Uranian principle is freedom. Modern astrology's emphasis on free will and self-empowerment is in stark contrast to the more deterministic nature of its ancient predecessors. Synchronously, modern astrology gained increased momentum in the 1960s, a decade that emphasized the triumph of the self against stultifying structural forces and expected norms of behavior.

So an astrology student may ask the question: Should astrology be associated with Saturn or with Uranus? How about the broader question of which system of astrology (ancient or modern) is valid? Certainly practitioners of both older and newer forms claim that their methods bring consistent, positive results. Perhaps a variety of systems are relevant and applicable, depending on an individual's reference point, perspectives, and assumptions. Those drawn more to orderliness, and who view life in reward/punishment terms, are likely to find traditional systems to be supportive of this perspective. Those who question paradigms, see infinite shades of gray, and continually attempt personal reinvention tend to welcome the greater complexity, but also uncertainty, indicative of modern astrology. We view all of life with certain glasses, and we look for evidence to confirm our ideas; it is no different with astrology and its various systems. It seems quite plausible to suggest that astrology would be more Saturnian or Uranian depending on the approach of the astrologer. Therefore, depending on what paradigm is preferred, Saturn or Uranus is the ruler of astrology.

Uranus did introduce a wildcard to the traditional model. Some traditional approaches disregard the outer planets in order to preserve orderliness, and to respect and adhere to the way things have previously been done. There is in fact a clear dividing line between the classical planets and the transpersonal (Uranus,

Neptune, Pluto) since the latter tend to be removed from our everyday conscious experience. Modern approaches are more inclusive of these planets, but the traditionalist is still correct in stating that the territory they represent is beyond what we could know. Therefore, those who use the traditional seven planets consider their astrology more "real," and the techniques used within these systems are thought to have greater precision. True to the myth and spirit of Saturn, Uranus is castrated, and a protective and conservative approach becomes increasingly calcified. This sets up the tension whereby modern astrology is considered heretical, speculative and lacking consistency, and traditional astrology is viewed as prehistoric, rigid and suffocating. Some adherents might even consider the opposing form of astrology to be harmful.

"Transpersonal," by definition, is beyond the personal, what we could know. Modern approaches attempt to move closer to this knowing in full awareness that they may never fully arrive. In terms of growth, the journey or process is more important than the destination. In the same way that a Uranus contact with an inner planet stretches the inner planet to break through into further regions of evolution, the planet Uranus itself represents the enduring process of change, adaptation and, ultimately, awakening. If the approach of an astrologer is more about the here-and-now, mundane interests and whether something is "good" or "bad," then the outer planet energies may get in the way. Uranus isn't "better" than Saturn—it's just operating at a different frequency. As we'll explore in greater depth later, these two planets actually need each other—viewing them as competitive will only extend this illusion of fragmentation.

The Rulership of Aquarius

These different approaches would then construe Aquarius as being associated with or ruled by either Saturn or Uranus. The traditional approach is accurate in seeing both Saturn and Aquarius as sociological in scope, pertaining to systems and having a more neutral or removed quality. As mentioned before, life in general was less progressive before the discovery of Uranus. For the most part, conformity garnered success and attaining stature in society was generally prized. Deviation from the prevailing norms was not pragmatic. When Saturn was dominant, people were forced to compromise their personal freedom. This was the price one paid to be accepted as part of the collective.

Today, many are not willing to pay this price. For many, personal freedom is more important than social affiliation or status. The typical modern person aspires toward liberation; and in the typical modern astrological view, Aquarius ruled by Saturn equates to stifled progress and limited freedom. Aquarius is unconventional and makes no distinctions about people's worth, nor does it pass judgment on how they live their lives. Whereas Aquarius represents a collective, a unified "us," Saturn wants to divide that "us" into hierarchies. At the extreme, a Saturn-ruled Aquarius makes advancement impossible. It separates (Saturn) the known from the unknown and sets up a dynamic of fear and blockage in terms of integrating broader truths.

The rulership question is best worked out in actual charts. Do both astrologers who use Saturn and who use Uranus as the ruler of Aquarius find that it works? From what I've gathered, both approaches claim that it works! Again, there is no right or wrong answer, just different approaches stemming from different qualities of consciousness. My personal view is that astrology reflects the astrologer, so we see ourselves through it. Perhaps there is no objective astrology—perhaps it changes and evolves and has utility and meaning at a variety of levels and dimensions. This sounds awfully Uranian! A traditionalist would likely say that astrology doesn't change that much and can be used objectively. It is possible that both of these approaches have merit and application.

Uranus and Aquarius

Some refuse to designate Uranus the ruler of Aquarius because its scope is seen as generational or collective—removed from personal concerns or issues. The classical system of rulership remains intact, and the course of natal chart interpretations stay consistent. Many of these astrologers use Uranus and the outer planets, but see them as adding to the system, much like the asteroids, Black Moon Lilith or Chiron, which usually are not considered to rule signs.

Many modern astrologers find great consistency between Uranus and Aquarius—so much so that the rulership issue is a moot point. In fact, the spirit of Uranus is to break the mold in order for evolution to continue, so it's quite appropriate that the elegance of the more Saturnian traditional model be disrupted. The sections in Part 1 that address Uranus in connection with the inner planets show how personal this planet can be. Uranus often has an uncanny but often quizzical or even paradoxical effect in natal charts. Grasping and working with Uranus is, for many, an undertaking that is foreign, uncomfortable, difficult to fathom, and even bewildering. Therefore, if one's approach to astrology is not naturally Uranian, then the planet would appear to function in more generational ways.

Perhaps those who are natally more aligned with Uranus want to try to understand the unknown and ineffable and, by their nature, are more comfortable with the territory. Uranus appears strongly in charts of those who are ready to venture, or in need of venturing, into unmarked territory. Those who are fascinated by Uranus are simply wired to be, and it's an appropriate part of the soul growth to embrace this fact. They understand, feel, and use the experience of this transpersonal connection to arrive at greater individuation. These people are often the ones who assign rulership of Aquarius to Uranus, and who find new ways for astrology to grow.

Aquarius is considered a fixed sign. It has much to do with the notion that the only thing unchangeable or enduring (fixed) is change itself. Uranus, as the modern ruler of Aquarius, continually introduces the elements of innovation, breakthrough and change to align the present with the potentials of the future. Therefore, in reference to astrology itself, the modern-day Uranian views the system as constantly open to reform. In fact, the failure to reform it would be irresponsible to the very idea of progress that Uranus so champions. Only by making clear distinctions based on thorough investigation, by surviving the tests of time and scrutiny, should Uranian ideas be allowed through Saturn's barrier. It appears to this writer that the question of Uranus ruling Aquarius passes this important test.

Uranus/Saturn Interplay

The integration (considering the mythic tale of castration, we may say reconciliation) of Saturn and Uranus is a most formidable undertaking, but one that is essential to address. It is so easy for these two energies to become antagonistic to each other. The eternal polarization between conservative and progressive forces is but one example of this antagonism.

From the viewpoint of Saturn, the establishment of order is paramount. The level of evolution a society functions at determines how life is organized. From laws and governance to institutions and infrastructures, the social fabric reflects an agreed-upon consensus. Without the cementing of common norms, there is chaos. When society is functional there is a reasonable tendency to preserve what is working. In other words, "If it ain't broke, don't fix it."

Thus, conservative ideology is laudable and plays an important role for the maintenance of order, and for people to have a sense of security. Relying on the tried-and true-breeds trust and furthers one's confidence in not only the collective, but also in the self. By playing by the rules and contributing to society, we attain a solid place within the framework. There is absolutely nothing wrong with any of this. In fact, without it, there could be no civilization.

The great thorn that pierces this protective skin is the emergence of evidence that, in some ways, things are broken or at least outdated. When we evolve beyond the level of consciousness that solidified into social structures, there is great tension. For example, a transportation system that serves a city at a certain population level is functional. When growth or change reaches a certain point, a traffic nightmare ensues. There must be expansion to accommodate the new reality. Likewise, when everyone shares the same religion, has the same skin color or agrees upon specific gender roles, a consensus is established that works impressively, until these conditions no longer exist. The enduring social and communal structures firmly in place only work in a vacuum-sealed environment that is impervious to change. This of course is impossible. As sure as the rising and setting of the Sun, time marches onward, bringing unforeseen changes. Everything is in a dynamic and perpetual state of evolution. And here we see the titanic clash of Saturnian structure and Uranian progress.

Saturn governs the status quo—it solidifies what works for maximal utility. Equal to its reliability is an undercurrent of fear. Absolutely nothing in this universe is constant, except for change itself. Saturn can choose to respect or to repress this reality. Since the awareness of Uranian reformation is relatively new, and since using its progressive scope adeptly is still a largely undeveloped skill, our history up to this point has mostly been to repress it. As a result, the antagonism between convention and future potentials gradually rises towards a series of climactic battles. Saturn is positioned as the inevitable loser in this endless game of continual evolution. The farther a planet is from the Sun, the broader is its scope for collective evolution. Therefore, Uranian progress trumps Saturnian preservation—though integration of the two is the goal. In dealing with Uranus, the question is not whether adaptation is warranted, but, rather, how it can be implemented.

Part of the scope of Uranus is to deliver a progressive jolt to any stultifying or worn-out structures. It allows for broader and more complex truths to be downloaded and potentially integrated into society. As a mental and metaphysical energy, it crackles with dizzying and fascinating possibilities, all designed to keep evolution marching forward.

Opening the Vise Grip

Picture a laser beam extending indefinitely into the future, which is analogous to our eternal evolutionary circumstance (Uranus). Then picture someone coming along and putting a vise grip on it (Saturn). The application of the vise allows the line to be contained, so we can work with it. It's not uncontrollable or endlessly speculative anymore. This is essential—however, the tighter the vise is, the more restrictive. How much do we want to strangle infinity? As soon as we think we know something, the vise grip stifles everything else that our understanding doesn't account for.

If we never apply the vise, we never show up here. There is always a bargain between Saturn and Uranus, but in the end, Uranus holds the upper hand. Evolution will always proceed. Uranus is a broader truth than Saturn. As stated, it orbits farther out and encapsulates unending possibilities. We can take it further and see that Neptune is an even broader truth: that fostering emotional interconnectedness throughout our oneness gives us an even greater perspective. Pluto then provides the impetus to dig into our power and use the broader intellectual (Uranus) and emotional (Neptune) understandings for our collective survival. All of the outer planet interchanges with Saturn are designed to loosen the grip, so that greater collective advancement may proceed.

Due to the fact that (modern) astrology itself is Uranian, and that evolution continually advances in some form, it is only a matter of time before the Saturnian status quo meets an onslaught of the greater truth that astrology offers. It is as if the plan all along was to confront the limitations of our worldly assumptions and grasp the dazzling array of implications revealed for our contemplation. Within the field of astrology a similar dynamic is being played out between more Saturnian versus Uranian approaches. Indeed, we can see this in a variety of fields, in all cultures.

Saturn has quite the role, like a two-way evolutionary valve. It must always yield or open for evolution to continue. If it refuses to open, the pressure that will confront it will build, until dramatic or cataclysmic means of release become necessary. At this point of evolution, collectively, we have a hard time letting go of the ego in order to realize the transpersonal. As a result, outer planet clashes with Saturn have been really spectacular. This is perhaps the greatest masterwork of the human condition: integrating outer planet energies into the status quo. What an elusive and delicate balance. Err on one side, and there will be problems. With too much Saturn, we strangle infinity. Not enough Saturn—chaos.

We may think of the laser beam as stemming from a magnificent source of energy, Spirit itself. Through the application of the vise grip, the temporary closing of the valve, we bring manifestation, a direct illumination of Spirit. However, it's still pretty dark out. There are leagues of problems in this world, collective challenges without easy solutions. We must continue to find ways to open the vise grip. At this moment in history, it appears that evolution will be threatened if we don't. The upcoming Uranus activity (2008-2012 and beyond) is of the highest import, and when this Uranus/Saturn dynamic will be quite noticeable. Let's approach it with wisdom, perspective, and always an eye toward progress.

Exposing Hypocrisy

One of the ways in which we can pry open the vise grip is by realizing that it restricts growth by amplifying divisions. Saturn is a separating force that is necessary to create order in the familiar world. We have restrooms for men and restrooms for women. Borders allow us to know what country we're in. Laws are passed to differentiate acceptable and unacceptable behavior.

Uranus pertains to unification beyond all divisions. As discussed in the last chapter, the Uranian matrix acts like a magnificent theater of mirrors. Every divided part in the Saturnian world sees itself in a variety of ways. Through recognition of self, we may join with what has been estranged. The alternative is not to recognize self in the other and to solidify a divisive dynamic. This often leads to one disparaging the other. Since the other is really mirroring a part of the self, this disparagement takes the form of hypocrisy. Upon seeing this hypocrisy, we can take measures to unify with what has been separated. Below are some examples of hypocrisy as seen in the divisions of world views, cultural issues, morality, behavior, race, gender, and class.

One of the greatest divisions of world views is between science and religion. Each sees the other as dogmatic, closed-minded and clueless about the big picture. Each produces "evidence" to affirm its viewpoint, and the failure of the other to take into account this evidence is considered a serious character flaw. Many who ask us to "love thy neighbor as thyself" want to erect a 700-foot-long wall on the United States/Mexico border to keep Mexicans out of the country. They are afraid that Hispanics will exploit America financially, while they support laws that greatly favor their own pocketbook. Progressives can also be overly Saturnian. Consider the liberal "health nut" who believes that conservatives are fanatics, while he counts the calories of his tofu while running on his treadmill. There are animal rights activists who claim that those who wear fur coats are inconsiderate—as they throw ink or blood on them. Mel Gibson went on an anti-Semitic rant, though his personal savior is a Jewish man. Israel considers its Arab neighbors to be preoccupied with securing land—as it arms an area about the size of New Jersey into one of the premier military powers in history. Religious zealots go door-to-door to help those they believe are misguided.

Some of the most dramatic hypocrisy is found in sexual domains. Mark Foley abused his congressional authority by pursuing male pages while working toward protecting children from sexual predators. Ted Haggard preached against homosexuality and sinful lifestyles, and was found to have illegally paid for drug-fueled homosexual dalliances. Catholic priests are trained to be paragons of virtue, while the pedophilia scandal that rocked the church is of epic proportions. Ken Starr said that Bill Clinton is obsessed with sex, yet he put out a report detailing a cigar entering a vagina, and semen stains on a dress.

Many people are not integrated with their own violent tendencies. The father who hits his children insists that they are "out of line." One of the murderous rationales of the Nazis was the belief that Jews are bloodthirsty and want to control the world. Slave owners justified their behavior with the belief that blacks are savages, while they whipped and sometimes raped them. George W. Bush said that Saddam Hussein was a threat to international peace as he launched an unprovoked war. Also, the invasion was "justified" because of the tyrannical abuse Hussein inflicted on his people. Later we learned of the torture at the Abu Ghraib prison at the hands of U.S. personnel. There tends to be a rather high correlation between those who describe themselves as "pro-life" and those who support going to war. A more subtle form of hypocrisy is found in how we apply names. The Civil War was anything but civil and the United States is a collection of many diverse states (red and blue, north and south) that want nothing to do with each other.

Groups are often formed to rally and organize people around a common purpose. The establishment of a group positions it in relation to other groups and the differences between outlook and agenda become magnified. Ultimately, these differences may catalyze awareness and integration. On the road there, hypocrisy is likely to emerge. Consider the "Hippies," who prize individual expression and freedom but who tend to have a uniform appearance. There is pressure to adhere to a specific lifestyle and mindset—to be "cool" or liberal enough. The group has as many Saturnian rules for conformity as for what it rebels against!

What we involve ourselves in says much about what we're working on. It's been recognized that many who enter the helping professions are in need of help themselves. They benefit from the work, and there is nothing wrong with this—we teach what we are learning. The problem arises when this isn't recognized or embraced. Hypocrisy emerges, as depicted in a cartoon of a psychiatrists' convention: The speaker says,

"Everybody's crazy except for us…any questions?" Since this dynamic is universal, we can even apply it to astrologers. As a group, astrologers seem to have as many problems as anyone—yet they tell people how they can live their lives better.

Gender sets up another in-group versus out-group dynamic. An example is the man who thinks that women are weak and needy, but pleads with his wife when she mentions divorce. There's the woman who claims that men are selfish but she demands more gifts and attention. Sometimes men deride women for vanity, though many men enjoy driving around in fancy sport cars. There are women who believe men are controlling, though sex is a way some women seek to control a partner.

We can even see this hypocrisy dynamic in terms of class. Some poor people decry how rich people put up gates to keep them out, while these poor people are adamant that no one step foot on their turf. There are rich people who call the poor lazy while they themselves plan for early retirements to sail on yachts. Some poor people complain that the wealthy don't appreciate what they have, while there are many incidents of abuse, neglect and absent-parenthood among the poor.

The Aquarian Dilemma

Since Uranus/Aquarius is future-oriented, how can we work with it in the present? Catching lightning is a temporary triumph—there'll be a more incredible storm tomorrow. So, there's always a bargain when we discover new truths—and that's just the way of it. Though we can see that giving form to Uranus is a pyrrhic victory, we're still better off than we were yesterday.

The Uranian field of astrology faces this dilemma. Times when it has taken hold of the collective imagination, it has been stripped down to a level palatable for the masses. The obvious example of this is Sun sign astrology and the common simplification of knowing a person's Sun, Moon and Ascendant. These simplifications circumvent the greater depth available.

Though they can invite greater exploration, it also creates an astrology that is packaged.

Certainly it's not so bad to have a basic form of astrology alive in the collective consciousness. In fact, many have been stimulated to explore the field further. However, a particular culture has been established that influences further inquiry. As a result, many assumptions of popular astrology, whether pointing to deeper understandings or not, are not questioned. The lack of questioning of these basic tenets stifles the continual advancement that Uranus insists upon. Can we really be sure that the perspectives that informed basic astrology are sound and impervious to change? Or, could it be that they reflect the mindset of their times?

When a Uranian challenge to the basic framework is presented, it shouldn't be immediately accepted wholesale without scrutiny. In every field, from the engineering of cars, to the technology of making music, to the application of laws to society, gradual adjustments are made to fit the times. Since Uranian and Saturnian forces are functional in all fields, this seems like a healthy compromise. Change—but not too fast. Scrutiny, of both the older ways and the newer, seems essential for progress.

Since astrology is gaining in validity and has the potential to be used in the broader collective, shouldn't we seek to integrate astrology with academia, institutions, and popular culture? If we are all in pursuit of truth, and if astrology reveals a greater truth, what is stopping us from structuring society around astrology?

In contemplating this question, a little voice emerges that says, "Not so fast." I believe this mechanism of restraint exists because of the Aquarian dilemma. If we are not truly ready to have astrology become this mainstream, it would be disastrous to reform sociological structures in accordance with what we presently know. At least to me, it seems that we would need to change some of our paradigms and update our everyday living.

Perhaps someday we'll be closer to a more universal, non-denominational approach that honors psycho-spiritual depth and complexity. Until then, we should show restraint in having astrology occupy a prominent place in mainstream culture. Since modern astrology is Uranian, perhaps its rightful place is on the fringe. Even someday in the future when it appears that we're *collectively* more ready for astrology, the same issue of applying the vise grip and limiting the reach of the field would be relevant. This is an unresolvable dilemma—one that continually asks us to question, reform, and not become too comfortable with how things are. The only way to solve the Aquarian dilemma might be to apply the vise grip loosely.

Evolution and the Inner Planets

We are continually attempting to close the great divide between the four-dimensional Saturnian experience and the multi-dimensional Uranian experience. In order to do this at the individual level, we must dissolve the personal story, the egoic mind—the sense of a separate self. This is a very advanced proposition. Many don't have the solidity of self to release it, or the understanding that when we release it, we are held by a larger container. All the inner planet functions can take us away from the transpersonal—and they also can connect us to it. All are traps and aids for the transpersonal mind to use. Here, we'll connect back to the other planets in the system.

The Sun, being the life force itself, can either serve the self or seek to contribute to the greater cause of the collective. It depends how satisfied one is with one's growth. Certainly in the formative years, it is necessary and useful to bolster the sense of the individual self. We all need to figure out who we are, cultivate our uniqueness, and master the fine points of everyday living. As development proceeds, there comes a point when the individual needs to ask himself if there is something more. The Sun is able to shine more strongly when we are enthused by life and eager to meet it. As personal development proceeds, the accumulation of youthful experience no longer satisfies. Filling up this void can unfold in a number of ways. Those who experience an existential crisis, a confrontation with the question of personal meaning, will struggle. Those who pass this trial find ways to contribute.

The Moon is the most regressive planet in the system and therefore the one that limits transpersonal utilization the most. From a spiritual perspective, the Moon shows what is unconscious within the soul, the defensive and protective strategies used for survival. It's personal to the core, unresolved and contracted. Nevertheless, we can become conscious of the Moon, learn to untangle and detach from its clutching, and use it proactively. The Moon is motivated by love. When it's not preoccupied with unresolved needs within the self, the tenderness of the Moon gives us the impetus to care about evolution. Whereas the Sun lights and warms, the Moon fuels this radiance from an underground well of feeling. We can choose to live from the heart and thereby find ways to heal the world.

Mercury presents quite the dilemma. In service to the self, it knows what it knows, perceives what it does, and is unable to attain a loftier, more complete understanding. Mercury uses logic and reason and is resistant to multi-dimensional, including right-brain, perspectives. Only when the brain discovers how limited its scope really is can it then integrate with the transpersonal. When it does, it becomes the ideal instrument to teach and to give voice to spiritual phenomena. It must guard against simplification and continually check whether its messages are really stemming from personal preferences. The curious zest for knowledge and learning, though, may certainly lead to broader truths.

Like the other planets, Venus, too, is a double-edged sword. Involved in sensory, social, aesthetic, and artistic domains, it conveys one's connection to the material world and other beings. The undeveloped Venus seeks to fortify the self through personal accumulation and manipulate others for gain. Sensing incompleteness, it tries to bolster the self by proving its worth. Venus may also be used intentionally to connect purposely with one's surroundings by infusing one's body, art or relationships with greater inspiration. Venus displays beauty—and the ways in which we live our lives can be more akin to artwork. Venus allows us to experience Spirit in the other and throughout the natural world.

The undeveloped Mars is the most selfish of all. It's necessary to be self-serving—to feed hungers and see to the fitness of "me", or "number one." We are given free will, and there is autonomy for us to seize. Along with Aries and the 1st House, we notice the movement from the womb (Pisces, 12th House) into separateness. The individual must decide whether he wants to then reintegrate with oneness or simply champion "number one." With the transpersonal intention, behavior (Mars) can be directed in ways that promote this reintegration. In equal measure to living selfishly, an individual can impact this life through courage, informed action and being a champion of evolution. This can happen with the realization that the individual behavior connects to a larger source.

Jupiter and Saturn are social planets. They channel the inner planet functions into a directed life path (Jupiter) and solid vocational contribution (Saturn). Many do live by a philosophy (Jupiter) of climbing the mountain of achievement (Saturn). Some have personal belief systems (Jupiter) they wish to have cemented into the social structure (Saturn). Informed by Uranus and the transpersonal planets, Jupiter and Saturn take on much different dimensions. Jupiter pertains to mission; the outer planets provide a holistic, non-denominational and all-inclusive scope. In other words, "We're all in this together, so let's do something about the state of the world." The integration of Uranus and Saturn is of paramount importance and has been addressed in detail throughout this chapter.

The Uranus/Nodes Cycle

This section provides some evidence in support of modern astrology's connection to Uranus. At *The Blast* astrology conference in Sedona, Arizona (March 29-April 2, 2007), Robert Blaschke lectured on the Uranus/Nodes cycle—as he explained, roughly every 15.5 years Uranus forms a conjunction with the North Node. During the conference, Uranus formed an exact conjunction with the North Node in Pisces, as well as with Mercury. Blaschke spoke of the significance of this event: a new chapter in the history of astrology was being born. Here, we'll review, add to, and comment upon some of the information presented by Blaschke.

The North Node is a statement of what, collectively, we are working on and moving toward. Blaschke reasons that when Uranus makes a conjunction with the North Node, the field of astrology begins movement toward the sign of the conjunction, as well as other planets with the North Node. Because the recent conjunction in 2007 took place in Pisces, astrology is now moving in a transpersonal direction, and the boundaries among the various forms of astrology are dissolving. Furthermore, Mercury was closely conjoined Uranus, so new spiritual ideas are a large part of this. Jupiter in Sagittarius squares the Nodes, suggesting that using astrology to understand the universe in a meaningful way will be further explored. The Virgo Moon was in conjunction with the Virgo South Node. This suggests that we are maturing away from the pull of our emotional limitations by liberating (Uranus) the unconscious (opposed Moon).

The previous conjunction of Uranus with the North Node occurred in 1991, in Capricorn. At this time, interest in traditional, medieval and Hellenistic systems of astrology was taking hold. Project Hindsight and ARAHAT were founded to rediscover ancient texts and bring this wisdom to the field. Also, astrology made inroads with accreditation and inclusion in educational institutions. During this phase, Kepler College began to graduate students with advanced degrees in astrology. Serious (Capricorn) astrology based on methodology and tradition was in vogue.

In 1976 Uranus was in conjunction with the North Node in Scorpio. Psychological or depth astrology was flourishing. Liz Greene, Stephen Arroyo, Donna Cunningham, and many others helped make astrology a powerful tool for understanding the unconscious. Jeffrey Wolf Green and Steven Forrest were dubbed the "Pluto Brothers"—indeed, there was a profound emphasis on the tiny planet in their work. Within this mysterious Scorpio aura, occult dimensions of astrology were also explored. Far from being just entertainment, astrology was now understood to be a powerful tool that could illuminate the unconscious, the artifacts that reside in the shadow.

In contrast, in 1961 the Uranus/North Node conjunction was in Leo. Sun sign astrology was in its heyday, punctuated by Linda Goodman's *Sun Signs*. Astrology was seen as entertainment, as a way of understanding the personality rather than deeper soul processes. "What's your sign?" became a popular pick-up line, simplified "pop" astrology filled magazines and newspapers, and the field was not taken seriously by most. Blaschke has also noted that in 1946, Uranus and the North Node formed a conjunction in Gemini. During this time frame, the Siderealist movement came to the West, led by Cyril Fagan. The idea of dual Zodiacs (Gemini) was a challenging concept for students to learn. During this phase, modern astrology was in a fledgling phase, though the ideas were being developed for the flowering that soon followed.

These prior astrological phases have cemented into the collective consciousness. Now we have entered a new phase, one that promises greater spiritual uplift, a plethora of new ideas, revitalized spiritual direction and emotional liberation. The focus will be on understanding the breadth of the field and joining together in collective purpose (Pisces). Astrology is going to further inform our place in the cosmos and provide perspective and meaning (the influence of Jupiter in Sagittarius) and freedom from the bondage of limited paradigms (Uranus opposed Virgo Moon).

After the Pisces period, Uranus will form a conjunction with the North Node and Mars in Taurus in 2022, with Saturn in Aquarius and Mercury in Leo squaring it. This conjunction in Taurus may begin a chapter about grounding astrology, bringing it to the "everyday" after the transpersonal phase. Saturn in Aquarius suggests that our institutions will be modernizing. The inclusion of Mars could indicate that a newfound approach (Uranus/Mars), based on understanding the intelligence of nature, may be applied to how we steward the environment (Taurus).

Mercury in Leo adds a spirited and colorful vocal quality. In contrast to the superficial side of Leo (the proliferation of Sun signs in the 1960s), Mercury in this chart is in aspect to both Saturn and Uranus, which inflects it with more serious and transpersonal components. Astrology may enter mass communications in a more informed way.

Uranian Wisdom and Paradoxes

For the final section, some quizzical Uranian statements will be introduced and explained. Uranus challenges our assumptions, turns things inside out and often yields greater truths that are completely unexpected. For example, you may have heard, "we are spiritual beings having human experiences," which turns the idea that we are human beings able to have spiritual experiences on its head. Several of the statements below will sound familiar to some readers. First, the subtitle of this book is *the constant of change*. Change by its very definition denotes a lack of constancy, but since change always endures, we have our first paradox.

When we figure out who we are, it turns out to be nobody. Uranus invites us to the transpersonal, to energetically join with the collective. In order to merge from the most informed and healthy place, we need to bust through prior limitations and claim our individual truth. Then we are able to have self-knowledge and raise consciousness, and we find that we are a part of Spirit—the personal falls away. Self-development eventually turns into self-transcendence.

Mind thinks us. We are so accustomed to the individual mind thinking about larger frameworks, such as God or nature. The Uranian perspective sees the individual mind as being a part of Spirit and informed by it. Since the energy of Spirit runs through everything, Spirit is the prime mover, the generator of life. We are a product of these larger energetic occurrences and enveloped within its functioning. The larger spiritual mind is actually responsible for our vitality. The Universal Mind *thought up* each of us.

We awaken to the dream. Commonly we think of waking out of sleep and into everyday living. We take a shower, have a bite to eat and go to work. The Uranian view is that reality as we experience it is a colossal, multi-dimensional exchange of energy. We are globs of energy bouncing off each other, stimulating greater awareness through addressing lessons. The next step after Uranus is Neptune—when we awaken, we participate in life from this multi-dimensional awareness, which has the condition of fluidity, timelessness and impermanence. We are mystics swimming in a dream.

Liberation is found through surrender, life is found through death. In the familiar realms, liberation is found through strength, freedom and autonomy, while life is found through an active engagement with life itself. At the transpersonal level, liberation into Spirit is found through surrendering the personal ego. When we die, we shed the confines of the body and have an unmitigated reunion with the source of life. Without egoic surrender, another paradox emerges: *(Egoic) freedom is bondage*.

Once we notice the trick, we become the trickster. We've been tricked by the familiar dimensions of reality into believing that this is all there is. When we transcend this limitation (Saturn) and see existence multi-dimensionally, we are then able to be an agent of progress (Uranus). Becoming Uranian naturally catalyzes and challenges others to grow using innovative methods. There is increased psychic awareness to Uranus, along with the overarching view of the cosmic dance into incarnation and back. Those who see the trick release personal concerns in favor of instigating evolutionary advancement using extra-sensory perception and other forms of wizardry, riddles and tools of the trickster.

Once nothing matters anymore, everything is precious. When individual concerns are subjugated to the broader transpersonal or universal, there is an opening to gratitude. One may erroneously suspect that nonattachment leads to deadening removal and observation rather than participation. Rather, nonattached consciousness becomes more sensitive to the subtleties and nuances of life and appreciates how precious everything really is. When we release our stories of what life should be, we embrace what life is.

Saying "I don't know" shows the most knowledge. Within the Saturnian world, we may subscribe to binary black-and-white thinking. This preserves order but also contracts Uranian possibilities. At the multi-dimensional or transpersonal level, knowledge is not so clear-cut. All the rules are broken with Uranus, all possibilities are relevant, and all dimensions are engaged. The rational mind can never fully grasp the scope of this. The ability to say "I don't know" is not ignorant. Rather, it shows a willingness not to constrict the infinite, to remain open to its reach. The rational mind may say that the opposite of a truth is a lie, but the Uranian view is that the opposite of a truth is another truth—an observation made by many talented thinkers.

You can't think outside the box because the box is thinking. The activity of the brain is personal. Individual thoughts, ideas and ruminations are part of Mercury's functioning, which operates within the Saturnian boundary. Mercury is able to conceive of the transpersonal but not truly experience it because it reduces the territory to language, logic and some semblance of order. As it's written in the Tao te Ching, "The Tao that can be told is not the eternal Tao." Mercury functions within the box of reason—Uranus (and the other transpersonal planets) transcends it.

We get out by going in, we leave by arriving. In order to elevate consciousness and grasp the transpersonal, we must fully arrive into ourselves and the world that hosts us. The idea of egoic surrender is not to abandon the self, but rather to embrace it fully while also recognizing its limitations. The methodology of transcendence is to integrate outer planet functioning into the confines of the inner planet or personal energies. Then we straddle both worlds and notice another Uranian paradox: *Heaven is on Earth.*

Nature tames people. The triumph of the individual has included a sense of mastery over nature. We have made impressive gains through refining and utilizing natural resources. In short, we have civilized ourselves through taming nature. The broader view turns it around: Nature is connecting to itself *through* us. When we cooperate with this evolutionary unfolding, we learn about ourselves and may consciously contribute. When we align with the intelligence of nature, the personal story collapses, and the wilder parts of us become tamed.

Failing is growing, losing is winning. The ego wants to succeed, whereas the soul wants to grow. Situations the ego may construe as failures or losses may in fact introduce rich and necessary spiritual lessons. The most trying situations are actually *gifts,* no matter how much the ego rolls its eyes at such a notion.

Accidents are on purpose. In a meaningful universe, there is meaning in everything. Randomness is a product of the skeptical mind that cannot fathom a larger design. The Uranian view is that all energy is interconnected. Accidents or coincidences are actually synchronicities—how the universe connects to itself in order to stimulate awakening. The ego often dismisses accidents and thereby stays contracted and oblivious to what purpose may be underlying such events.

The imperfections of the world are perfect. Evolution is proceeding on its own course, in its own way, in its own time. In approaching the realization of some form of "perfect" future, what is perceived as imperfect now alerts us to what needs to be changed. We all have imperfections, and these, too, are perfect for us to address. We may lament that the world is filled with many social, political or even spiritual ills or imperfections, but these *perfectly* catalyze growth. Spirit knows what it's doing, and doesn't have to be corrected by us. Instead, when we correct ourselves we can experience Spirit's perfection.

Our view of the world is really our view of the self. Infinite mirrors in unending guises reflect back who we are so that we can awaken to the authentic self—which, of course, is the universe itself. We are microcosms embedded in a far larger body and mind. Whatever frequency we resonate at will attract and connect to a similar wavelength. Therefore, the echoes that return show us who we are. From the personal standpoint it may sound narcissistic to think that the world is who we are; that everything "out there" is really inside. The transpersonal view yields another paradox. *Not accepting that the world is the self is narcissism* because it indicates entrapment in the personal story.

We vanish into thick air. The common view is that air is empty—we snap our fingers to suggest that something can disappear into it. We are now learning that air or space is teeming with a network of transrational connections, the matrix. Furthermore, if Dr. Krasnoholovets is correct, then this network is literally everywhere around us, embedded within the gravitational interplay of the planetary bodies. As many Eastern paths and wisdom traditions teach us, the physical world is impermanent, while the unseen world is what endures. There is no vanishing, just changing. Air is only thin from one perspective.

I don't care about you because I love you. From the Uranian view, *all* experiences are necessary no matter what value judgments we assign. The deeper spiritual love we may have towards each others' growth is unwavering and unconditional. There is less care about the everyday narrative that tends to organize experiences as positive or negative. Instead of coddling or investing in so-called "positive" outcomes for another, we can love them as they struggle—to not wish for any alteration of these necessary and rich experiences, however painful to the personality. This usage of "care" goes along with what is personal while "love" is equated with the soul.

Seriously, don't take it all so seriously! The Uranian view that integrates the trickster learns to see the endless dance of energy. All of life is constantly changing, transforming, evolving. It's a fascinating carnival, a spectacle on the largest possible scale. The show will never be cancelled. So, don't get so caught up in it! We can relax with the knowledge that the cliché may be right, all **is** good. This is a wondrous, interconnected world. When we take this idea of oneness seriously, then we don't have to take it all so seriously. In the end, we ***are*** Spirit. *So smile…and realize that it's not (only) you who is happy.* ☺

Conclusion

A common thought experiment asks what would happen if an irresistible force (Uranus) meets an immovable object (Saturn). It turns out that the material world is impermanent, so the object isn't so immovable after all—the irresistible force is the victor. The world of ideas and the concept of progress are eternal—never to be squashed or compromised by the fleeting world of form contained in the bottle of time.

And it is form and time that give a temporary home to such revolutionary ideas. So, who is it that destroys what is outdated, calcified and restrictive? Is it a wild uncontrollable force from the outside, or is it us? All of us contain the spark of the irresistible force. It appears that all along, it's been an inside job. What many fear most (unforeseen changes, annihilation, perceived chaos) is our ticket to liberation. As Barack Obama echoes Gandhi, "we are the change we seek."

This Uranian force gives us nothing less than immortality, which is not found at an elusive fountain of youth—it's by conquering the fear of death. Uranus teaches us how we can reinvent the self to align with our unadulterated spiritual promise—the realization of the timeless soul. By so doing, we leave a mark on the manifest world that echoes for eternity. By so doing, our souls are let loose on a limitless multi-dimensional playground.

Endnotes

1. The quandary any author faces in discussing Uranus is the limitation of the writer's perspective. Uranus is an overarching metaphysical principle that transcends time and the nuances of any given culture. Any attempt at discussing the full scope of the planet is bound to fail. Nevertheless, we must play the hand we're given. This book is written from a modern, western view that primarily focuses on people and events of the twentieth century.

2. Note that the exact birth time of charts is unnecessary to see what aspects are evident as the planets don't move very far on any given day. The special case is the Moon, which does travel about 12 degrees a day. For people whose birth time is unknown, charts were cast at 12 noon in the birth area of the native. If the Uranus/Moon aspect was within orbs at this time, the person was included. Certainly, the Moon may be outside of the listed orb if the true birth time was near midnight. However, the Uranus/Moon aspect was either applying to, or just separating from, being in aspect. Considering the Moon is a luminary, astrologers generally allow a larger orb which would broaden the times the planets were technically in aspect. So please note that a few examples listed in the Uranus/Moon section might be out of orb. However, it seems to this writer that the issue of unknown birth times is something we all have to address. Throwing out these charts seems to be a drastic step. Including them with this caveat seems to be a workable solution.

3. Chart Notes: All charts use the Porphyry house system, True Node, Tropical; all dates are NS, and are consistent with the listing in Astrodatabank.
Galileo Galilei: February 25, 1564, 3:31 p.m. Pisa, Italy. Rating: A
Abraham Lincoln: February 12, 1809, 6:54 a.m. Hodgenville, KY Rating: B
Marie Curie: November 7, 1867, 10:36 a.m. Warsaw, Poland. Rating: AA
Anne Frank: June 12, 1929, 7:30 a.m. Frankfurt, Germany. Rating: AA
Jackie Robinson: January 31, 1919, 6:30 p.m. Cairo, GA. Rating: B
Margaret Sanger: September 14, 1879, 2:30 a.m. Corning, NY. Rating: C
Neil Armstrong: August 5, 1930, 12:31 a.m. Washington, OH. Rating: AA
David Kopay: June 28, 1942, 9:57 a.m. Evergreen Park, IL. Rating: AA
Jerry Rubin: July 14, 1938, 10:34 a.m. Cincinnati, OH. Rating: AA
Andy Warhol: August 6, 1928, 6:30 a.m. Pittsburgh, PA. Rating: B
Jimi Hendrix: November 27, 1942, 10:15 a.m. Seattle, WA. Rating: AA
Toni Morrison: February 18, 1931, 11:00 a.m. Lorain, OH. Rating: AA
David Koresh: August 17, 1959, 8:49 a.m. Houston, TX. Rating: A
Ellen DeGeneres: January 26, 1958, 3:30 a.m. Metairie, LA. Rating: C
Cindy Sheehan: July 10, 1957, 1:40 p.m. Inglewood, CA. Rating: AA

4. Some interesting notes: Albert Einstein's Sun is also at 23 degrees Pisces, so it's precisely conjoined the Sun in the Uranus discovery chart. He is perhaps the greatest Uranian figure in history. We are approaching a time when transiting Uranus will hit the Uranus discovery chart's Sun (in early

2009) during a very dramatic Uranian time (reviewed in Part 2). Like the Discovery chart, William Herschel (November 15, 1738) has a Uranus/Saturn opposition. In fact, he has a Uranus/Venus/Moon stellium in Capricorn opposed Saturn/Neptune in Cancer (Uranus is also sextile Pluto). Grounding the planet and sharing a new vision of the solar system with others is very much the idea.

John Flamsteed's (August 29, 1646) natal chart also features a Uranus/Saturn opposition, with Uranus in aspect to Mercury, Jupiter, Venus, and Neptune as well. Le Monnier's (November 23, 1715) chart is overwhelmingly Uranian: a Uranus/Jupiter/Mars Grand Trine, Uranus square Mercury, and Uranus in conjunction with Saturn. His Sun in early Sagittarius is widely sextile Uranus in late Virgo. And Flamsteed, Le Monnier and Herschel all have Uranus in aspect to Saturn.

5. For a more comprehensive discussion on planetary cycles please see *Cosmos & Psyche* by Richard Tarnas. These sections are intentionally brief—to give an introduction to these cycles and provide some examples. What Tarnas has accomplished is epic in scope and thoroughness. The canon of astrological thinking is expanding from pat descriptions into a broader understanding of evolutionary issues—and the intention here is to add to the discussion.

Acknowledgments

Many thanks go to Evelyn Terranova, who did a superb job with the cover artwork. I'm thrilled to have your images represent my work. The detailed eye of Sarah Myers has been invaluable in tightening up my writing—thank you so much for being an excellent editor. To my Uranian comrade, Bill Streett, who wrote such an eloquent forward, handled the graphic design impeccably, and was my main sounding board for the content—thank you! And thanks to Josh Levin, who gets credit for the photograph, and for helping to catalyze my Uranian side.

I want to thank the astrological community for keeping the field vibrant and relevant. The elders I've been honored to connect with and learn from have been exceptional (and I'm glad I found the Forrest through the trees, thank you Steven), the support and interest in my work is greatly appreciated. I've had the privilege of working with wonderful clients and students, who have truly made me the astrologer I am. Most of all, I want to acknowledge my peers, and the new wave of youngsters, who bring fresh perspectives to the field. The fellowship and community being created is essential for bringing astrology to the twenty-first century. We are certainly having a blast, led by Moses (Siregar) in the desert.

Being a writer is possible only with the support and understanding of friends and family (and a special acknowledgment to my dear, and quite Uranian, son). Though some of you still wonder why I spend so much time doing this, thank you for accepting that I choose to. Thank you to those who directly and indirectly influence and inspire my work: the astrologers, philosophers, scientists, artists, mystics, misfits, skeptics, playmates, sparring partners, and even the extraordinary ordinary men and women who fill in the gaps. And thank you to nature itself for being so intelligent, enticing, hilarious, and filled with endless awe and mystery. I'm humbled to help give voice to your designs.

About the Author

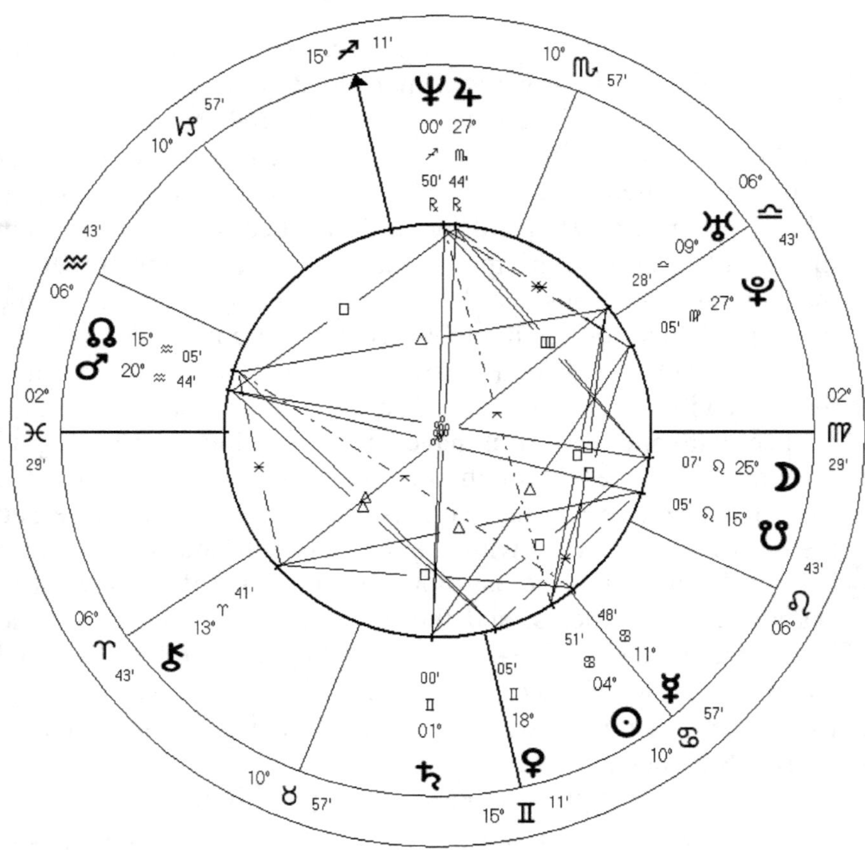

Eric Meyers
June 26, 1971
11:29 p.m.
New Haven, CT

Eric has Uranus (in the 8th House in Libra) square the Sun and Mercury (in Cancer), and trine (and ruling) his 12th House Aquarius North Node. Mars is also in Aquarius in the 12th House. This book was written (late 2006-early 2008) with transiting Uranus trine natal Mercury, square the MC, and square Venus (3rd House ruler), while his progressed Sun was sextile Uranus.

www.ingramcontent.com/pod-product-compliance
Lightning Source LLC
LaVergne TN
LVHW020540100826
845148LV00010B/1550